Anonymous

Report of the Committee Secondary School Studies

Anonymous

Report of the Committee Secondary School Studies

ISBN/EAN: 9783744667098

Printed in Europe, USA, Canada, Australia, Japan

Cover: Foto ©Thomas Meinert / pixelio.de

More available books at **www.hansebooks.com**

REPORT OF THE COMMITTEE OF TEN ON SECONDARY SCHOOL STUDIES ❦ WITH THE REPORTS OF THE CONFERENCES ARRANGED BY THE COMMITTEE

PUBLISHED FOR THE NATIONAL EDUCATIONAL ASSOCIATION BY THE AMERICAN BOOK COMPANY ❦ NEW YORK, CINCINNATI, CHICAGO M D CCC XC IV

PREFATORY NOTE.

The Report of the Committee of Ten on Secondary School Studies is now generally known among the leading educators of the country, and, while there is much diversity of opinion respecting many of its recommendations, there is substantial agreement that it is the most important educational document ever issued in the United States.

Prepared under the auspices of the National Educational Association, this Report was first published by the Bureau of Education, at Washington, and distributed at public expense to the extent of the funds available for that purpose. In spite of this liberal distribution, many thousands of instructors and educators could not receive a copy from that source.

In view of the importance of the Report, and the increasing demand for copies, the National Educational Association has arranged with the American Book Company to print and publish another edition, and to furnish it at a nominal price, that its beneficial influence may be extended still more widely.

In issuing the new edition, it has been thought best to make certain improvements in the make-up of the book, and to insert an Analytical and Topical Index, by which convenient and instant reference may be had to any subject mentioned in the Report of the Committee, or in those of the nine conferences.

Friends of the Association may be interested to know that any profit which may be derived from the sale of the Report in this form, will accrue to the benefit of the Association, and re-imburse, in part, the very considerable expense involved in its preparation.

N. A. CALKINS,
Chairman of Board of Trustees, of
National Educational Association.

TABLE OF CONTENTS.

	Page.
Report of the Committee of Ten	3
Origin of the Conferences	3
Members of the Committee of Ten	4
Subjects of the Conferences	5
List of Eleven Questions	6
Places of holding Conferences	7
Members of the Nine Conferences	8
Composition of Conferences	11
Program for Twelve Years' Course	34
Program for High Schools	37
Classical Program for High Schools	41
Minority Report of President Baker	56
Report of Latin Conference	60
Report of Greek Conference	76
Report of English Conference	86
Report of Other Modern Languages Conference	96
Report of Mathematics Conference	104
Report of Physics, Chemistry, and Astronomy Conference	117
Minority Report of W. J. Waggoner	123
Minority Report of Alfred P. Gage	123
Report of the Committee on Experiments	124
Report of Natural History Conference	138
Nature Study for Grades below the High School	142

V

Page.

Botany for Common Schools......................................151

Zoölogy for Secondary Schools..................................154

Physiology in Primary and Secondary Schools....................158

Report of History, Civil Government, and Political Economy Con-

   ference ....162.

Appendix to Report of History, Civil Government, and Political Econ-

   omy Conference..202

Report of Geography Conference.................................204

Minority Report of Edwin J. Houston............................237

ANALYTICAL INDEX.

I. AIMS OF EDUCATION,

BOTANY, result of first four years' work, 148—of first six years' work, 150. ENGLISH, objects of teaching, 86—formal grammar, 89. GEOGRAPHY, as mental discipline, 214—observational purpose of, 211. GEOMETRY, purpose of, 115. GERMAN AND FRENCH in grammar schools, 99—German or French in high schools, 99. GREEK, grammatical knowledge not an end, 82 —purpose of study, 83. HISTORY, aim of teaching, 164, 168, 169, 170— examinations in, for college entrance, 165. LATIN, purpose of study, 61, 62. MATHEMATICS, discipline of, 114. MODERN LANGUAGES, educational value of, 96. NATURAL HISTORY, object of, in lowest grades, 139—nature study in primary schools, objects of, 142—results of first two years' work, 146. PHYSICS AND CHEMISTRY, rediscovery of laws not the aim, 118. PHYSIOLOGY as personal help, 159. PRODUCTIVE ABILITY, the great end of education is to create, 213. ZOÖLOGY as means of discipline, intellectual growth, broad culture, 158.

II. BOOKS, TEXT-BOOKS, REFERENCE-BOOKS, AND MATERIALS.

ARITHMETIC, abuse of text-books, 108. BOTANY, text-books in, defective in certain respects, 205. ENGLISH, Trench "On the Study of Words" recommended, 92. GEOGRAPHY, libraries for, 217—photographs and lantern slides, 218—simply memorizing from text-books should be avoided, 219—illustrative material, 223, 224—maps, 213, 217—relief maps, 219. GREEK, recommendations as to text-books, 77. HISTORY, text-books used in third year, 164—collection of reference-books, 165—text-books, dry and lifeless instruction by, 167, 184—libraries for teaching, 184—text-books, 188—criteria of a good text-book, 189—parallel text-books: sets of books, 189—material for reading: school libraries, reference-books, 193—historical novels, 194—wall-maps and atlases, 199. LATIN, Cato Major, 63—manuals of composition discouraged, 63—Gradatim, Eutropius, and the Viri Romæ recommended as easy reading, 64—Bucolics not recommended, 64— Froude's Cæsar, Forsyth's Cicero, Trollope's Cicero, Sellar's Virgil, and Wilkins's Primer of Roman Literature recommended, 73. NATURE STUDY, materials, 143—physical science, study of books and phenomena compared, 119. PHYSICS AND CHEMISTRY, one-half time to text-book, 118—chemistry and physics, study of text-books without laboratory work of little value, 119—physics and chemistry, more abundant material for former, 122—chemistry, text-books in, 137. READING-BOOK may be discarded at the beginning of the seventh year, 89. WEATHER-MAPS, 207. ZOÖLOGY, text-books in, defective in certain respects, 205.

III. CLASS EDUCATION.

Seventh Question: " *Should the subject be treated differently for pupils who are going to college, for those who are going to a scientific school, and for those who, presumably, are going to neither ?* "

ANSWERED UNANIMOUSLY in the negative by all the conferences, 17. BAD FOR ALL classes of pupils, 173. ENGLISH conference, specific answer to seventh question, 93. HISTORY, instruction precisely the same for all pupils, 165, 167, 203. MODERN LANGUAGES, conference on, 98. NATURAL HISTORY conference, differentiation unwise, 141. PHYSICS, CHEMISTRY, AND ASTRONOMY, no difference in treatment for those not going to college, 118.

IV. COLLEGES.

AVERAGE AGE of admission lowered, 14. ASTRONOMY not required, 118. CLOSE ARTICULATION with high schools, 53. ENGLISH, requirements in, should be made uniform in kind, 93—recommendations for admission, 93—admission, essays to be on the main subjects, 94—English should be a "final " subject, 95. GEOGRAPHY, examinations in, for admission, 234—field-work in geography, 236. GEOMETRY, admission to solid and plane, 116. GREEK, admission sight examinations, 80—examinations in grammar upon text, 80—Greek composition, 81. HISTORY, examinations for entrance, 165—work done in preparatory school taken as evidence, 165—colleges, relations with lower schools, 167—cram for entrance, 171—"Whatever improves the schools must improve the college," 174—regular written tests accepted as evidence, 184—a "final " subject, 185. LATIN, standard of admission raised in point of quality, 60—translation at sight, 74. MODERN LANGUAGES, admission to, 99, 102. NATURAL HISTORY, entrance and final examinations, 141—superiority of laboratory test to written examination, 140—natural science and history, habits of study painfully acquired by students, 15. PHYSICS AND CHEMISTRY required, 118 —admission, laboratory work as a test, 118—certificates from approved schools the ideal method, 118.

V. CONCENTRATION OF STUDIES.

ARITHMETIC AND PHYSICS, 109, 111—mathematical knowledge necessary to physics, 119. BOTANY, careful examination of, specimens best secured by careful sketching, 152. ENGLISH, relation of, to all studies, 87—formal grammar not a necessity to the use of good English, 89—English, history, and geography, 91—and other languages, 92—every subject should help every other, 16. GEOGRAPHY, relations of history and natural sciences to, 205, 219—geography, meteorology, and geology, relations of, 205, 206, 207, 208—relation to all modes of expression, 219—geography and drawing, 220 —elementary geography identical with elementary science, 239. GEOMETRY, drawing and modeling, 111—concrete geometry, relation to drawing, modeling, and arithmetic, 24. GREEK, geography, history, mythology, antiquities, 80. HISTORY, intimately connected with English, ancient and modern languages, topography, political, historical, and commercial geography, and the drawing of historical maps, 164—history and civil government, 165—history and English, 172, 195—inter-relation of subjects, 176—history and ethics, 180, 186—history and literature, 190, 193—history and geography, 199. MODERN LANGUAGES and English, 96. NATURE STUDY correlated with language; literature, drawing, and all other modes of expression, 139—natural history, careful drawings and good language in, 140—nature study, coördination with modes of expression, 144—relation to geography and arithmetic, 145—plant study related to geography, meteorology, zoölogy, anthropology, 143—nature studies the best means of teaching reading and writing, 221—natural science as means of teaching language, 240—natural sciences, geography and drawing, 49—physical science introduced by the study of geography, 240. POLITICAL ECONOMY related to U. S. history, civil government, and commercial geography, 165. SPELLING learned incidentally in combination with the subject studied, and not from a spelling-book, 88. SUBJECTS, interlacing of, 24.

VI. COURSES OF STUDY.

ALGEBRA, systematic study of, in high schools, 106—special report on, 111. ARITHMETIC, course to be abridged and enriched, 105—commercial arithmetic discussed, 107. BOTANY preferred to zoölogy in high schools, 139—botany and zoölogy, suggestions for courses of study, 140—plants, study to be continued throughout the year, 145—botany, course of study in first and second grades, 145—third and fourth grades, 146—fifth and sixth grades, 148—seventh and eighth grades, 150—for common schools, discussion and course of work, 151—year of work in, should be continuous, 153. CHEMISTRY, experiments in, 127. ENGLISH, elementary course of study, 87, 88—formal grammar, 88—English in high schools, 90—rhetoric in high schools, 90—English language, history of, not recommended for high schools, 91—phonetics, 91. FRENCH OR GERMAN in grammar schools, 96—modern languages, 97—German or French in grammar schools, 99—German and French in high schools, 99. GEOGRAPHY, order of subjects, 241 —physical geography, arrangement of topics, 242—physical geography analyzed, 246—geographic subjects, natural order of, 209. GEOMETRY, concrete, in grammar schools, 106—demonstrative geometry, 112. GREEK, time of study, 77. HISTORY, subjects included in an eight years' course, 162—courses of study suggested, 162—oral instruction in biography and mythology, 164—uniform programs not recommended, 167—time to begin:

question of consecutive study, 170—topics for intensive study, 177. LATIN, age of beginning, 60, 61—time of study, 61. PHYSICAL SCIENCE, natural phenomena, study of, in elementary schools, 117—in elementary schools, one period per day, 117—nature studies, one-quarter of the time in high schools given to, 123—natural history in primary schools should begin in kindergarten and lowest grades, 138, 139—nature studies one hour per week throughout the whole course below high school, 139—one-fourth of time in high school devoted to, 141—experiments in physics in high schools, 125—chemistry to precede physics, 200 hours to each, 117, 118—minority report, physics before chemistry, 121. POLITICAL ECONOMY discussed, 181. PHYSIOLOGY in later years of high school course, 138. ZOÖLOGY for secondary schools, 154—dissection should be postponed, 154.

VII. EXAMINATIONS.

GREEK, sight examinations, 80—examinations in grammar upon textbooks, 80. HISTORY, purpose of examinations in, 183. NATURAL HISTORY, entrance and final examinations for college, 141. ORAL OR WRITTEN, 120. TRANSLATIONS at sight, 62.

VIII. HIGH SCHOOLS.

ALGEBRA, systematic study of, in, 106. BOTANY preferred to zoölogy in, 139—morphology, comparative, in, 140—botany and zoölogy suggestions for courses of study, 140. CHEMISTRY to precede physics, 200 hours to each, 117, 118—physical science, secondary education that ignores the study of nature highly objectionable, 119—minority report, physics before chemistry, 120—experiments in physics, 125—experiments in chemistry, 127—nature studies, one-quarter of the time to, 123—three-fifths of the time employed in laboratory work, 139—one-fourth of the time devoted to, 141. ENGLISH, 90—rhetoric, 90. HISTORY, course of study, 163—topics for intensive study, 163. METEOROLOGY, high school course in, 231. MODERN LANGUAGES, 97. PHYSIOLOGY in later years of high school course, 138. POLITICAL ECONOMY, no formal instruction in, 165. NO PREPARATION for high school in botany, zoölogy, chemistry, physics, and mathematics, outside of arithmetic, 15. SECONDARY SCHOOLS do not exist for college preparation, 51. ZOÖLOGY, course of study in, 154—time for study, 154.

IX. LABORATORY AND FIELD-WORK.

CHEMISTRY, experiments in, 127—physics and chemistry, one-half time to laboratory work, 118—importance of laboratory work : loose work harmful, 119—value of keeping records, 119—physical experiments in elementary schools, 116—physics and chemistry, more abundant material for former, 122—experiments in physics in high school, 125. CIVICS, field studies in, 181. GEOGRAPHY, excursions, 212—materials for, 215. GEOLOGICAL field-work, 223. HISTORY, as a laboratory science, 169—field excursions, 181, 198. NATURE STUDIES, three-fifths of time employed in laboratory work, 139—materials, 143—natural science and geography, field-work, 59 —natural history must consist largely of laboratory work, 139—laboratory tests, superiority of, over written examinations, 140.

X. METHODS OF TEACHING.

ARITHMETIC, radical change in the teaching of, 23, 105—metric system to be taught by actual measurements, 105—method of teaching, should be, throughout, objective, 105—text-books subordinate to the living teacher, 105—rules should be taught inductively at the end of the subject, 105. ASTRONOMY by observation, 118. ENGLISH, elementary study, 87—composition writing criticised, 88—bad English, correction of, not recommended, 94. GERMAN AND FRENCH, methods of teaching, translation at sight, 100—modern languages, method of instruction, 100, 101, 102. GEOGRAPHY, methods of presentation, 216—topical recitation, 219—methods in lowest grades, 220—map drawing, 221—geography, methods in grammar grades, 222. GEOMETRY, demonstrative, 113—oral exercises in, 24—in grammar grades, 110. GREEK, inductive method criticised, 82—translation at sight, 83—first translation in the order of the original, 84—translation at sight, 19, 62. HISTORY, topical method recommended, 164—lectures, 188—written work in, 194—debates as a means of teaching, 198—illustrative methods, pictures, 197—devices for teaching, 191—better omit, than teach in the old-fashioned way, 189—historical teaching, methods of, 185. LATIN, composition limited to text read, 63—sounds, 66, 67—reading aloud, 68—understanding at sight, 71—caution as to inductive method, 75. METEOROLOGY, 227. NATURAL HISTORY, observational study with specimens in the hands of each pupil, 141—children must study the plant as a whole, and as a living organism, 142, 143—nature study, 143—guide to, 144. PHYSICS AND CHEMISTRY, re-discovery of laws not the aim, 118—scientific method important, 119. PHYSIOGRAPHY, methods in, 223.

XI. PRINCIPLES OF TEACHING.

BOTANY for primary schools, central thought, care and protection, 145. ENGLISH, purpose of, 87. FRENCH AND GERMAN, reason for introducing, into grammar schools, 96. GEOGRAPHY, general elementary, applied, physical geography and physiography, meteorology, geology, 204-209—physiography defined, 206—geography, order of observational and representative, descriptive, and rational, 211-214—as mental discipline, 214. GREEK COMPOSITION, 79—Homer, 78. HISTORY, 175—intensive study of eight years' course, 176—glib recitations devoid of thought, 190. LATIN, quality *versus* quantity, 62—cramming mode useless, 62—writing of, 62—undue prominence of rules, 65. YOUNG CHILDREN cannot generalize, 143.

XII. RELATIVE VALUES OF STUDIES.

CHEMISTRY to precede physics, 117. GEOGRAPHY, relations of, 204—physiography, objections to the term in minority report, 244. GREEK, Latin should precede, 77. HISTORY, relative value, 168. PHYSICAL SCIENCE, secondary education that ignores the study of nature highly objectionable, 119—relations of science, history, and geography to Latin, Greek, and mathematics, 13. PHYSIOLOGY, relation to other studies, 158.

XIII. SUPERVISION.

PHYSICAL SCIENCE, special teachers of, 117—special science superintendents, 119. SUPERINTENDENTS and principals should be teachers of teachers, 54.

XIV. TEACHERS, TRAINING OF TEACHERS, AND NORMAL SCHOOLS.

ENGLISH, special teachers of, 90. GEOGRAPHY, selection of new teachers, 217. GREEK, poor teaching of, 78. HISTORY, teachers of, 164—teaching by rote from text-books in grammar schools, 185—training of teachers, 186, 187—special teachers, 187. LATIN, teaching of, by untrained teachers, 64. MODERN LANGUAGES, preparation of teachers, 103. NORMAL SCHOOLS and colleges should supply better trained teachers, 18—normal schools should be better equipped, 54. PHYSICAL SCIENCE, necessity for intelligent teachers in, 119. PHYSIOLOGY, qualifications of teachers for, 161. SUMMER SCHOOLS, 54. TRAINED TEACHERS necessary, 18—teachers in elementary schools ill-prepared, 25—need of more highly trained teachers, 53—attitude of teacher's mind, 70—colleges and universities should assist in training teachers, 54—universities should establish training courses, 187.

REPORT OF THE COMMITTEE OF TEN

REPORT OF THE COMMITTEE OF TEN.

To the National Council of Education :

The Committee of Ten appointed at the meeting of the National Educational Association at Saratoga on the 9th of July, 1892, have the honor to present the following report : —

At the meeting of the National Council of Education in 1891, a Committee appointed at a previous meeting made a valuable report through their Chairman, Mr. James H. Baker, then Principal of the Denver High School, on the general subject of uniformity in school programmes and in requirements for admission to college.) The Committee was continued, and was authorized to procure a Conference on the subject of uniformity during the meeting of the National Council in 1892, the Conference to consist of representatives of leading colleges and secondary schools in different parts of the country. This Conference was duly summoned, and held meetings at Saratoga on July 7th, 8th, and 9th, 1892. There were present between twenty and thirty delegates. Their discussions took a wide range, but resulted in the following specific recommendations, which the Conference sent to the National Council of Education then in session.

1. That it is expedient to hold a conference of school and college teachers of each principal subject which enters into the programmes of secondary schools in the United States and into the requirements for admission to college — as, for example, of Latin, of geometry, or of American history — each conference to consider the proper limits of its subject, the best methods of instruction, the most desirable allotment of time for the subject, and the best methods of testing the pupils' attainments therein, and each conference to represent fairly the different parts of the country.

2. That a Committee be appointed with authority to select the members of these conferences and to arrange their meetings, the results of all the conferences to be reported to this Committee for such action as it may deem appropriate, and to form

the basis of a report to be presented to the Council by this Committee.

3. That this Committee consist of the following gentlemen :

CHARLES W. ELIOT, President of Harvard University, Cambridge, Mass., *Chairman.*

WILLIAM T. HARRIS, Commissioner of Education, Washington, D. C.

JAMES B. ANGELL, President of the University of Michigan, Ann Arbor, Mich.

JOHN TETLOW, Head Master of the Girls' High School and the Girls' Latin School, Boston, Mass.

JAMES M. TAYLOR, President of Vassar College, Poughkeepsie, N. Y.

OSCAR D. ROBINSON, Principal of the High School, Albany, N. Y.

JAMES H. BAKER, President of the University of Colorado, Boulder, Colo.

RICHARD H. JESSE, President of the University of Missouri, Columbia, Mo.

JAMES C. MACKENZIE, Head Master of the Lawrenceville School, Lawrenceville, N. J.

HENRY C. KING, Professor in Oberlin College, Oberlin, Ohio.

These recommendations of the Conference were adopted by the National Council of Education on the 9th of July, and the Council communicated the recommendations to the Directors of the National Educational Association, with the further recommendation that an appropriation not exceeding $2500 be made by the Association towards the expenses of these conferences. On the 12th of July the Directors adopted a series of resolutions under which a sum not exceeding $2500 was made available for this undertaking during the academic year 1892–93.

Every gentleman named on the above Committee of Ten accepted his appointment ; and the Committee met, with every member present, at Columbia College, New York City, from the 9th to the 11th of November, 1892, inclusive.

In preparation for this meeting, a table had been prepared by means of a prolonged correspondence with the principals of selected secondary schools in various parts of the country, which showed the subjects taught in forty leading secondary schools in the United States, and the total number of recitations, or exercises, allotted to each subject. Nearly two hundred schools were applied to for this information ; but it did not prove practicable to obtain within three months verified statements from more than forty schools. This table proved con-- clusively, first, that the total number of subjects taught in these secondary schools was nearly forty, thirteen of which, however, were found in only a few schools; secondly, that many of these subjects were taught for such short periods that little training could be derived from them; and thirdly, that the time allotted to the same subject in the different schools varied widely. Even for the older subjects, like Latin and algebra, there appeared to be a wide diversity of practice with regard to the time allotted to them. Since this table was comparative in its nature,—that is, permitted comparisons to be made between different schools,—and could be easily misunderstood and misapplied by persons who had small acquaintance with school programmes, it was treated as a confidential document; and was issued at first only to the members of the Committee of Ten and the principals of the schools mentioned in the table. Later, it was sent—still as a confidential paper—to the members of the several conferences organized by the Committee of Ten.

The Committee of Ten, after a preliminary discussion on November 9th, decided on November 10th to organize conferences on the following subjects:— 1. Latin; 2. Greek; 3. English; 4. Other Modern Languages; 5. Mathematics; 6. Physics, Astronomy, and Chemistry; 7. Natural History (Biology, including Botany, Zoölogy, and Physiology); 8. History, Civil Government, and Political Economy; 9. Geography (Physical Geography, Geology, and Meteorology). They also decided that each Conference should consist of ten members. They then proceeded to select the members of each of these Conferences, having regard in the selection to the scholarship and experience of the gentlemen named, to the fair division of the members between colleges on the one hand and schools on the other, and to the proper geographical distribution of the total membership. After selecting ninety members for the nine Conferences, the Committee decided on an additional number of names to be used as substitutes for persons originally chosen who should decline to serve, from two to four substitutes being selected for each Conference. In the selection of substitutes the Committee found it difficult to regard the geographical distribution of the persons selected with as much strictness as in the original selection; and, accordingly, when it became necessary to call on a considerable number of substitutes, the accurate geographical distribution of membership was somewhat impaired. The lists of the members of the several Conferences were finally adopted at a meeting of the Committee on November 11th; and the Chairman and Secretary of the Committee were then empowered to fill any vacancies which might occur.

The Committee next adopted the following list of questions as a guide for the discussions of all the Conferences, and directed that the Conferences be called together on the 28th of December:—

1. In the school course of study extending approximately from the age of six years to eighteen years — a course including the periods of both elementary and secondary instruction — at what age should the study which is the subject of the Conference be first introduced?

2. After it is introduced, how many hours a week for how many years should be devoted to it?

3. How many hours a week for how many years should be devoted to it during the last four years of the complete course; that is, during the ordinary high school period?

4. What topics, or parts, of the subject may reasonably be covered during the whole course?

5. What topics, or parts, of the subject may best be reserved for the last four years?

6. In what form and to what extent should the subject enter into college requirements for admission? Such questions as the sufficiency of translation at sight as a test of knowledge of a language, or the superiority of a laboratory examination in a scientific subject to a written examination on a text-book. are intended to be suggested under this head by the phrase "in what form."

7. Should the subject be treated differently for pupils who are going to college, for those who are going to a scientific school, and for those who, presumably. are going to neither?

8. At what stage should this differentiation begin, if any be recommended?

9. Can any description be given of the best method of teaching this subject throughout the school course?

10. Can any description be given of the best mode of testing attainments in this subject at college admission examinations?

11. For those cases in which colleges and universities permit a division of the admission examination into a preliminary and a final examination, separated by at least a year, can the best limit between the preliminary and final examinations be approximately defined?

The Committee further voted that it was expedient that the Conferences on Latin and Greek meet at the same place. Finally, all further questions of detail with regard to the calling and the instruction of the Conferences were referred to the Chairman with full power.

During the ensuing six weeks, the composition of the nine Conferences was determined in accordance with the measures adopted by tne Committee of Ten. Seventy persons originally selected by the Committee accepted the invitation of the Committee, and sixty-nine of these persons were present at the meetings of their respective Conferences on the 28th of December. Twenty substitutes accepted service, of whom twelve were persons selected by the Committee of Ten, and eight were selected under the authority granted to the Chairman and Secretary of the Committee in emergencies. One of these eight gentlemen was selected by a Conference at its first meeting. Two gentlemen who accepted service — one of the original members and one substitute — absented themselves from the meetings of their respective Conferences without giving any notice to the Chairman of the Committee of Ten, who was therefore unable to fill their places. With these two exceptions, all the Conferences met on December 28th with full membership.

The places of meeting were as follows : — for the Latin and Greek Conferences, the University of Michigan, Ann Arbor, Mich. ; for the English Conference, Vassar College, Poughkeepsie, N. Y. ; for the Conference on Other Modern Languages, the Bureau of Education, Washington, D. C. ; for the Conference on Mathematics, Harvard University, Cambridge, Mass. ; for the Conferences on Physics, Astronomy, and Chemistry, and on Natural History, the University of Chicago, Chicago, Ill. ; for the Conference on History, Civil Government, and Political Economy, the University of Wisconsin, Madison, Wis. ; for the Conference on Geography, the Cook

County Normal School, Englewood, Ill. The Committee of Ten and all the Conferences enjoyed the hospitality of the several institutions at which they met, and the members were made welcome at private houses during the sessions. Through the exertions of Mr. N. A. Calkins, Chairman of the Trustees of the National Educational Association, important reductions of railroad fares were procured for some members of the Committee and of the Conferences; but the reductions obtainable were less numerous and considerable than the National Council of Education had hoped. In filling a few vacancies of which notice was received shortly before December 28th, it was necessary to regard as one qualification nearness of residence to the appointed places of meeting; but on the whole the weight and effectiveness of the several Conferences were not impaired by the necessary replacement of twenty of the members originally selected by the Committee of Ten. The list of the members of the Conferences on the 28th of December was as follows: —

1. LATIN.

Professor CHARLES E. BENNETT, Cornell University, Ithaca, N. Y.

FREDERICK L. BLISS, Principal of the Detroit High School, Detroit, Mich.

JNO. T. BUCHANAN, Principal of the Kansas City High School, Kansas City, Mo.

WILLIAM C. COLLAR, Head Master of the Roxbury Latin School, Roxbury, Mass.

JOHN S. CROMBIE, Principal of the Adelphi Academy, Brooklyn, N. Y.

Professor JAMES H. DILLARD, Tulane University, New Orleans, La.

Rev. WILLIAM GALLAGHER, Principal of Williston Seminary, Easthampton, Mass.

Professor WILLIAM G. HALE, University of Chicago, Chicago, Ill.

Professor JOHN C. ROLFE, University of Michigan, Ann Arbor, Mich.

JULIUS SACHS, Principal of the Collegiate Institute for Boys, 38 West 59th Street, New York City.

2. GREEK.

E. W. COY, Principal of the Hughes High School, Cincinnati, O.

Professor MARTIN L. D'OOGE, University of Michigan, Ann Arbor, Mich.

A. F. FLEET, Superintendent of the Missouri Military Academy, Mexico, Mo.

ASHLEY D. HURT, Head Master of the High School, Tulane University, New Orleans, La.

ROBERT D. KEEP, Principal of the Free Academy, Norwich, Conn.
Professor ABBY LEACH, Vassar College, Poughkeepsie, N. Y.
CLIFFORD H. MOORE, Phillips Academy, Andover, Mass.
WILLIAM H. SMILEY, Principal of the High School, Denver, Colo.
Professor CHARLES F. SMITH, Vanderbilt University, Nashville, Tenn.
Professor BENJAMIN I. WHEELER, Cornell University, Ithaca, N. Y.

3. ENGLISH.

Professor EDWARD A. ALLEN, University of Missouri, Columbia, Mo.
F. A. BARBOUR, Michigan State Normal School, Ypsilanti, Mich.
Professor FRANK A. BLACKBURN, University of Chicago, Chicago, Ill.
Professor CORNELIUS B. BRADLEY, University of California, Berkeley, Calif.
Professor FRANCIS B. GUMMERE, Haverford College, Pa.
Professor EDWARD E. HALE, Jr., University of Iowa, Iowa City, Iowa.
Professor GEORGE L. KITTREDGE, Harvard University, Cambridge, Mass.
CHARLES L. LOOS, Jr., High School, Dayton, Ohio.
W. H. MAXWELL, Superintendent of Schools, Brooklyn, N. Y.
SAMUEL THURBER, Master in the Girls' High School, Boston, Mass.

4. OTHER MODERN LANGUAGES.

Professor JOSEPH L. ARMSTRONG, Trinity College, Durham, N. C.
THOMAS B. BRONSON, Lawrenceville School, Lawrenceville, N. J.
Professor ALPHONSE N. VAN DAELL, Massachusetts Institute of Technology, Boston, Mass.
CHARLES H. GRANDGENT, Director of Modern Language Instruction in the Public Schools, Boston, Mass.
Professor CHARLES HARRIS, Oberlin College, Oberlin, Ohio.
WILLIAM T. PECK, High School, Providence, R. I.
Professor SYLVESTER PRIMER, University of Texas, Austin, Texas.
JOHN J. SCHOBINGER, Principal of a Private School for Boys, Chicago, Ill.
ISIDORE H. B. SPIERS, William Penn Charter School, Philadelphia, Pa.
Professor WALTER D. TOY, University of North Carolina, Chapel Hill, N. C.

5. MATHEMATICS.

Professor WILLIAM E. BYERLY, Harvard University, Cambridge, Mass.
Professor FLORIAN CAJORI, Colorado College, Colorado Springs, Colo.
ARTHUR H. CUTLER, Principal of a Private School for Boys, New York City.
Professor HENRY B. FINE, College of New Jersey, Princeton, N. J.
W. A. GREESON, Principal of the High School, Grand Rapids, Mich.
ANDREW INGRAHAM, Swain Free School, New Bedford, Mass.
Professor SIMON NEWCOMB, Johns Hopkins University, and Washington, D. C.

Professor GEORGE D. OLDS, Amherst College, Amherst, Mass.
JAMES L. PATTERSON, Lawrenceville School, Lawrenceville, N. J.
Professor T. H. SAFFORD, Williams College, Williamstown, Mass.

6. PHYSICS, ASTRONOMY, AND CHEMISTRY.

Professor BROWN AYERS, Tulane University, New Orleans, La.
IRVING W. FAY, The Belmont School, Belmont, Calif.
ALFRED P. GAGE, English High School, Boston, Mass.
GEORGE WARREN KRALL, Manual Training School, Washington University, St. Louis, Mo.
Professor WILLIAM W. PAYNE, Carleton College, Northfield, Minn.
WILLIAM McPHERSON, Jr,, 2901 Collinwood Avenue, Toledo, Ohio.
Professor IRA REMSEN, Johns Hopkins University, Baltimore, Md.
Professor JAMES H. SHEPARD, South Dakota Agricultural College, Brookings, So. Dak.
Professor WILLIAM J. WAGGENER, University of Colorado, Boulder, Colo.
GEORGE R. WHITE, Phillips Exeter Academy, Exeter, N. H.

7. NATURAL HISTORY (BIOLOGY, INCLUDING BOTANY, ZOÖLOGY, AND PHYSIOLOGY).

Professor CHARLES E. BESSEY, University of Nebraska, Lincoln, Neb.
ARTHUR C. BOYDEN, Normal School, Bridgewater, Mass.
Professor SAMUEL F. CLARKE, Williams College, Williamstown, Mass.
Professor DOUGLAS H. CAMPBELL, Leland Stanford Jr. University, Palo Alto, Calif.
President JOHN M. COULTER, Indiana University, Bloomington, Ind.
Principal S. A. MERRITT, Helena, Montana.
W. B. POWELL, Superintendent of Schools, Washington, D. C.
CHARLES B. SCOTT, High School, St. Paul, Minn.
Professor ALBERT H. TUTTLE, University of Virginia, Charlottesville, Va.
O. S. WESTCOTT, Principal of the North Division High School, Chicago, Ill.

8. HISTORY, CIVIL GOVERNMENT, AND POLITICAL ECONOMY.

President CHARLES K. ADAMS, University of Wisconsin, Madison, Wis.
Professor EDWARD G. BOURNE, Adelbert College, Cleveland, Ohio.
ABRAM BROWN, Principal of the Central High School, Columbus, Ohio.
Professor A. B. HART, Harvard University, Cambridge, Mass.
RAY GREENE HULING, Principal of the High School, New Bedford, Mass.
Professor JESSE MACY, Iowa College, Grinnell, Iowa.
Professor JAMES HARVEY ROBINSON, University of Pennsylvania, Philadelphia, Pa.
Professor WILLIAM A. SCOTT, University of Wisconsin, Madison, Wis.
HENRY P. WARREN, Head Master of the Albany Academy, Albany, N. Y.
Professor WOODROW WILSON, College of New Jersey, Princeton, N. J.

9. GEOGRAPHY (PHYSICAL GEOGRAPHY, GEOLOGY, AND
METEOROLOGY).

Professor THOMAS C. CHAMBERLIN, University of Chicago, Chicago, Ill.
Professor GEORGE L. COLLIE, Beloit College, Beloit, Wis.
Professor W. M. DAVIS, Harvard University, Cambridge, Mass.
DELWIN A. HAMLIN, Master of the Rice Training School, Boston, Mass.
Professor EDWIN J. HOUSTON, Central High School, Philadelphia, Pa.
Professor MARK W. HARRINGTON, The Weather Bureau, Washington,
D. C.
CHARLES F. KING, Dearborn School, Boston, Mass.
FRANCIS W. PARKER, Principal of the Cook County Normal School,
Englewood, Ill.
G. M. PHILIPS, Principal of the State Normal School, West Chester, Pa.
Professor ISRAEL C. RUSSELL, University of Michigan, Ann Arbor, Mich.

The ninety members of the Conferences were divided as
follows, — forty-seven were in the service of colleges or universities, forty-two in the service of schools, and one was a
government official formerly in the service of a university.   A
considerable number of the college men, however, had also had
experience in schools.   Each Conference, in accordance with a
recommendation of the Committee of Ten, chose its own
Chairman and Secretary ; and these two officers prepared the
report of each Conference.   Six of the Chairmen were college
men, and three were school men ; while of the Secretaries, two
were college men and seven school men.   The Committee of
Ten requested that the reports of the Conferences should be
sent to their Chairman by the 1st of April, 1893 — three
months being thus allowed for the preparation of the reports.
Seven Conferences substantially conformed to this request of
the Committee ; but the reports from the Conferences on
Natural History and Geography were delayed until the second
week in July.   The Committee of Ten, being of course unable
to prepare their own report until all the reports of the December
Conferences had been received, were prevented from presenting
their report, as they had intended, at the Education Congress
which met at Chicago July 27th–29th.

All the Conferences sat for three days ; their discussions
were frank, earnest, and thorough ; but in every Conference an
extraordinary unity of opinion was arrived at.   The nine
reports are characterized by an amount. of agreement which

quite surpasses the most sanguine anticipations. Only two Conferences present minority reports, namely, the Conference on Physics, Astronomy, and Chemistry, and the Conference on Geography; and in the first case, the dissenting opinions touch only two points in the report of the majority, one of which is unimportant. In the great majority of matters brought before each Conference, the decision of the Conference was unanimous. When one considers the different localities, institutions, professional experiences, and personalities represented in each of the Conferences, the unanimity developed is very striking, and should carry great weight.

Before the 1st of October, 1893, the reports of the Conferences had all been printed, after revision in proof by the chairmen of the Conferences respectively, and had been distributed to the members of the Committee of Ten, together with a preliminary draft of a report for the Committee. With the aid of comments and suggestions received from members of the Committee a second draft of this report was made ready in print to serve as the ground-work of the deliberations of the Committee at their final meeting. This meeting was held at Columbia College from the 8th to the 11th of November, 1893, inclusive, every member being present except Professor King, who is spending the current academic year in Europe. The points of view and the fields of work of the different members of the Committee being fortunately various, the discussions at this prolonged meeting were vigorous and comprehensive, and resulted in a thorough revision of the preliminary report. This third revise having been submitted to the members of the Committee, a cordial agreement on both the form and the substance of the present report, with the exceptions stated in the minority report of President Baker, was arrived at after a correspondence which extended over three weeks. The report itself embodies the numerous votes and resolutions adopted by the Committee.

Professor King, having received in Europe the Conference reports, the two preliminary drafts of the Committee's report, and the third revise, desired to have his name signed to the final report.

The Council and the public will doubtless be impressed, at first sight, with the great number and variety of important changes urged by the Conferences; but on a careful reading of the appended reports it will appear that the spirit of the Conferences was distinctly conservative and moderate, although many of their recommendations are of a radical nature. The Conferences which found their tasks the most difficult were the Conferences on Physics, Astronomy, and Chemistry; Natural History; History, Civil Government, and Political Economy; and Geography; and these four Conferences make the longest and most elaborate reports, for the reason that these subjects are to-day more imperfectly dealt with in primary and secondary schools than are the subjects of the first five Conferences. The experts who met to confer together concerning the teaching of the last four subjects in the list of Conferences all felt the need of setting forth in an ample way what ought to be taught, in what order, and by what method. They ardently desired to have their respective subjects made equal to Latin, Greek, and Mathematics in weight and influence in the schools; but they knew that educational tradition was adverse to this desire, and that many teachers and directors of education felt no confidence in these subjects as disciplinary material. Hence the length and elaboration of these reports. In less degree, the Conferences on English and Other Modern Languages felt the same difficulties, these subjects being relatively new as substantial elements in school programmes.

The Committee of Ten requested the Conferences to make their reports and recommendations as specific as possible. This request was generally complied with; but, very naturally, the reports and recommendations are more specific concerning the selection of topics in each subject, the best methods of instruction, and the desirable appliances or apparatus, than concerning the allotment of time to each subject. The allotment of time is a very important matter of administrative detail; but it presents great difficulties, requires a comprehensive survey of the comparative claims of many subjects, and in different parts of the country is necessarily affected by the various local conditions and historical developments. Nevertheless, there will be found in the Conference reports recommendations of a fundamental and far-reaching character concerning the allotment of programme time to each subject.

It might have been expected that every Conference would have demanded for its subject a larger proportion of time than is now commonly assigned to it in primary and secondary schools; but, as a matter of fact, the reports are noteworthy for their moderation in this respect, — especially the reports on the old and well-established subjects. The Latin Conference declares that, — " In view of the just demand for more and better work in several other subjects of the preparatory course, it seemed clear to the Conference that no increase in the quantity of the preparation in Latin should be asked for." Among the votes passed by the Greek Conference will be noticed the following : — " That in making the following recommendations, this Conference desires that the average age at which pupils now enter college should be lowered rather than raised; and the Conference urges that no addition be made in the advanced requirements in Greek for admission to college." The Mathematical Conference recommends that the course in arithmetic in elementary schools should be abridged, and recommends only a moderate assignment of time to algebra and geometry. The Conference on Geography says of the present assignment of time to geography in primary and secondary schools that " it is the judgment of the Conference that too much time is given to the subject in proportion to the results secured. It is not their judgment that more time is given to the subject than it merits, but that either more should be accomplished, or less time taken to attain it."

Anyone who reads these nine reports consecutively will be struck with the fact that all these bodies of experts desire to have the elements of their several subjects taught earlier than they now are; and that the Conferences on all the subjects except the languages desire to have given in the elementary schools what may be called perspective views, or broad surveys, of their respective subjects — expecting that in later years of the school course parts of these same subjects will be taken up with more amplitude and detail. The Conferences on Latin, Greek, and the Modern Languages agree in desiring to have the study of foreign languages begin at a much earlier age than now, — the Latin Conference suggesting by a reference to European usage that Latin be begun from three to five years earlier than it commonly is now. The Conference on Mathematics wish to have given in elementary schools not only a general survey of arithmetic, but also the elements of algebra, and concrete geometry in connection with drawing. The Conference on Physics, Chemistry, and Astronomy urge that nature studies should constitute an important part of the elementary school course from the very beginning. The Conference on Natural History wish the elements of botany and zoölogy to be taught in the primary schools. The Conference on History wish the systematic study of history to begin as early as the tenth year of age, and the first two years of study to be devoted to mythology and to biography for the illustration of general history as well as of American history. Finally, the Conference on Geography recommend that the earlier course treat broadly of the earth, its environment and inhabitants, extending freely into fields which in later years of study are recognized as belonging to separate sciences.

In thus claiming entrance for their subjects into the earlier years of school attendance, the Conferences on the newer subjects are only seeking an advantage which the oldest subjects have long possessed. The elements of language, number, and geography have long been imparted to young children. As things now are, the high school teacher finds in the pupils fresh from the grammar schools no foundation of elementary mathematical conceptions outside of arithmetic; no acquaintance with algebraic language; and no accurate knowledge of geometrical forms. As to botany, zoölogy, chemistry, and physics, the minds of pupils entering the high school are ordinarily blank on these subjects. When college professors endeavor to teach chemistry, physics, botany, zoölogy, meteorology, or geology to persons of eighteen or twenty years of age, they discover that in most instances new habits of observing, reflecting, and recording have to be painfully acquired by the students, — habits which they should have acquired in early childhood. The college teacher of history finds in like manner that his subject has never taken

any serious hold on the minds of pupils fresh from the secondary
schools. He finds that they have devoted astonishingly little
time to the subject; and that they have acquired no habit of
historical investigation, or of the comparative examination of
different historical narratives concerning the same periods or
events. It is inevitable, therefore, that specialists in any one of
the subjects which are pursued in the high schools or colleges
should earnestly desire that the minds of young children
be stored with some of the elementary facts and principles of
their subject; and that all the mental habits, which the adult
student will surely need, begin to be formed in the child's
mind before the age of fourteen. It follows, as a matter of
course, that all the Conferences except the Conference on
Greek, make strong suggestions concerning the programmes of
primary and grammar schools, — generally with some reference
to the subsequent programmes of secondary schools. They
desire important changes in the elementary grades; and the
changes recommended are all in the direction of increasing
simultaneously the interest and the substantial training quality
of primary and grammar school studies.

If anyone feels dismayed at the number and variety of the
subjects to be opened to children of tender age, let him observe
that while these nine Conferences desire each their own subject
to be brought into the courses of elementary schools, they all
agree that these different subjects should be correlated and
associated one with another by the programme and by the
actual teaching. If the nine Conferences had sat all together
as a single body, instead of sitting as detached and even
isolated bodies, they could not have more forcibly expressed
their conviction that every subject recommended for introduction into elementary and secondary schools should help
every other; and that the teacher of each single subject should
feel responsible for the advancement of the pupils in all
subjects, and should distinctly contribute to this advancement.

On one very important question of general policy which
affects profoundly the preparation of all school programmes,
the Committee of Ten and all the Conferences are absolutely
unanimous. Among the questions suggested for discussion in
each Conference were the following: —

7. Should the subject be treated differently for pupils who are going to college, for those who are going to a scientific school, and for those who, presumably, are going to neither?

8. At what age should this differentiation begin, if any be recommended?

The 7th question is answered unanimously in the negative by the Conferences, and the 8th therefore needs no answer. The Committee of Ten unanimously agree with the Conferences. Ninety-eight teachers, intimately concerned either with the actual work of American secondary schools, or with the results of that work as they appear in students who come to college, unanimously declare that every subject which is taught at all in a secondary school should be taught in the same way and to the same extent to every pupil so long as he pursues it, no matter what the probable destination of the pupil may be, or at what point his education is to cease. Thus, for all pupils who study Latin, or history, or algebra, for example, the allotment of time and the method of instruction in a given school should be the same year by year. Not that all the pupils should pursue every subject for the same number of years; but so long as they do pursue it, they should all be treated alike. It has been a very general custom in American high schools and academies to make up separate courses of study for pupils of supposed different destinations, the proportions of the several studies in the different courses being various. The principle laid down by the Conferences will, if logically carried out, make a great simplification in secondary school programmes. It will lead to each subject's being treated by the school in the same way by the year for all pupils, and this, whether the individual pupil be required to choose between courses which run through several years, or be allowed some choice among subjects year by year.

Persons who read all the appended reports will observe the frequent occurrence of the statement that, in order to introduce the changes recommended, teachers more highly trained will be needed in both the elementary and the secondary schools. There are frequent expressions to the effect that a higher grade of scholarship is needed in teachers of the lower classes, or that the general adoption of some method urged by a Conference

2

must depend upon the better preparation of teachers in the high schools, model schools, normal schools, or colleges in which they are trained. The experienced principal or superintendent in reading the reports will be apt to say to himself, — "This recommendation is sound, but cannot be carried out without teachers who have received a training superior to that of the teachers now at my command." It must be remembered, in connection with these admissions, or expressions of anxiety, that the Conferences were urged by the Committee of Ten to advise the Committee concerning the best possible — almost the ideal — treatment of each subject taught in a secondary school course, without, however, losing sight of the actual condition of American schools, or pushing their recommendations beyond what might reasonably be considered attainable in a moderate number of years. The Committee believe that the Conferences have carried out wisely the desire of the Committee, in that they have recommended improvements, which, though great and seldom to be made at once and simultaneously, are by no means unattainable. The existing agencies for giving instruction to teachers already in service are numerous; and the normal schools and the colleges are capable of making prompt and successful efforts to supply the better trained and equipped teachers for whom the reports of the Conferences call.

Many recommendations will be found to be made by more' than one Conference. Thus, all the Conferences on foreign languages seem to agree that the introduction of two foreign languages in the same year is inexpedient; and all of them insist on practice in reading the foreign language aloud, on the use of good English in translating, and on practice in translating the foreign language at sight, and in writing it. Again, all the Conferences on scientific subjects dwell on laboratory work by the pupils as the best means of instruction, and on the great utility of the genuine laboratory note-book; and they all protest that teachers of science need at least as thorough a special training as teachers of languages or mathematics receive. In reading the reports, many instances will be noticed in which different Conferences have reached similar conclusions without any consultation, or have followed a common line of thought.

Your Committee now proceed to give summaries of the most important recommendations made by the Conferences as regards topics and methods, reserving the subject of time-allotment. But in so doing, they desire to say that the reading of these summaries should not absolve anyone interested in the general subject from reading with care the entire report of every Conference. The several reports are so full of suggestions and recommendations concisely and cogently stated that it is impossible to present adequate abstracts of them.

1. Latin.

An important recommendation of the Latin Conference is the recommendation that the study of Latin be introduced into American schools earlier than it now is. They recommend that translation at sight form a constant and increasing part of the examinations for admission to college and of the work of preparation. They next urge that practice in writing Latin should not be dissociated from practice in reading and translating; but, on the contrary, that the two should be carried on with equal steps. The Conference desire the schools to adopt a greater variety of Latin authors for beginners, and they give good reasons against the exclusive use of Caesar's Gallic War. They object to the common practice of putting the teaching of beginners into the hands of the youngest teachers, who have the slenderest equipment of knowledge and experience. They dwell on the importance of attending to pronunciation and reading aloud, to forms, vocabulary, syntax, and order, and to the means of learning to understand the Latin before translating it; and they describe and urge the importance of a higher ideal in translation than now prevails in secondary schools. The formal recommendations of the Conference, fourteen in number, will be found concisely stated in numbered paragraphs at the close of their report.

2. Greek.

The Conference on Greek agree with the Conference on Latin in recommending the cultivation of reading at sight in schools, and in recommending that practice in translation into the foreign language should be continued throughout the school course. They urge that three years be the minimum time for the study of Greek in schools; provided that Latin be studied four years. They would not have a pupil begin the study of Greek without a knowledge of the elements of Latin. They recommend the substitution of portions of the Hellenica for two books of the Anabasis in the requirements for admission to college, and the use of some narrative portions of Thucydides in schools. They urge that Homer should continue to be studied in all schools which provide instruction in Greek through three years, and they suggest that the Odyssey is to be preferred to the Iliad. They regret " that so few colleges through their admission examinations encourage reading at sight in schools." Like the Latin Conference, the Greek Conference urge that the reading of the text be constantly practiced by both teacher and pupil, " and that teachers require from their pupils no less intelligent reading of the text than accurate translation of the same." The Greek Conference also adopted a vote " to concur with the Latin Conference as to the age at which the study of Latin should be begun." The specific recommendations of the Conference will be found in brief form in the paragraphs at the head of the eleven numbered sections into which their report is divided.

3. ENGLISH.

The Conference on English found it necessary to deal with the study of English in schools below the high school grade as well as in the high school. Their opening recommendations deal with the very first years of school, and one of the most interesting and admirable parts of their report relates to English in the primary and the grammar schools.

The Conference are of the opinion that English should be pursued in the high school during the entire course of four years; but in making this recommendation the Conference have in mind both study of literature and training in the expression of thought. To the study of rhetoric they assign one hour a week in the third year of the high school course. To the subject of historical and systematic grammar they assign one hour a week

in the fourth year of the high school course. The intelligent
reader of the report of this Conference will find described in it
the means by which the study of English in secondary schools
is to be made the equal of any other study in disciplinary or
developing power. The Conference claim for English as much
time as the Latin Conference claim for Latin in secondary
schools ; and it is clear that they intend that the study shall be
in all respects as serious and informing as the study of Latin.
One of the most interesting opinions expressed by the Conference is " that the best results in the teaching of English in high
schools cannot be secured without the aid given by the study
of some other language ; and that Latin and German, by reason
of their fuller inflectional system, are especially suited to this
end." In the case of high schools, as well as in schools of lower
grade, the Conference declare that every teacher, whatever his
department, should feel responsible for the use of good English
on the part of his pupils. In several passages of this report
the idea recurs that training in English must go hand in hand
with the study of other subjects. Thus the Conference hope
for the study of the history and geography of the English-
speaking people, so far as these illustrate the development
of the English language. They mention that " the extent
to which the study of the sources of English words can be
carried in any school or class will depend on the acquaintance
the pupils possess with Latin, French, and German." They
say that the study of words should be so pursued as to illustrate the political, social, intellectual, and religious development of the English race ; and they urge that the admission of
a student to college should be made to depend largely on his
ability to write English, as shown in his examination books on
other subjects./ It is a fundamental idea in this report that the
study of every other subject should contribute to the pupil's
training in English ; and that the pupil's capacity to write
English should be made available, and be developed, in every
other department. The very specific recommendations of the
Conference as to English requirements for admission to colleges
and scientific schools are especially wise and valuable.

4. OTHER MODERN LANGUAGES.

The most novel and striking recommendation made by the Conference on Modern Languages is that an elective course in German or French be provided in the grammar school, the instruction to be open to children at about ten years of age. The Conference made this recommendation "in the firm belief that the educational effects of modern language study will be of immense benefit to all who are able to pursue it under proper guidance." They admit that the study of Latin presents the same advantages; but living languages seem to them better adapted to grammar school work. The recommendations of this Conference with regard to the number of lessons a week are specific. They even construct a table showing the time which should be devoted to modern languages in each of the last four years of the elementary schools and in each year of the high school. They plead that "all pupils of the same intelligence and the same degree of maturity be instructed alike, no matter whether they are subsequently to enter a college or scientific school, or intend to pursue their studies no farther." The Conference also state with great precision what in their judgment may be expected of pupils in German and French at the various stages of their progress. An important passage of the report treats of the best way to facilitate the progress of beginners; — pupils should be lifted over hard places; frequent reviews are not to be recommended; new texts stimulate interest and enlarge the vocabulary. Their recommendations concerning translation into English, reading aloud, habituating the ear to the sounds of the foreign language, and translating into the foreign language, closely resemble the recommendations of the Conferences on Latin, Greek, and English regarding the best methods of instruction in those languages. In regard to college requirements, the Conference agree with several other Conferences in stating "that college requirements for admission should coincide with the high school requirements for graduation." Finally, they declare that "the worst obstacle to modern language study is the lack of properly equipped instructors; and that it is the duty of universities, states, and cities to provide opportunities for the special preparation of modern language teachers."

5. MATHEMATICS.

The form of the report of the Conference on Mathematics differs somewhat from that of the other reports. This report is subdivided under five headings : — 1st, General Conclusions. 2nd, The Teaching of Arithmetic. 3rd, The Teaching of Concrete Geometry. 4th, The Teaching of Algebra. 5th, The Teaching of Formal or Demonstrative Geometry.

The first general conclusion of the Conference was arrived at unanimously. The Conference consisted of one government official and university professor, five professors of mathematics in as many colleges, one principal of a high school, two teachers of mathematics in endowed schools, and one proprietor of a private school for boys. The professional experience of these gentlemen and their several fields of work were various, and they came from widely separated parts of the country ; yet they were unanimously of opinion "that a radical change in the teaching of arithmetic was necessary." They recommend " that the course in arithmetic be at once abridged and enriched ; abridged by omitting entirely those subjects which perplex and exhaust the pupil without affording any really valuable mental discipline, and enriched by a greater number of exercises in simple calculation, and in the solution of concrete problems." They specify in detail the subjects which they think should be curtailed, or entirely omitted ; and they give in their special report on the teaching of arithmetic a full statement of the reasons on which their conclusion is based. They map out a course in arithmetic which, in their judgment, should begin about the age of six years, and be completed at about the thirteenth year of age.

The Conference next recommend that a course of instruction in concrete geometry with numerous exercises be introduced into the grammar schools ; and that this instruction should, during the earlier years, be given in connection with drawing. They recommend that the study of systematic algebra should be begun at the age of fourteen ; but that, in connection with the study of arithmetic, the pupils should earlier be made familiar with algebraic expressions and symbols, including the method of solving simple equations. " The Conference

believe that the study of demonstrative geometry should begin
at the end of the first year's study of algebra, and be carried on
by the side of algebra for the next two years, occupying about
two hours and a half a week." They are also of opinion "that
if the introductory course in concrete geometry has been well
taught, both plane and solid geometry can be mastered at this
time." Most of the improvements in teaching arithmetic which
the Conference suggest "can be summed up under the two
heads of giving the teaching a more concrete form, and paying
more attention to facility and correctness in work. The concrete system should not be confined to principles, but be
extended to practical applications in measuring and in physics."

In regard to the teaching of concrete geometry, the Conference urge that while the student's geometrical education should
begin in the kindergarten, or at the latest in the primary school,
systematic instruction in concrete or experimental geometry
should begin at about the age of ten for the average student,
and should occupy about one school hour a week for at least
three years. From the outset of this course, the pupil should
be required to express himself verbally as well as by drawing
and modelling. He should learn to estimate by the eye, and
to measure with some degree of accuracy, lengths, angular
magnitudes, and areas; to make accurate plans from his own
measurements and estimates; and to make models of simple
geometrical solids. The whole work in concrete geometry will
connect itself on the one side with the work in arithmetic, and
on the other with elementary instruction in physics. With the
study of arithmetic is therefore to be intimately associated the
study of algebraic signs and forms, of concrete geometry, and
of elementary physics. Here is a striking instance of the interlacing of subjects which seems so desirable to every one of the
nine Conferences.

Under the head of teaching algebra, the Conference set forth
in detail the method of familiarizing the pupil with the use of
algebraic language during the study of arithmetic. This part
of the report also deals clearly with the question of the time
required for the thorough mastery of algebra through quadratic
equations. The report on the teaching of demonstrative geometry is a clear and concise statement of the best method of

teaching this subject. It insists on the importance of elegance and finish in geometrical demonstration, for the reason that the discipline for which geometrical demonstration is to be chiefly prized is a discipline in complete, exact, and logical statement. If slovenliness of expression, or awkwardness of form, is tolerated, this admirable discipline is lost. The Conference therefore recommend an abundance of oral exercises in geometry — for which there is no proper substitute — and the rejection of all demonstrations which are not exact and formally perfect. Indeed throughout all the teaching of mathematics the Conference deem it important that great stress be laid by the teacher on accuracy of statement and elegance of form as well as on clear and rigorous reasoning. Another very important recommendation in this part of the report is to be found in the following passage, — "As soon as the student has acquired the art of rigorous demonstration, his work should cease to be merely receptive. He should begin to devise constructions and demonstrations for himself. Geometry cannot be mastered by reading the demonstrations of a text-book; and while there is no branch of elementary mathematics in which purely receptive work, if continued too long, may lose its interest more completely, there is also none in which independent work can be made more attractive and stimulating." These observations are entirely in accordance with the recent practice of some colleges in setting admission examination papers in geometry which demand of the candidates some capacity to solve new problems, or rather to make new application of familiar principles.

6. PHYSICS, CHEMISTRY, AND ASTRONOMY.

The Conference on this subject were urgent that the study of simple natural phenomena be introduced into elementary schools; and it was the sense of the Conference that at least one period a day from the first year of the primary school should be given to such study. Apparently the Conference entertained the opinion that the present teachers in elementary schools are ill prepared to teach children how to observe simple natural phenomena; for their second recommendation was that special science teachers or superintendents be appointed to instruct the teachers of elementary schools in the methods of teaching natural phenomena. The Conference was clearly of opinion that from the beginning this study should be pursued by the pupil chiefly, though not exclusively, by means of experiments and by practice in the use of simple instruments for making physical measurements. The report dwells repeatedly on the importance of the study of things and phenomena by direct contact. It emphasizes the necessity of a large proportion of laboratory work in the study of physics and chemistry, and advocates the keeping of laboratory note-books by the pupils, and the use of such note-books as part of the test for admission to college. At the same time the report points out that laboratory work must be conjoined with the study of a text-book and with attendance at lectures or demonstrations; and that intelligent direction by a good teacher is as necessary in a laboratory as it is in the ordinary recitation or lecture room. The great utility of the laboratory note-book is emphatically stated. To the objection that the kind of instruction described requires much time and effort on the part of the teacher, the Conference reply that to give good instruction in the sciences requires of the teacher more work than to give good instruction in mathematics or the languages; and that the sooner this fact is recognized by those who have the management of schools the better for all concerned. The science teacher must regularly spend much time in collecting materials, preparing experiments, and keeping collections in order; and this indispensable labor should be allowed for in programmes and salaries. As regards the means of testing the progress of the pupils in physics and chemistry, the Conference were unanimously of opinion that a laboratory examination should always be combined with an oral or written examination, neither test taken singly being sufficient. There was a difference of opinion in the Conference on the question whether physics should precede chemistry, or chemistry physics. The logical order would place physics first; but all the members of the Conference but one advised that chemistry be put first for practical reasons which are stated in the majority report. A sub-committee of the Conference has prepared lists of experiments in physics and chemistry for the use of secondary schools, — not, of course, as a prescription, but only as a suggestion, and a somewhat precise indication of the topics which the Conference had in mind, and of the limits of the instruction.

7. NATURAL HISTORY.

The Conference on Natural History unanimously agreed that the study of botany and zoölogy ought to be introduced into the primary schools at the very beginning of the school course, and be pursued steadily, with not less than two periods a week, throughout the whole course below the high school. In the next place they agreed that in these early lessons in natural science no text-book should be used; but that the study should constantly be associated with the study of literature, language, and drawing. It was their opinion that the study of physiology should be postponed to the later years of the high school course; but that in the high school, some branch of natural history proper should be pursued every day throughout at least one year. Like the report on Physics, Chemistry, and Astronomy, the report on Natural History emphasizes the absolute necessity of laboratory work by the pupils on plants and animals; and would have careful drawing insisted on from the beginning of the instruction. As the laboratory note-book is recommended by the Conference on Physics, so the Conference on Natural History recommends that the pupils should be made to express themselves clearly and exactly in words, or by drawings, in describing the objects which they observe; and they believe that this practice will be found a valuable aid in training the pupils in the art of expression. They agree with the Conference on Physics, Chemistry, and Astronomy that science examinations should include both a written and a laboratory test, and that the laboratory note-books of the pupils should be produced at the examination. The recommendations of this Conference are therefore very similar to those of the sixth Conference, so far as methods go; but there are appended to the general report of the Conference on Natural History sub-reports which describe the proper topics, the best order of topics, and the right methods of instruction in botany for schools below the high school, and for the high

school itself, and in zoölogy for the secondary schools.
Inasmuch as both the subject matter and the methods of
instruction in natural history are much less familiar to ordinary
school teachers than the matter and the methods in the languages and mathematics, the Conference believed that descriptive details were necessary in order to give a clear view of
the intentions of the Conference. In another sub-report the
Conference give their reasons for recommending the postpone-
ment to the latest possible time of the study of physiology and
hygiene. Like the sixth Conference, the Conference on Natural
History protest that no person should be regarded as qualified
to teach natural science who has not had special training for
this work, — a preparation at least as thorough as that of their
fellow teachers of mathematics and the languages.

8. History, Civil Government, and Political Economy.

The Conference on History, Civil Government, and Political
Economy had a task different in some respects from those of
other Conferences. It is now-a-days admitted that language,
natural science, and mathematics should each make a substantial part of education; but the function of history in education
is still very imperfectly apprehended. Accordingly, the eighth
Conference were at pains to declare their conception of the
object of studying history and civil government in schools, and
their belief in the efficiency of these studies in training the
judgment, and in preparing children for intellectual enjoyments
in after years, and for the exercise at maturity of a salutary
influence upon national affairs. They believed that the time
devoted in schools to history and the allied subjects should be
materially increased; and they have therefore presented arguments in favor of that increase. At the same time, they state
strongly their conviction that they have recommended " nothing
that was not already being done in some good schools, and that
might not reasonably be attained wherever there is an efficient
system of graded schools." This Conference state quite as
strongly as any other their desire to associate the study of their
particular subject with that of other subjects which enter into
every school programme. They declare that the teaching of

history should be intimately connected with the teaching of
English; that pupils should be encouraged to avail themselves
of their knowledge of ancient and modern languages; and that
their study of history should be associated with the study of
topography and political geography, and should be supplemented by the study of historical and commercial geography,
and the drawing of historical maps. They desire that historical
works should be used for reading in schools, and that subjects
of English composition should be drawn from the lessons in
history. They would have historical poems committed to
memory, and the reading of biographies and historical novels
encouraged. While they are of opinion that political economy
should not be taught in secondary schools, they urge that, in
connection with United States history, civil government, and
commercial geography, instruction should be given in the most
important economic topics. The Conference would therefore
have the instruction in history made contributary to the work
in three other school departments, namely, English, geography,
and drawing. The subject of civil government they would
associate with both history and geography. They would introduce it into the grammar school by means of oral lessons, and
into the high school by means of a text-book with collateral
reading and oral lessons. In the high school they believe that
the study of civil government may be made comparative, —
that is, that the American method may be compared with
foreign systems.

Although the Conference was made up of very diverse
elements, every member of the Conference was heartily in
favor of every vote adopted. This remarkable unanimity was
not obtained by the silence of dissentients, or the withdrawal
of opposition on disputed points. It was the natural result of
the strong conviction of all the members, that history, when
taught by the methods advocated in their report, deserves a
position in school programmes which would give it equal
dignity and importance with any of the most favored subjects,
and that the advantages for all children of the rational study of
history ought to be diffused as widely as possible. On one
point they made a clearer declaration than any other Conference; although several other Conferences indicate similar

opinions. They declared that their interest was chiefly " in the school children who have no expectation of going to college, the larger number of whom will not even enter a high school," and that their " recommendations are in no way directed to building up the colleges, or increasing the number of college students." Like every other Conference, they felt anxious about the qualifications of the teachers who are to be entrusted with the teaching of history, and they urged that only teachers who have had adequate special training should be employed to teach history and civil government. In their specific recommendations they strongly urge that the historical course be made continuous from year to year, and extend through eight years, and in this respect be placed upon the same footing with other substantial subjects.

The answers of this Conference to the questions contained in the memorandum sent to the Conferences by the Committee of Ten were specific and clear. They will be found in an appendix to the report of the Conference.

In regard to the time to be devoted to history in school programmes, this Conference ask for not less than three periods a week throughout a course of eight years; and they suggest that some of this time can be found by contracting the course in arithmetic, and using for history a part of the time now given to political geography and to language study. Of these eight years they suggest that four should be in the high school and four in the grammar school. They " especially recommend such a choice of subjects as will give pupils in the grammar schools an opportunity of studying the history of other countries, and to the high schools one year's study on the intensive method."

A large portion of the report is necessarily taken up with the description of what the Conference consider the most suitable historical topics and the best methods of teaching history. This portion of the report does not admit of any useful presentation in outline; it must be read in full.

With regard to examinations in history for admission to college, the Conference protest " against the present lax and inefficient system," and seem to sum up their own desires on this subject in the statement that " the requirements for college ought to be so framed that the methods of teaching best adapted to meet them will also be best for all pupils."

Like the Conferences on scientific subjects the Conference on History insist on note-books, abstracts, special reports, and other written work, as desirable means of teaching. If the recommendations of the nine Conferences should be carried out in grammar and high schools, there would certainly be at least one written exercise a day for every pupil, — a result which persons interested in training children to write English deem it important to accomplish.

The observations of the Conference on geographical training in connection with history are interesting and suggestive, as are also the recurring remarks on the need of proper apparatus for teaching history, such as maps, reference-libraries, historical pictures, and photographs. It is not the natural sciences alone which need school apparatus.

9. Geography.

Considering that geography has been a subject of recognized value in elementary schools for many generations, and that a considerable portion of the whole school time of children has long been devoted to a study called by this name, it is somewhat startling to find that the report of the Conference on Geography deals with more novelties than any other report; exhibits more dissatisfaction with prevailing methods; and makes, on the whole, the most revolutionary suggestions. This Conference had but nine members present at its sessions; and before the final revision of its report had been accomplished, one of the most valued of its members died. Seven members sign the majority report, and the minority report is presented by one member. The dissenting member, however, while protesting against the views of the majority on many points, concurs with the majority in some of the most important conclusions arrived at by the Conference.

It is obvious on even a cursory reading of the majority and minority reports that geography means for all the members of this Conference something entirely different from the term geography as generally used in school programmes. Their definition of the word makes it embrace not only a description

of the surface of the earth, but also the elements of botany,
zoölogy, astronomy, and meteorology, as well as many considerations pertaining to commerce, government, and ethnology.
"The physical environment of man" expresses as well as any
single phrase can the Conference's conception of the principal
subject which they wish to have taught. No one can read the
reports without perceiving that the advanced instruction in
geography which the Conference conceive to be desirable and
feasible in high schools cannot be given until the pupils have
mastered many of the elementary facts of botany, zoölogy,
geometry, and physics. It is noteworthy also that this ninth
Conference, like the seventh, dealt avowedly and unreservedly
with the whole range of instruction in primary and secondary
schools. They did not pretend to treat chiefly instruction in
secondary schools, and incidentally instruction in the lower
schools; but, on the contrary, grasped at once the whole problem, and described the topics, methods, and apparatus appropriate to the entire course of twelve years. They recognized that
complete descriptions would be necessary in all three branches
of the subject, — topics, methods, and equipment; and they
have given these descriptions with an amplitude and force
which leave little to be desired. More distinctly than any
other Conference, they recognized that they were presenting an
ideal course which could not be carried into effect everywhere
or immediately. Indeed at several points they frankly state
that the means of carrying out their recommendations are not
at present readily accessible; and they exhibit the same anxiety
which is felt by several other Conferences about training
teachers for the kind of work which the Conference believe to
be desirable. After the full and interesting descriptions of the
relations and divisions of geographical science, as the Conference define it, the most important sections of their report relate
to the methods and means of presenting the subject in schools,
and to the right order in developing it. The methods which
they advocate require not only better equipped teachers, but
better means of illustrating geographical facts in the schoolroom, such as charts, maps, globes, photographs, models,
lantern slides, and lanterns. Like all the other Conferences
on scientific subjects, the ninth Conference dwell on the im-

portance of forming from the start good habits of observing correctly and stating accurately the facts observed. They also wish that the instruction in geography may be connected with the instruction in drawing, history, and English. They believe that meteorology may be taught as an observational study in the earliest years of the grammar school, the scholars being even then made familiar with the use of the thermometer, the wind-vane, and the rain-gauge ; and that it may be carried much farther in the high school years, after physics has been studied, so that the pupils may then attain a general understanding of topographical maps, of pressure and wind charts, of iso-thermal charts, and of such complicated subjects as weather prediction, rainfall and the distribution of rain, storms, and the seasonal variations of the atmosphere. Their conception of physiography is a very comprehensive one. In short, they recommend a study of physical geography which would em-brace in its scope the elements of half-a-dozen natural sciences, and would bind together in one sheaf the various gleanings which the pupils would have gathered from widely separated fields. There can be no doubt that the study would be interest-ing, informing, and developing, or that it would be difficult and in every sense substantial.

It already appears that the nine Conferences have attended carefully to three out of the five subjects which it was the intention of the National Council of Education that they should examine. They have discussed fully the proper limits of the several subjects of instruction in secondary schools, the best methods of instruction, and the best methods of testing pupils' attainments. The Conferences were equally faithful in dis-cussing the other two subjects committed to them by the Council, namely, the most desirable allotment of time for each subject, and the requirements for admission to college.

The next subject which the Committee of Ten, following the guidance of the Conferences, desire to present to the Council is, therefore, the allotment of school time among the various subjects of study. It is the obvious duty of the Committee, in the first place, to group together in tabular form the numer-ous suggestions on this subject made by the Conferences.

3

TABLE I.

SUBJECT.	Elementary Grades.—Primary and Grammar School.								Secondary School.—High School or Academy.			
	1st Year. Age. 6–7.	2d Year. 7–8.	3d Year. 8–9.	4th Year. 9–10.	5th Year. 10–11.	6th Year. 11–12.	7th Year. 12–13.	8th Year. 13–14.	9th Year. 14–15.	10th Year. 15–16.	11th Year. 16–17.	12th Year. 17–18.
1. LATIN.	Reasons given for beginning Latin earlier than is now the custom.								5 p. a wk.	5 p. a wk.	5 p. a wk.	5 p. a wk.
2. GREEK.							Latin to be begun a year before Greek.			5 p. a wk.	4 p. a wk.	4 p. a wk.
3. ENGLISH.	Pupils to reproduce orally stories told them, to invent stories and describe objects.		Supplementary reading begun — and continued through all the grades. Composition begun — writing narratives and descriptions — oral and written exercises on forms and the sentence.				From this grade no reader to be used.	Grammar, 3 p. a wk.	Literature, 3 p. a wk. Composition, 2 p. a wk.	Literature, 3 p. a wk. Composition, 2 p. a wk.	Literature, 3 p. a wk. Composition, 1 p. a wk. Rhetoric, 1 p. a wk.	Literature, 3 p. a wk. Composition, 1 p. a wk. Grammar, 1 p. a wk.
4. MODERN LANGUAGES.					Elective German or French, 5 p. a wk.	Elective German or French, 4 p. a wk.	Elective German or French, 3 p. a wk. at least.	Elective German or French, 3 p. a wk. at least.	The language begun below, 4 p. a wk.	The same language, 4 p. a wk. Second language, 4 p. a wk.	The same language, 4 p. a wk. Second language, 4 p. a wk.	The same language, 4 p. a wk. Second language, 4 p. a wk.

	First eight years					High-school years			
5. MATHEMATICS.	Arithmetic during first eight years, with algebraic expressions and symbols and simple equations — no specific number of hours being recommended.	Concrete Geometry, 1 p. a wk.	Concrete Geometry, 1 p. a wk.	Concrete Geometry, 1 p. a wk.	Concrete Geometry, 1 p. a wk.	Algebra, 5 p. a wk.	Algebra or Book-keeping and Commercial Arithmetic, 2½ p. a wk. Geometry, 2½ p. a wk.	Algebra or Book-keeping and Commercial Arithmetic, 2½ p. a wk. Geometry, 2½ p. a wk.	Trigonometry and higher Algebra for candidates for scientific schools.
6. PHYSICS, CHEMISTRY, AND ASTRONOMY.	Study of natural phenomena 5 p. a wk. through first eight years by experiments, including physical measurements and the recommendations of Conferences 7 and 9.					Elective Astronomy, 5 p. a wk. 12 wks.		Chemistry, 5 p. a wk.	Physics, 5 p. a wk.
7. NAT. HISTORY.	Through first eight years 2 p. a wk., of not less than 30 minutes each, devoted to plants and animals; the instruction to be correlated with language, drawing, literature, and geography.					One yr. (which yr. not specified) 5 p. a wk. for botany or zoölogy. Half-yr. (late in course) anatomy, physiology, and hygiene, 5 p. a wk.			
8. HISTORY.		Biography & Mythology, 3 p. wk.	American History and elements of civil government, 3 p. a wk.	Greek and Roman History, 3 p. a wk.		French History, 3 p. a wk.	English History, 3 p. a wk.	American History, 3 p. a wk.	A special period intensively, and civil government, 3 p. a wk.
9. GEOGRAPHY.	Time allotted in first eight years to equal that given to number work. The subject — the earth, its environment and inhabitants, including the elements of astronomy, meteorology, zoölogy, botany, history, commerce, races, religions, and governments.			Physical Geography.		(Physiography, geology, or meteorology at some part of the high school course. Possibly more than one of these where election is allowed.)		Elective Meteorology, ½ this year or next	Elective geology or physiography, ½ yr.

Abbreviations: p. = a recitation period of 40–45 minutes; wk. = week; yr. = year.

Having exhibited the programme-time suggestions of the Conferences, it will remain for the Committee to construct a flexible and comprehensive schedule of studies, based on the recommendations of the Conferences.

The preceding table exhibits the demands for programme time made by all the Conferences. It will be seen at once that this table does not yield, without modification, a practical programme. The nine Conferences acted separately, and were. studying each its own needs, and not the comparative needs of all the subjects. It was not for them to balance the different interests, but for each to present strongly one interest. It will further be noticed that some of their demands are not specific, — that is, they do not call for any specified number of recitation periods for a definite number of weeks during a stated number of years. The Conferences on Languages and History are the most definite in their recommendations, the Conferences on Mathematics and the Sciences being much less definite. Table I. is therefore not a programme, but the materials from which serviceable programmes may be constructed.

The Committee of Ten deliberately placed in this one table the recommendations of the Conferences for the elementary grades and the recommendations for secondary schools, in order that the sequence of the recommendations for each subject might be clearly brought out. The recommendations made for the secondary schools presuppose in many cases that the recommendations made for the elementary schools have been fulfilled; or, at least, in many cases the Conferences would have made different recommendations for the secondary schools, if they had been compelled to act on the assumption that things must remain just as they are in the elementary schools.

At this point it is well to call attention to the list of subjects which the Conferences deal with as proper for secondary schools. They are: 1. languages — Latin, Greek, English, German, and French, (and locally Spanish); 2. mathematics — algebra, geometry, and trigonometry; 3. general history, and the intensive study of special epochs; 4. natural history — including descriptive astronomy, meteorology, botany, zoölogy, physiology, geology, and ethnology, most of which subjects may be conveniently grouped under the title of physical geography; and 5. physics and chemistry. The Committee of Ten assent to this list, both for what it includes and for what it excludes, with some practical qualifications to be mentioned below.

Table II. exhibits the total amount of instruction (estimated by the number of weekly periods assigned to each subject) to be given in a secondary school during each year of a four years' course, on the supposition that the recommendations of the Conferences are all carried out.

TABLE II.

1ST SECONDARY SCHOOL YEAR.

Latin . . . . 5 p.
English Literature, 3 p. }
" Composition, 2 p. } . . . 5 p.
German or French . . . . 4 p.
Algebra . . . . 5 p.
History . . . . 3 p.

                                    22 p.

2ND SECONDARY SCHOOL YEAR.

Latin . . . . 5 p.
Greek . . . . 5 p.
English Literature, 3 p. }
" Composition, 2 p. } . . . . 5 p.
German . . . . 4 p.
French . . . . 4 p.
Algebra,* 2½ p. }
Geometry, 2½ p. } . . . . 5 p.
Astronomy (12 weeks) . . . . . 5 p.
Botany or Zoölogy . . . . 5 p.
History . . . . 3 p.

                                    37½ p.

* Option of book-keeping and commercial arithmetic.

3RD SECONDARY SCHOOL YEAR.

Latin . . . . 5 p.
Greek . . . . 4 p.
English Literature, 3 p. }
" Composition, 1 p. } . . . 5 p.
Rhetoric, 1 p. }
German . . . . 4 p.
French . . . . 4 p.
Algebra* . . . . 2½ p.
Geometry . . . . 2½ p.
Chemistry . . . . 5 p.
History . . . . 3 p.

                                    35 p.

* Option of book-keeping and commercial arithmetic.

4TH SECONDARY SCHOOL YEAR.

Latin . . . . 5 p.
Greek . . . . 4 p.
English Literature, 3 p. }
" Composition, 1 p. } . . . 5 p.
" Grammar, 1 p. }
German . . . . 4 p.
French . . . . 4 p.
Trigonometry, 2 p. ½ yr. }
Higher Algebra, 2 p. ½ yr. } . . . 2 p.
Physics . . . . 5 p.
Anatomy, Physiology, and Hygiene, ½ yr. . . . . 5 p.
History . . . . 3 p.
Geol. or Physiography, 3 p. ½ yr. }
Meteorology, 3 p. ½ yr. } 3 p.

                                    37½ p.

The method of estimating the amount of instruction offered
in any subject by the number of recitation periods assigned to
it each week for a given number of years or half years is in
some respects an inadequate one, for it takes no account
of the scope and intensity of the instruction given during
the periods; but so far as it goes, it is trustworthy and instructive. It represents with tolerable accuracy the proportional expenditure which a school is making on a given
subject, and therefore the proportional importance which the
school attaches to that subject. It also represents roughly
the proportion of the pupil's entire school time which he can
devote to a given subject, provided he is free to take all the
instruction offered in that subject. All experience shows
that subjects deemed important get a large number of weekly
periods, while those deemed unimportant get a small number.
Moreover, if the programme time assigned to a given subject
be insufficient, the value of that subject as training cannot be
got, no matter how good the quality of the instruction.

Every one of these years, except the first, contains much
more instruction than any one pupil can follow; but, looking
at the bearing of the table on the important question of educational expenditure, it is encouraging to observe that there are
already many secondary schools in this country in which
quite as many subjects are taught as are mentioned in this
table, and in which there are more weekly periods of instruction provided for separate classes than are found in any year of
the table. In some urban high schools which provide from
five to nine different courses of three to five years each, and
in some endowed secondary schools which maintain two or
three separate courses called Classical, Latin-scientific, and
English, or designated by similar titles, the total number of
weekly periods of unrepeated instruction given to distinct
classes is even now larger than the largest total of weekly
periods found in Table II. The annual expenditure in such
schools is sufficient to provide all the instruction called for by
Table II. The suggestions of the Conferences presuppose that
all the pupils of like intelligence and maturity in any subject
study it in the same way and to the same extent, so long as
they study it at all,—this being a point on which all the

Conferences insist strongly. No provision is made, therefore, for teaching Latin, or algebra, or history to one portion of a class four times a week, and to another portion of the same class only thrice or twice a week. Such provisions are very common in American schools; but the recommendations of the Conferences, if put into effect, would do away with all expenditures of this sort.

It clearly appears from Table II. that the recommendations of the Conferences on scientific subjects have been moderate so far as the proposed allotment of time to them is concerned. The Conferences on Physics, Chemistry and Astronomy, Natural History, and Geography held one combined session in Chicago, and passed a resolution that one-fourth of the whole high school course ought to be devoted to natural science, their intention doubtless being that each pupil should devote one quarter of his time to science; yet if all the time asked for in secondary schools by the scientific Conferences be added together, it will appear, first, that the rare pupil who should take all the scientific instruction provided would need for it only one quarter of his time, and secondly, that less than one-sixth of the whole instruction to be given in accordance with the combined recommendations of all the Conferences is devoted to subjects of natural science. The first year of the secondary school course according to Table II. will contain no science at all; and it is only in the last year of the secondary school that the proportion of natural science teaching rises to one-fourth of the whole instruction.

In studying these two tables which result from the recommendations of the Conferences, the Committee of Ten perceived at once, that if the recommendations are to be carried out, so far as offering the instruction proposed is concerned, a selection of studies for the individual pupil must be made in the second, third, and fourth years of the secondary school course. This selection will obviously be made in different ways in different schools. Any school principal may say, — "With the staff at my command I can teach only five subjects out of those proposed by the Conferences in the manner proposed. My school shall therefore be limited to these five." Another school may be able to teach in the thorough manner proposed five subjects, but some or all of these five may be different from those selected by the first school. A larger or richer school may be able to teach all the subjects mentioned, and by the methods and with the apparatus described. In the last case, each pupil, under the supervision of the teachers, and with the advice of parents or friends, may make choice between several different four-years' courses arranged by the school; or, if the school authorities prefer, the pupil may be allowed to make year by year a carefully guided choice among a limited number of subjects; or these two methods may be combined. Selection for the individual is necessary to thoroughness, and to the imparting of power as distinguished from information; for any large subject whatever, to yield its training value, must be pursued through several years and be studied from three to five times a week, and if each subject studied is thus to claim a considerable fraction of the pupil's school time, then clearly the individual pupil can give attention to only a moderate number of subjects.

In Table II. the number of weekly periods assigned to a single subject varies from two to five, about half of the assignments being made for five periods a week. There is an obvious convenience in the number five because it ordinarily gives one period a day for five days in the week; but there is also an obvious disadvantage in making too free use of the number five. It practically limits to three or, at most, four, the number of subjects which the individual pupil may pursue simultaneously; and this limit is inexpedient in a four years' programme.

The Committee have therefore prepared the following modification of Table II., using four as the standard number of weekly periods, except in the first year of a new language, and in the few cases in which the Conferences advise a number smaller than four. By this means the total number of periods is somewhat reduced, except in the first year, and the numbers of periods allotted to different subjects are made more consonant, each with the others. The result is only a correlation and adjustment of the recommendations of the Conferences, no judgment or recommendation of the Committee being expressed in it.

TABLE III. *4. p. Scheme*

1st Secondary School Year.		2nd Secondary School Year.	
Latin	5 p.	Latin	4 p.
English Literature, 2p.		Greek	5 p.
" Composition, 2 p.	4 p.	English Literature, 2 p.	4 p.
German [or French]	5 p.	" Composition, 2 p.	
Algebra	4 p.	German, continued	4 p.
History of Italy, Spain, and France	3 p.	French, begun	5 p.
Applied Geography (European political — continental and oceanic flora and fauna)	4 p.	Algebra,* 2 p.	4 p.
		Geometry, 2 p.	
		Botany or Zoölogy	4 p.
	25 p.	English History to 1688	3 p.
			33 p.
		* Option of book-keeping and commercial arithmetic.	

3rd Secondary School Year.		4th Secondary School Year.	
Latin	4 p.	Latin	4 p.
Greek	4 p.	Greek	4 p.
English Literature, 2 p.		English Literature, 2 p.	
" Composition, 1 p.	4 p.	" Composition, 1 p.	4 p.
Rhetoric, 1 p.		" Grammar, 1 p.	
German	4 p.	German	4 p.
French	4 p.	French	4 p.
Algebra,* 2 p.	4 p.	Trigonometry,	2 p.
Geometry, 2 p.		Higher Algebra,	
Physics	4 p.	Chemistry	4 p.
History, English and American	3 p.	History (intensive) and Civil Government	3 p.
Astronomy, 3 p. 1st ½ yr.	3 p.	Geology or Physiography, 4 p. 1st ½ yr.	4 p.
Meteorology, 3 p. 2nd ½ yr.		Anatomy, Physiology, and Hygiene, 4 p. 2nd ½ yr.	
	34 p.		33 p.
* Option of book-keeping and commercial arithmetic.			

The adoption of the number four as the standard number of weekly periods will not make it impossible to carry into effect the fundamental conception of all the Conferences, namely, — that all the subjects which make part of the secondary school course should be taught consecutively enough and extensively enough to make every subject yield that training which it is best fitted to yield, — provided that the proposed correlation and association of subjects are carried out in practice. With regard to the arrangement or sequence of subjects, the Committee follow in this table the recommendations of the Conferences with only slight modifications. They insert in the first year applied geography, using the term in the sense in which it is used by the Conference on Geography; and they make this insertion in order that natural science may be represented in the programme of that year, and that a complete break of continuity, as regards science subjects, between the eighth grade and the second year of the secondary school may be avoided. They have felt obliged to put physics into the third year, and chemistry into the fourth, in order that the subject of physics may precede meteorology and physiography; and they have slightly increased the number of lessons in astronomy. With regard to the proportions of school time to be devoted to the different subjects, Table III. reduces somewhat the proportional time devoted to Latin, English, and mathematics, and increases the proportional time to be devoted to natural science. In a secondary school which teaches all the subjects recommended by the Conferences, and to the extent contemplated in Table III., nearly one-fifth of the whole instruction given will be devoted to natural science.

The Committee regard Table III. not, of course, as a feasible programme, but as the possible source of a great variety of good secondary school programmes. It would be difficult to make a bad programme out of the materials contained in this table, unless indeed the fundamental principles advocated by the Conferences should be neglected. With some reference to Table I., excellent six years' and five years' programmes for secondary schools can readily be constructed by spreading the subjects contained in Table III. over six or five years instead of four, — of course with some changes in the time-allotment.

The details of the time-allotment for the several studies which enter into the secondary school programme may seem to some persons mechanical, or even trivial—a technical matter to be dealt with by each superintendent of schools, or by each principal of a secondary school, acting on his own individual experience and judgment; but such is not the opinion of the Committee of Ten. The Committee believe that to establish just proportions between the several subjects, or groups of allied subjects, on which the Conferences were held, it is essential that each principal subject shall be taught thoroughly and extensively, and therefore for an adequate number of periods a week on the school programme. If twice as much time is given in a school to Latin as is given to mathematics, the attainments of the pupils in Latin ought to be twice as great as they are in mathematics, provided that equally good work is done in the two subjects; and Latin will have twice the educational value of mathematics. Again, if in a secondary school Latin is steadily pursued for four years with four or five hours a week devoted to it, that subject will be worth more to the pupil than the sum of half a dozen other subjects, each of which has one sixth of the time allotted to Latin. The good effects of continuous study in one subject will be won for the pupil through the Latin, and they will not be won through the six other subjects among which only so much time as is devoted to the single language has been divided. If every subject studied at all is to be studied thoroughly and consecutively, every subject must receive an adequate time-allotment. If every subject is to provide a substantial mental training, it must have a time-allotment sufficient to produce that fruit. Finally, since selection must be exercised by or on behalf of the individual pupil, all the subjects between which choice is allowed should be approximately equivalent to each other in seriousness, dignity, and efficacy. Therefore they should have approximately equal time-allotments. The Conferences have abundantly shown how every subject which they recommend can be made a serious subject of instruction, well fitted to train the pupil's powers of observation, expression, and reasoning. It remains for makers of school programmes to give every subject the chance of developing a good training capacity by giving it an adequate time-allotment.

The schedule of studies contained in Table III. permits flexibility and variety in three respects. First, it is not necessary that any school should teach all the subjects which it contains, or any particular set of subjects. Secondly, it is not necessary that the individual pupil should everywhere and always have the same number of periods of instruction per week. In one school the pupils might have but sixteen periods a week, in another twenty; or in some years of the course the pupils might have more periods a week than in other years. Within the schedule many particular arrangements for the convenience of a school, or for the welfare of an individual pupil would be possible. Thirdly, it is not necessary that every secondary school should

begin its work at the level which is assumed as the starting point
of secondary instruction in Tables I., II., and III.   If in any
community the high school has no such grammar school foundation beneath it as is imagined in Table I. it will simply have to
begin its work lower down in the table. The sequence of studies
recommended by the Conferences would still serve as a guide;
but the demarcation between the elementary schools and the
high school would occur in that community at a lower point.
From this point of view, Tables I., II., and III. may be considered to set a standard towards which secondary schools should
tend; and not a standard to which they can at once conform.

The adoption of a programme based on Table III. would not
necessarily change at all the relation of a school to the colleges
or universities to which it habitually sends pupils. Any such
programme would lend itself either to the examination method
of admission to college, or to the certificate method; and it
could be slightly modified in such a way as to meet the present
admission requirements of any college in the country. Future
changes in admission requirements might fairly be made with a
view to the capabilities of programmes based on Table III.

As samples of school programmes constructed within the
schedules of Table III., the Committee present the following
working programmes, which they recommend for trial wherever
the secondary school period is limited to four years. All four
combined might, of course, be tabulated as one programme
with options by subject.

These four programmes taken together use all the subjects
mentioned in Table III., and usually, but not always, to about
the amounts there indicated. History and English suffer
serious contraction in the Classical programme. All four
programmes conform to the general recommendations of the
Conferences, that is, — they treat each subject in the same
way for all pupils with trifling exceptions; they give time
enough to each subject to win from it the kind of mental
training it is fitted to supply; they put the different principal
subjects on an approximate equality so far as time-allotment is
concerned; they omit all short information courses; and they
make sufficiently continuous the instruction in each of the main

lines, namely, language, science, history and mathematics. With slight modifications, they would prepare the pupils for admission to appropriate courses in any American college or university on the existing requirements; and they would also meet the new college requirements which are suggested below.

In preparing these programmes, the Committee were perfectly aware that it is impossible to make a satisfactory secondary school programme, limited to a period of four years, and founded on the present elementary school subjects and methods. In the opinion of the Committee, several subjects now reserved for high schools, — such as algebra, geometry, natural science, and foreign languages, — should be begun earlier than now, and therefore within the schools classified as elementary; or, as an alternative, the secondary school period should be made to begin two years earlier than at present, leaving six years instead of eight for the elementary school period. Under the present organization, elementary subjects and elementary methods are, in the judgment of the Committee, kept in use too long.

The most striking differences in the four programmes will be found, as is intimated in the headings, in the relative amounts of time given to foreign languages. In the Classical programme the foreign languages get a large share of time; in the English programme a small share. In compensation, English and history are more developed in the English programme than in the Classical.

Many teachers will say, at first sight, that physics comes too early in these programmes and Greek too late. One member of the Committee is firmly of the opinion that Greek comes too late. The explanation of the positions assigned to these subjects is that the Committee of Ten attached great importance to two general principles in programme making: — In the first place they endeavored to postpone till the third year the grave choice between the Classical course and the Latin-Scientific. They believed that this bifurcation should occur as late as possible, since the choice between these two roads often determines for life the youth's career. Moreover, they believed that it is possible to make this important decision for a boy on good grounds, only when he has had opportunity to exhibit his quality and discover his tastes by making excursions into all the principal fields of knowledge. The youth who has never studied any but his native language cannot know his own capacity for linguistic acquisition; and the youth who has never made a chemical or physical experiment cannot know whether or not

TABLE IV.

YEAR.	CLASSICAL. Three foreign languages (one modern).		LATIN-SCIENTIFIC. Two foreign languages (one modern).	
I.	Latin	5 p.	Latin	5 p.
	English	4 p.	English	4 p.
	Algebra	4 p.	Algebra	4 p.
	History	4 p.	History	4 p.
	Physical Geography	3 p.	Physical Geography	3 p.
		20 p.		20 p.
II.	Latin	5 p.	Latin	5 p.
	English	2 p.	English	2 p.
	*German [or French] begun	4 p.	German [or French] begun	4 p.
	Geometry	3 p.	Geometry	3 p.
	Physics	3 p.	Physics	3 p.
	History	3 p.	Botany or Zoölogy	3 p.
		20 p.		20 p.
III.	Latin	4 p.	Latin	4 p.
	*Greek	5 p.	English	3 p.
	English	3 p.	German [or French]	4 p.
	German [or French]	4 p.	Mathematics { Algebra 2 / Geometry 2 }	4 p.
	Mathematics { Algebra 2 / Geometry 2 }	4 p.	Astronomy ½ yr. & Meteorology ½ yr.	3 p.
		20 p.	History	2 p.
				20 p.
IV.	Latin	4 p.	Latin	4 p.
	Greek	6 p.	English { as in Classical 2 / additional 2 }	4 p.
	English	2 p.	German [or French]	3 p.
	German [or French]	3 p.	Chemistry	3 p.
	Chemistry	3 p.	Trigonometry & Higher Algebra / or / History }	3 p.
	Trigonometry & Higher Algebra / or / History }	3 p.	Geology or Physiography ½ yr. / and / Anatomy, Physiology, & Hygiene ½ yr. }	3 p.
		20 p.		20 p.

* In any school in which Greek can be better taught than a modern language, or in which local public opinion or the history of the school makes it desirable to teach Greek in an ample way, Greek may be substituted for German or French in the second year of the Classical programme.

he has a taste for exact science. The wisest teacher, or the most observant parent, can hardly predict with confidence a boy's gift for a subject which he has never touched. In these considerations the Committee found strong reasons for postponing bifurcation, and making the subjects of the first two

TABLE IV. (*continued*).

YEAR.	MODERN LANGUAGES. Two foreign languages (both modern).	ENGLISH. One foreign language (ancient or modern).
I.	French [*or* German] begun . . . . 5 p. English . . . . 4 p. Algebra . . . . 4 p. History . . . . 4 p. Physical Geography . . . . . . 3 p. ——— 20 p.	Latin, or German, or French . . . 5 p. English . . . . 4 p. Algebra . . . . 4 p. History . . . . 4 p. Physical Geography. . . . . . . 3 p. ——— 20 p.
II.	French [*or* German] . . . . . . 4 p. English . . . . 2 p. German [*or* French] begun . . . . 5 p. Geometry . . . . 3 p. Physics . . . . 3 p. Botany or Zoölogy . . . . 3 p. ——— 20 p.	Latin, or German, or French . . 5 or 4 p. English . . . . 3 or 4 p. Geometry . . . . 3 p. Physics . . . . 3 p. History . . . . 3 p. Botany or Zoölogy . . . . 3 p. ——— 20 p.
III.	French [*or* German] . . . . . . 4 p. English . . . . 3 p. German [*or* French] . . . . . . 4 p. Mathematics { Algebra 2 / Geometry 2 } . . . . 4 p. Astronomy ½ yr. & Meteorology ½ yr. 3 p. History . . . . 2 p. ——— 20 p.	Latin, or German, or French . . . 4 p. English { as in others 3 / additional 2 } . . . . . 5 p. Mathematics { Algebra 2 / Geometry 2 } . . . 4 p. Astronomy ½ yr. & Meteorology ½ yr. 3 p. History { as in the Latin-Scientific 2 / additional / 2 } 4 p. ——— 20 p.
IV.	French [*or* German] . . . . . . 3 p. English { as in Classical 2 / additional 2 } . . . . 4 p. German [*or* French] . . . . . . 4 p. Chemistry . . . . 3 p. Trigonometry & Higher Algebra 3 } or } 3 p. History } Geology or Physiography ½ yr. } and } 3 p. Anatomy, Physiology,&Hygiene ½ yr. } ——— 20 p.	Latin, or German, or French . . . 4 p. English { as in Classical 2 / additional 2 } . . . . 4 p. Chemistry . . . . 3 p. Trigonometry & Higher Algebra . . 3 p. History . . . . 3 p. Geology or Physiography ½ yr. } and } 3 p. Anatomy, Physiology,&Hygiene ½ yr. } ——— 20 p.

years as truly representative as possible. Secondly, inasmuch as many boys and girls who begin the secondary school course do not stay in school more than two years, the Committee thought it important to select the studies of the first two years in such a way that linguistic, historical, mathematical, and scientific subjects should all be properly represented. Natural history being represented by physical geography, the Committee wished physics to represent the inorganic sciences of precision. The first two years of any one of the four programmes presented above will, in the judgment of the Committee, be highly profitable by themselves to children who can go no farther.

Although the Committee thought it expedient to include among the four programmes, one which included neither Latin nor Greek, and one which included only one foreign language (which might be either ancient or modern), they desired to affirm explicitly their unanimous opinion that, under existing conditions in the United States as to the training of teachers and the provision of necessary means of instruction, the two programmes called respectively Modern Languages and English must in practice be distinctly inferior to the other two.

In the construction of the sample programmes the Committee adopted twenty as the maximum number of weekly periods, but with two qualifications, namely, that at least five of the twenty periods should be given to unprepared work, and that laboratory subjects should have double periods whenever that prolongation should be possible.

The omission of music, drawing, and elocution from the programmes offered by the Committee was not intended to imply that these subjects ought to receive no systematic attention. It was merely thought best to leave it to local school authorities to determine, without suggestions from the Committee, how these subjects should be introduced into the programmes in addition to the subjects reported on by the Conferences.

The Committee were governed in the construction of the first three programmes by the rule laid down by the language Conferences, namely, that two foreign languages should not be begun at the same time. To obey this rule is to accept strict limitations in the construction of a four years' Classical programme. A five years' or six years' programme can be made much more easily under this restriction. The Committee were anxious to give five weekly periods to every foreign language in the year when it was first attacked; but did not find it possible to do so in every case.

The four programmes can be carried out economically in a single school; because, with a few inevitable exceptions, the several subjects occur simultaneously in at least three programmes and with the same number of weekly periods. '

Numerous possible transpositions of subjects will occur to every experienced teacher who examines these specimen programmes. Thus, in some localities it would be better to transpose French and German; the selection and order of science subjects might be varied considerably to suit the needs or circumstances of different schools; and the selection and order of historical subjects admit of large variety.

Many subjects now familiar in secondary school courses of study do not appear in Table III. or in the specimen programmes given above; but it must not be supposed that the omitted subjects are necessarily to be neglected. If the recommendations of the Conference were carried out, some of the omitted subjects would be better dealt with under any one of the above programmes than they are now under familiar high school and academy programmes in which they figure as separate subjects. Thus, drawing does not appear as a separate subject in the specimen programmes; but the careful reader of the Conference reports will notice that drawing, both mechanical and free-hand, is to be used in the study of history, botany, zoölogy, astronomy, meteorology, physics, geography, and physiography, and that the kind of drawing recommended by the Conferences is the most useful kind, — namely, that which is applied to recording, describing, and discussing observations. This abundant use of drawing might not prevent the need of some special instruction in drawing, but it ought to diminish the number of periods devoted exclusively to drawing. Again, neither ethics nor economics, neither metaphysics nor aesthetics appear in the programmes; but in the large number of periods devoted to English and history there would be some time for incidental instruction in the elements of these subjects. It is through the reading and writing required of pupils, or

4

recommended to them, that the fundamental ideas on these important topics are to be inculcated. Again, the industrial and commercial subjects do not appear in these programmes; but book-keeping and commercial arithmetic are provided for by the option for algebra designated in Table III. ; and if it were desired to provide more amply for subjects thought to have practical importance in trade or the useful arts, it would be easy to provide options in such subjects for some of the science contained in the third and fourth years of the "English" programme.

The Committee of Ten think much would be gained if, in addition to the usual programme hours, a portion of Saturday morning should be regularly used for laboratory work in the scientific subjects. Laboratory work requires more consecutive time than the ordinary period of recitation affords; so that an hour and a half is about the shortest advantageous period for a laboratory exercise. The Committee venture to suggest further that, in addition to the regular school sessions in the morning, one afternoon in every week should be used for out-of-door instruction in geography, botany, zoölogy, and geology, these afternoon and Saturday morning exercises being counted as regular work for the teachers who conduct them. In all laboratory and field work, the Committee believe that it will be found profitable to employ as assistants to the regular teachers, — particularly at the beginning of laboratory and field work in each subject, — recent graduates of the secondary schools who have themselves followed the laboratory and field courses; for at the beginning the pupil will need a large amount of individual instruction in the manipulation of specimens, the use of instruments, and the prompt recording of observations. One teacher without assistants cannot supervise effectively the work of thirty or forty pupils, either in the laboratory or in the field. The laboratory work on Saturday mornings could be maintained throughout the school year; the afternoon excursions would of course be difficult, or impossible, for perhaps a third of the school year.

In general, the Committee of Ten have endeavored to emphasize the principles which should govern all secondary school programmes, and to show how the main recommendations of the several Conferences may be carried out in a variety of feasible programmes.

One of the subjects which the Committee of Ten were directed to consider was requirements for admission to college; and particularly they were expected to report on uniform requirements for admission to colleges, as well as on a uniform secondary school programme. Almost all the Conferences have something to say about the best mode of testing the attainments of candidates at college admission examinations; and some of them, notably the Conferences on History and Geography, make very explicit declarations concerning the nature of college examinations. The improvements desired in the mode of testing the attainments of pupils who have pursued in the secondary schools the various subjects which enter into the course will be found clearly described under each subject in the several Conference reports; but there is a general principle concerning the relation of the secondary schools to colleges which the Committee of Ten, inspired and guided by the Conferences, feel it their duty to set forth with all possible distinctness.

The secondary schools of the United States, taken as a whole, do not exist for the purpose of preparing boys and girls for colleges. Only an insignificant percentage of the graduates of these schools go to colleges or scientific schools. Their main function is to prepare for the duties of life that small proportion of all the children in the country — a proportion small in number, but very important to the welfare of the nation — who show themselves able to profit by an education prolonged to the eighteenth year, and whose parents are able to support them while they remain so long at school. There are, to be sure, a few private or endowed secondary schools in the country, which make it their principal object to prepare students for the colleges and universities; but the number of these schools is relatively small. A secondary school programme intended for national use must therefore be made for those children whose education is not to be pursued beyond the secondary school. The preparation of a few pupils for college or scientific school should in the ordinary secondary school be the

incidental, and not the principal object.   At the same time, it
is obviously desirable that the colleges and scientific schools
should be accessible to all boys or girls who have completed
creditably the secondary school course.   Their parents often do
not decide for them, four years before the college age, that they
shall go to college, and they themselves may not, perhaps, feel
the desire to continue their education until near the end of their
school course.   In order that any successful graduate of a good
secondary school should be free to present himself at the gates
of the college or scientific school of his choice, it is necessary
that the colleges and scientific schools of the country should
accept for admission to appropriate courses of their instruction
the attainments of any youth who has passed creditably through
a good secondary school course, no matter to what group of
subjects he may have mainly devoted himself in the secondary
school.   As secondary school courses are now too often
arranged, this is not a reasonable request to prefer to the
colleges and scientific schools; because the pupil may now go
through a secondary school course of a very feeble and scrappy
nature — studying a little of many subjects and not much of any
one, getting, perhaps, a little information in a variety of fields,
but nothing which can be called a thorough training.   Now the
recommendations of the nine Conferences, if well carried out,
might fairly be held to make all the main subjects taught in the
secondary schools of equal rank for the purposes of admission to
college or scientific school.   They would all be taught consecutively and thoroughly, and would all be carried on in the same
spirit; they would all be used for training the powers of observation, memory, expression, and reasoning; and they would all
be good to that end, although differing among themselves in
quality and substance.   In preparing the programmes of Table
IV., the Committee had in mind that the requirements for
admission to colleges might, for schools which adopted a programme derived from that table, be simplified to a considerable
extent, though not reduced.   A college might say, — We will
accept for admission any groups of studies taken from the
secondary school programme, provided that the sum of the studies in each of the four years amounts to sixteen, or eighteen,
or twenty periods a week, — as may be thought best, — and

provided, further, that in each year at least four of the subjects presented shall have been pursued at least three periods a week, and that at least three of the subjects shall have been pursued three years or more. For the purposes of this reckoning, natural history, geography, meteorology, and astronomy might be grouped together as one subject. Every youth who entered college would have spent four years in studying a few subjects thoroughly; and, on the theory that all the subjects are to be considered equivalent in educational rank for the purposes of admission to college, it would make no difference which subjects he had chosen from the programme — he would have had four years of strong and effective mental training. The Conferences on Geography and Modern Languages make the most explicit statement to the effect that college requirements for admission should coincide with high-school requirements for graduation. The Conference on English is of opinion "that no student should be admitted to college who shows in his English examination and his other examinations that he is very deficient in ability to write good English." This recommendation suggests that an ample English course in the secondary school should be required of all persons who intend to enter college. It would of course be possible for any college to require for admission any one subject, or any group of subjects, in the table, and the requirements of different colleges, while all kept within the table, might differ in many respects; but the Committee are of opinion that the satisfactory completion of any one of the four years' courses of study embodied in the foregoing programmes should admit to corresponding courses in colleges and scientific schools. They believe that this close articulation between the secondary schools and the higher institutions would be advantageous alike for the schools, the colleges, and the country.

Every reader of this report and of the reports of the nine Conferences will be satisfied that to carry out the improvements proposed more highly trained teachers will be needed than are now ordinarily to be found for the service of the elementary and secondary schools. The Committee of Ten desire to point out some of the means of procuring these better

trained teachers.   For the further instruction of teachers in
actual service, three agencies already in existence may be much
better utilized than they now are.   The Summer Schools which
many universities now maintain might be resorted to by much
larger numbers of teachers, particularly if some aid, such as
the payment of tuition fees and travelling expenses, should be
given to teachers who are willing to devote half of their
vacations to study, by the cities and towns which these
teachers serve.   Secondly, in all the towns and cities in which
colleges and universities are planted, these colleges or universities may usefully give stated courses of instruction in the
main subjects used in the elementary and secondary schools
to teachers employed in those towns and cities.   This is a
reasonable service which the colleges and universities may
render to their own communities.   Thirdly, a superintendent
who has himself become familiar with the best mode of teaching
any one of the subjects which enter into the school course
can always be a very useful instructor for the whole body of
teachers under his charge.   A real master of any one subject
will always have many suggestions to make to teachers of
other subjects.   The same is true of the principal of a high
school, or other leading teacher in a town or city.   In every
considerable city school system the best teacher in each department of instruction should be enabled to give part of his time
to helping the other teachers by inspecting and criticising their
work, and showing them, both by precept and example, how
to do it better.

In regard to preparing young men and women for the
business of teaching, the country has a right to expect much
more than it has yet obtained from the colleges and normal
schools.   The common expectation of attainment for pupils of
the normal schools has been altogether too low the country
over.   The normal schools, as a class, themselves need better
apparatus, libraries, programmes, and teachers.   As to the
colleges, it is quite as much an enlargement of sympathies as an
improvement of apparatus or of teaching that they need.
They ought to take more interest than they have heretofore
done, not only in the secondary, but in the elementary schools:
and they ought to take pains to fit men well for the duties

of a school superintendent. They already train a considerable number of the best principals of high schools and academies; but this is not sufficient. They should take an active interest, through their presidents, professors, and other teachers, in improving the schools in their respective localities, and in contributing to the thorough discussion of all questions affecting the welfare of both the elementary and the secondary schools.

Finally, the Committee venture to suggest, in the interest of secondary schools, that uniform dates — such as the last Thursday, Friday, and Saturday, or the third Monday, Tuesday, and Wednesday of June and September — be established for the admission examinations of colleges and scientific schools throughout the United States. It is a serious inconvenience for secondary schools which habitually prepare candidates for several different colleges or scientific schools that the admission examinations of different institutions are apt to occur on different dates, sometimes rather widely separated.

The Committee also wish to call attention to the service which Schools of Law, Medicine, Engineering, and Technology, whether connected with universities or not, can render to secondary education by arranging their requirements for admission, as regards selection and range of subjects, in conformity with the courses of study recommended by the Committee. By bringing their entrance requirements into close relation with any or all of the programmes recommended for secondary schools, these professional schools can give valuable support to high schools, academies, and preparatory schools.

CHARLES W. ELIOT,
WILLIAM T. HARRIS,
JAMES B. ANGELL,
JOHN TETLOW,
JAMES M. TAYLOR,
OSCAR D. ROBINSON,
JAMES H. BAKER,
RICHARD H. JESSE,
JAMES C. MACKENZIE,
HENRY C. KING.

4 December, 1893.

President Baker signs the above report, but adds the following statement: —

To the National Council of Education:

I beg leave to note some exceptions taken to parts of the Report of the Committee of Ten. Had the Committee not been limited in time, doubtless fuller discussion would have resulted in modifying some statements embodied in the report. The great value of the reports of the Conferences upon the subjects referred to them, as to matter, place, time, methods, adequate and continuous work for each subject, and identity of work in different courses, and the masterly summary and tabulation of their recommendations, made by the Chairman of the Committee of Ten, can but invite cordial commendation. Objections are raised to parts of the special work of the Committee.

1. I cannot endorse expressions that appear to sanction the idea that the choice of subjects in secondary schools may be a matter of comparative indifference. I note especially the following sentences, referring the reader to their context for accurate interpretation.

"Any school principal may say: — ' With the staff at my command I can teach only five subjects out of those proposed by the Conferences in the manner proposed. My school shall, therefore, be limited to these five.' Another school may be able to teach in the thorough manner proposed five subjects, but some or all of these five may be different from those selected by the first school."

"If twice as much time is given in a school to Latin as is given to mathematics, the attainments of the pupils in Latin ought to be twice as great as they are in mathematics, provided that equally good work is done in the two subjects; and Latin will have twice the educational value of mathematics."

"The schedule of studies contained in Table III. permits flexibility and variety in three respects. First, it is not necessary that any school should teach all the subjects which it contains, or any particular set of subjects."

" Every youth who entered college would have spent four years in studying a few subjects thoroughly ; and on the theory that all the subjects are to be considered equivalent in educational rank for the purpose of admission to college, it would make no difference which subjects he had chosen from the programme — he would have had four years of strong and effective mental training."

All such statements are based upon the theory that, for the purposes of general education, one study is as good as another, — a theory which appears to me to ignore Philosophy, Psychology and Science of Education. It is a theory which makes education formal and does not consider the nature and value of the content. Power comes through knowledge ; we can not conceive of observation and memory in the abstract. The world which offers to the human mind several distinct views is the world in which our power that comes through knowledge is to be used, the world which we are to understand and enjoy. The relation between the subjective power and the objective — or subjective — knowledge is inseparable and vital. On any other theory, for general education, we might well consider the study of Egyptian hieroglyphics as valuable as that of physics, and Choctaw as important as Latin. Secondary school programmes can not well omit mathematics, or science, or history, or literature, or the culture of the ancient classics. An education which gives a view in all directions is the work of elementary and secondary schools. Such an education is the necessary preparation for the special work of the university student. If I rightly understood, the majority of the Committee rejected the theory of equivalence of studies for general education.

Studies vary in value for the training of the different powers, and for this additional reason the choice can not be regarded as a matter of indifference.

The training of "observation, memory, expression and reasoning" (inductive) is a very important part of education, but is not all of education. The imagination, deductive reasoning, the rich possibilities of emotional life, the education of the will through ethical ideas and correct habit, all are to be considered in a scheme of learning. Ideals are to be added to the scientific method.

The dilemma which appears on an examination of the time demands of the various conferences offers to the programme maker the alternatives of omitting essential subjects and of a rational adjustment of the time element, while retaining all essential subjects. Reason and experience point toward the latter alternative. By wise selection of matter within the lines of study adequate and consecutive time can be given to each.

2. The language of the second paragraph following Table II. might be misconstrued to mean that the Committee favor the multiplication of courses with a loss of the thoroughness attainable when the teaching force is devoted to one or two courses. Intension rather than extension of effort, both in respect to the number of courses and in respect to the number of studies or topics under each principal subject, is to be strongly recommended.

3. It may seem trivial to offer criticism of the specimen programmes made by the Committee, and yet I believe that each member felt that with ample deliberation results somewhat different would have been reached. Note for instance that in some of the programmes history is entirely omitted in the second year, and physics is given only three hours per week, — no more time than is allowed for botany or zoölogy. There are many symmetrical secondary school programmes in actual operation today which furnish continuous instruction in all important subjects throughout the four years, allowing to each an amount of time adequate to good results. For most high schools the first, the Classical programme, and the last programme, the one offering one foreign language, will commend themselves because they are economical, and they combine a good finishing course with adequate college preparation.

4. On the basis of the tabulated results of the Conferences I believe that by earnest scientific examination a scheme of work can be formulated that will meet the views of the members of the Committee and of most educators. As an afterthought it may be an occasion for regret that the strength of the discussion was not devoted to Table III. Instead of con-

sidering the work of the Committee as ended, I would recommend that the National Council hold itself responsible for further examination of the data furnished by the Conferences. I have not presumed to offer a substitute report, because I believe that the importance of the work demands further effort of an entire Committee.

Respectfully submitted,

JAMES H. BAKER.

REPORTS OF THE CONFERENCES.

LATIN.

President Charles W. Eliot, Chairman of the Committee of Ten of the National Council of Education : —

The Conference upon the subject of Latin respectfully submits the following report : —

In seven sessions of nearly three hours each the Conference discussed all the questions suggested in the circular of instructions, except the last, respecting the proper limit between the preliminary and the final examination for admission to college ; and on most of the points presented, as well as on several not suggested in the circular, arrived at unanimous or nearly unanimous conclusions, which will be found expressed in the Recommendations appended to this Report.

The first question considered was whether the requirements in Latin for admission to college ought to be increased.

It would be a very desirable gain to the study of Latin in our universities and colleges if the present standard of admission requirements could be raised ; and the experience of other countries would seem to indicate that a higher standard is feasible. But, in view of the just demands for more and better work in several other subjects of the preparatory course, it seemed clear to the Conference that no increase in the *quantity* of the preparation in Latin should be asked for. It is fully believed, however, that, through the careful choice of teachers, and the employment of better methods, a gain in the *quality* of the preparation can be secured without the expenditure of more time than is now generally given in the better schools. See Recommendations 1, 6, 11, and 14, at the end of this Report.

Upon the subject first suggested in the memorandum of the Committee of Ten, — namely, the question of the age at which the study of Latin should be begun, — a comparison of the customs existing in Europe and in this country will be suggestive. In the United States, the average age is about fifteen years, and probably above that number rather than below it.[1] In England and on the Continent the

---

[1] At some private and endowed public schools in this country, however, the age is not far from twelve. In Michigan, successful experiments have been made in introducing the study of Latin into the grammar-school; and the trial is also being made in certain grammar-schools in Massachusetts.

study is seldom begun so late as at the age of twelve, and much oftener between the ages of nine and eleven ; in other words, from four to six years earlier than with us. The reasons in favor of an early age are not far to seek. (1) Latin is a difficult language, and long study is needed to make it yield its best fruits. (2) The rudiments of the subject, and in particular the forms, can be more easily and quickly mastered at an early age ; and, conversely, the study of these things constitutes a less agreeable and less suitable discipline for a mind that is becoming conscious of its powers. A radical change cannot be brought about in this country at once ; but it is hoped that such a modification of grammar-school courses can be made without delay as to render it possible that the high-school course, — and with it the subject of Latin, — may be begun not later than at the age of fourteen. See Recommendations 2 and 3.

With regard to the number of years and the number of hours a week devoted to the study of Latin, the actual practice of the schools in this country varies greatly. In twenty-six representative schools having a four-year course, the aggregate of hours ranges from 580 to 1,009 ; and, in fourteen schools having a course of five or six years, from 740 to 1,925.[1] In the opinion of the Conference, Latin should claim about one-fifth of each school day, or five hours a week. This means a total of about 800 periods of forty-five or fifty minutes of actual work. If the course were to be one of five or six years, instead of four, the Conference would not recommend any diminution of the weekly allotment. The aggregate of 1,000 to 1,200 "hours" thus obtained, which might to some observers seem excessive, is much below the maximum amount already given in the fourteen representative schools having a course of five or six years, while it is identical with, or but little above, the average in those schools (viz., 1000 hours), and much below the average in the schools of England, France and Germany. The explanation of the undeniable fact that, in the countries just named, Latin has been more successfully employed than with us " as an instrument for training the mind to habits of intellectual conscientiousness, patience, discrimination, accuracy, and thoroughness, — in a word, to habits of clear and sound thinking," doubtless lies partly in the more liberal allowance of time. See Recommendations 3, 4, and 5.

The answer to the tenth question put before the Conference, with regard to the best method of testing attainments at the college examinations for admission, must turn mainly upon the general

---

[1] From statistics of forty representative schools gathered by the Committee of Ten.

character of the requirements held up before the schools. Up to the present time, the commoner form of requirement may be said to insist strongly upon the *quantitative* side. A certain number of books of certain authors are to be read, or certain defined substitutes, supposed to be equal in quantity ; a certain number of lessons in some manual of Latin composition must be studied ; and a certain amount of Latin grammar must be learned. After a preparation controlled by this quantitative conception, the test applied by colleges that do not use the certificate system must necessarily be directed to ascertaining what familiarity has been gained with the ground gone over. On the other hand, if the requirement be ability to translate " at sight " from Latin into English and from English into Latin, the test must necessarily be one of power. Its object is to show what the student is now capable of doing ; and it may therefore fairly be called a *qualitative* test. It has distinct and great advantages. What the student knows and what he can do is made manifest at once to the practised eye, and, on the other hand, ignorance and feebleness emerge with fatal clearness. " Cramming " is made nearly useless by it, and the steady gain of power becomes the student's necessary aim and sole means of salvation. Still, many shrink from adopting it as the sole test. The examination, they urge, may, especially in view of the fact that there are many students of mediocre natural gifts, but of faithfulness and staying powers, properly take account of the amount of work which the candidate has covered, and of the thoroughness with which he has performed a fixed task, as a means of judging, in the rough, of his fitness for higher study. Yet the importance of devoting a good deal of attention to translation at sight is now universally acknowledged among the best teachers in school and college, and the recommendation (included in No. 6) that translation at sight form a constant and increasing part of the examination for admission and of the work of preparation, is therefore regarded by the Conference as of especial moment.

Intimately connected with the same subject is the question of the writing of Latin, — its place in the study of the language, the subject-matter to be employed, and the method of development to be adopted.

The object is not the acquirement of the power for its own sake ; for this power, while once indispensable, is not to-day a necessity, nor even, for most men, an especially desirable accomplishment. The practice should be employed as a *means*, — as a powerful instrument for gaining a penetrating insight into the structure, idiom, and spirit of the Latin language, both in its agreement with, and in its differences from, the mother tongue. It is admitted, for example, that, in order to be able to read Latin, one must have a firm grasp of the principles of Latin syntax. But the experience of many teachers has shown that this grasp is to be gained with much more certainty through writing Latin than in any other way; and in this field, too, the student himself clearly sees the reasonableness and immediate utility of the same instruction which, when applied to a Latin text, often seems to him, and often is, needless and barren. Here, then, should fall the principal part of the syntactical instruction. And, for similar reasons, the writing of Latin affords the best field for the mastery of forms, of vocabulary, of idiom, and of order.

The majority of the Conference is of the belief that, instead of being dissociated from practice in reading and translating, as it still so commonly is, practice in writing should be regarded as the obverse and counterpart of reading, and therefore should be carried on *pari passu* with it. In no other way can direct advantage be taken of the threads of association woven in the mind by the reading of an author, and in no other way can the subject-matter, in the earlier stages, be made so interesting and so practical. It follows that the basis of all sentences and passages set for translation into English in the preparatory schools should be found in the Latin texts read. And it is also evidently desirable that the portions of the text chosen should be limited, — so limited, in fact, that they can gradually be committed to memory, and preserved as a permanent store. "This small treatise alone" says George Long, in the preface to his edition of the *Cato Major*, "if thoroughly mastered, . . . would make a man a good Latin scholar."

The use of manuals of composition based upon a plan of exercises having no connection with the texts read, and arranged in artificial sequence to illustrate syntactical rules, ought accordingly to be discouraged. See Recommendation 11.

The summoning of the Conference afforded a fortunate opportunity for the discussion of an important question not included in the memorandum, namely, what authors, and what parts of authors, should constitute the reading of the preparatory schools? Thus far, the colleges have in general left the schools very little liberty of choice. Three authors have been named by every college that prescribes set work. Of these three the easiest, or, as one should perhaps say, the least difficult, is Cæsar. Hence it has come about that the *Gallic War* is very commonly used as the first reading-book in Latin. Our American schools are probably the only ones in the world of which this is true. The choice is an unfortunate one. The book is altogether too difficult for beginners; it is too exclusively military in contents to be generally interesting; its vocabulary is too largely restricted, from the nature of the subject, to marches, sieges, and battles, to afford the best introduction to subsequent reading; and, finally, it touches human life at too few points to be morally helpful and significant. The Conference therefore makes two recommendations: first, that some easy reading, such as Gradatim, Eutropius, or the Viri Romae, be used as a transition from the introductory work of the beginner's book to the regular reading of a classic; and second, that at least a portion of the time now usually given to Cæsar be taken from him and given to Nepos. Against the "*Lives*" not one of the reasons urged against the use, or exclusive use, of the *Gallic War* can be brought. The objection that the Latinity of Nepos is inferior to that of Cæsar would be of weight only in case the chief object in the earlier years of the study of Latin were the immediate production of writers of an elegant Latin style. No such fear is felt by German, French, and English school-masters, who have found, as have also various experimenters in this country, that the use of the books mentioned above as bridges to and substitutes for Cæsar contributes to the pleasure and progress of the student. See Recommendation 9.

The Bucolics of Virgil constitute the least original, and, to the school-boy, least interesting, and most difficult, part of the poet's works. Their proper place is in an elective course for university students, in connection with the reading of Theocritus. It is advised that they be discontinued in the requirements for admission to college. See Recommendation 7.

Some teachers of learning, experience, and skill have believed that, in what is called the inductive method, they have found a shorter and better way of learning Latin than has heretofore been devised. The saving of time and the attainment of a more exact scholarship, which are the ends they have set themselves to bring about, are certainly greatly to be desired. Perhaps some good has been done by the publication of books calling attention strongly to a side of linguistic study which, even in the earlier years, should not be entirely ignored. But the Conference is of the opinion that it is an error to erect into the sole controlling principle what should, in the nature of things, be subordinate. On this subject, therefore, a word of caution seemed to nearly all its members to be desirable. See Recommendation 13.

In the judgment of the Conference, the greatest defects now existing in the instruction given in Latin in the schools are to be found in the elementary stages. It is a common practice to put the teaching of beginners into the hands of the youngest and most poorly paid teachers, that is to say, of those who have the slenderest equipment of knowledge and experience. The same thing is true in other subjects; but the danger seems to be especially great in Latin, partly because the field is so vast, covering as it does a great number and variety of topics, and partly because it is so difficult to determine practically the best distribution and appropriation of time along the several lines of study. To competent knowledge the teacher must add the clearest and most definite conceptions of the relative importance and the logical sequence of topics, of the ends to be reached in each stage, and of the best methods of arriving at these ends. If, then, the results of the study of Latin often seem absurdly meagre in proportion to the time spent upon the subject, we must look for the cause very largely in the fact that, at the most critical point in his study, the student is given over to an instructor of the least experience and knowledge.

To describe in full the best method of teaching Latin throughout the course, as was suggested in the memorandum of your Committee, would require the conversion of this Report into a treatise. But a brief summary may be made of the things to do and the things to avoid, and a few definite suggestions may be offered under each of the former heads.

The teacher of elementary Latin need not concern himself too much with the remoter ends of the study. To him the question should be: What knowledge is of prime importance, as the foundation for subsequent work? Stated generally, it may be said that the work of the first period should be (1) learning to pronounce accurately and to read fluently and intelligently the Latin text of what has been studied; (2) the mastery of inflection, so that number, case, person, mode, tense, etc., can be instantly recognized, and, conversely, can be formed without much hesitation by the student himself; (3) the acquisition of a working vocabulary of from one to two thousand words; (4) the mastery of the order of the Latin sentence; (5) the mastery of the simpler principles of syntax, regarded as a means of expression; (6) learning how to understand simple narrative in Latin; and (7) learning how to translate such narrative into true English. In necessary connection with the pursuit of these aims, a good deal of training of the ear should be employed, through listening to the reading or speaking of the teacher; and, in addition, a certain amount of practice in turning English into Latin will be necessary, as an indispensable instrument for fixing forms in the memory and establishing a feeling for their syntactical powers. On the other hand, the things to be avoided are (1) a dispersion of effort in consequence of the attempt to include too many parts of the study in the first stage; (2) an undue prominence of rules, and the treatment of syntax as an end in itself, rather than as an auxiliary to the penetration of the sense; and (3) the use of "translation English."

5

The more detailed suggestions that follow, under the head of the things to be done, apply in part, as will be seen, to the work of the later years of the preparatory course, as well as to the earlier.

1. PRONUNCIATION AND READING ALOUD. The Conference desires to emphasize the importance of a correct pronunciation of Latin from the very beginning of the study. A student who acquires the habit of pronouncing accurately in reading Latin prose will find little difficulty, and a genuine pleasure, in reading Latin verse. As practical aids to this end, the following suggestions are made with regard to certain peculiarities of the pronunciation of the Romans : —

(a) The long vowels received full length, not only in ultimas and penults, but in every syllable. (So, for example, the second a in amābāmus should occupy about as much time in the utterance as the second in amābam).

(b) An obstructed consonant (i. e., a consonant made more difficult to articulate fully, through being immediately followed by another, either in the same word or at the beginning of the next) was pronounced with a clearness and distinctness not known in similar cases in English, so that it occupied about as much time in the utterance as a short vowel. [A mute followed by a liquid, on the other hand, made a combination easy to pronounce both fully and rapidly, and so occupied no appreciable time in ordinary speech. In poetry, however, the first consonant was occasionally treated as obstructed, being pronounced as a distinct sound, out of combination].

(c) In verse, as in daily speech, a final vowel, before an initial vowel or vowel with h, was run as a glide into the next vowel.

Without a knowledge of quantities (and, of course, not merely in penults and ultimas, but in all syllables), correct reading is, in the nature of things, impossible. Yet to acquire this knowledge by looking up every word in the dictionary is, to the young student, a laborious, and, relatively, an unprofitable task. He should learn his quantities by the easiest and most direct way, namely, by the guidance of eye and ear. Hence books prepared for the first two years of a four-year course should, in the text proper, as well as in the paradigms, notes, and vocabulary, have the vowels long by nature marked (the unmarked ones being understood to be short). And the teacher, from whom, by unconscious imitation, class after class will largely take it pronunciation, should not feel at liberty to be careless in his own practice. He will find rules to be of little value, and example to be all-important.

For the sounds of the letters, the following scheme is recommended : —

ā as in *father*.

a like first *a* in *aha* (same quality as second but short), first vowel in *artistic* (of course with no *r* sound).

ē like the English *a*-sound as heard in *skein, cave, Cain*, but without the vanishing *ee*-element which ends the English sound.

e as in *net, bed*.

ī as in *machine*.

i as in *pin*.

ō like the English *ō*-sound heard in *note*, but without the vanishing *oo*-element which ends the English sound.

o as in the first syllable of *obey* and the second of *melody*. The sound is not the same as in *not, dot*.

ū as in *rule*.

u as in *pull*.

y like French *u*, German *ü*.

ae like *ai* in *aisle*.

oe like *oi* in *oil*.

au like *ow* in *how*.

eu by pronouncing both elements in rapid succession, — a combination not occurring in English.

ei as in *skein* (*with* the vanishing *ee*-element).

i consonantal (sometimes printed *j*) like *y* in *yet*.

ui occurs chiefly in *huic* and *cui*, which should be pronounced *wheek, kwee*.

b, d, f, h, k, l, m (not final), n, p, q, as in English, except that bs and bt should be pronounced *ps* and *pt*.

c always like *k*.

g always as in *get*; gu like *gw*, when preceded by *n* and followed by a vowel; ng like English *ng* in *anger*.

qu like English *qu* in *quick, queen*.

r trilled with the tip of the tongue.

s always as in *sin*; su like *sw* in *suavis, suadeo, suesco*, and in compounds and derivatives of these words.

z like *z*. (The evidence is as yet conflicting with regard to the sound of this consonant — probably *zd*, or *dz*, though possibly *z* — and for these reasons the English sound of *z* is for the present recommended).

t always as in *ten* (never with the sound of *sh*, as in English *creation*).

v like *w*.

x like *ks*.

ph, th, and ch not as in English, but nearly like *p, t*, and *k* (strictly with a slight explosive sound, as heard at the end of English words, *e. g., hop, hot, hock*).

Final m preceding an initial vowel (or vowel with *h*) should be pronounced as a faint nasal sound, the lips approaching the ordinary *m*-position, but not touching. The pronunciation before a consonant is doubtful, and, for the present, a change from the sound of English *m* is not recommended.

It is strongly recommended that abundant practice be given in the reading aloud of a continuous text already studied, which should be assigned in advance for the purpose, and carefully prepared. Not only is this an excellent literary exercise, which will add much to the interest and sense of reality of the subject-matter, but it will also contribute greatly to a feeling for forms (since in Latin so much depends upon word endings), and to a feeling for Latin order.

In this reading, while care should of course be taken with the individual sounds, it must not be supposed that pronunciation is the only or even the chief thing to aim at. The meaning of the text must not be subordinated to the sounds of the letters. The reader should endeavor to bring out the thought and literary art of his author, not only by a clear and full and easily-moving utterance, but by the grouping of words that constitute a phrase, by the suggestion of balance or antithesis wherever they are found, by a hint to the ear where the thought of the writer points back to something that has been said, or forward to something that is about to be said, and by emphasis in the expression wherever there is emphasis in the thought.

In this exercise the teacher himself (of course after careful preparation) should from time to time take part. And, whether it be the teacher or one of their own number who is reading, the pupils should be encouraged to try always to follow the sense by the ear alone, without the help of the book.

2. FORMS. The mastery of forms is indispensable as a basis of any sound knowledge and of any progress, and, if not acquired in the first year, is very rarely acquired later. The method must, in the main, be two-fold translation; first of single words, then of common combinations of adjective and noun, or pronoun and noun, or of all three; then of short phrases, as, e. g., a verb and its object, an adjective, preposition, and noun, forming a phrase, etc. Particularly should dependence not be made wholly or chiefly on the repetition of tabulated forms.

3. VOCABULARY. The mastery of the vocabulary of the language is a prodigious task. It confronts the learner at the outset, and it remains the last obstacle to be overcome. The fact seems not to be appreciated in elementary instruction, and accordingly many teachers think that text-books for the use of beginners should not contain more than a few hundred words, an error almost as great as to suppose that the words chosen should be largely taken from Caesar's *Gallic War*. It has already been said that this book is of too technical a character to constitute a good introduction to the reading of Latin ; and to plan the elementary work with especial reference to

it is, therefore, to heap mistake upon mistake. Copiousness and variety should characterize the vocabulary of the introductory book, not only for the sake of subsequent reading, but because both are a necessary condition of any human interest in the exercises, oral and written, which are indispensable for practice in elementary study.

Some suggestions for the easing of the young learner's task may be gathered from books that have appeared within a few years. (a) Special vocabularies attached to separate exercises or selections should in no case be committed to memory before the study of such *pensa*, but should be used for reference first, and memorized last of all; that is, words should be studied in a sentence before they are studied in isolation. Not only is the immediate tax upon the memory in this way lightened, but the impression made is more lasting. (b) Related words should be grouped together as fast as they occur. Five words obviously related in form and meaning can more easily be learned and remembered than one word in isolation. (c) The comparison and discrimination of nearly synonymous words (to be made, however, only as they occur in the learner's actual experience in reading) aids by giving definiteness and individuality to each. (d) And, finally, the greatest auxiliary is the habit of constant observation of the different applications of the same word. Students seldom know more than one English rendering for a Latin word, or more than one Latin rendering for an English word, — a state of things due in part to the want of the habit just referred to, but in part also to an undue insistence, at the earliest stage of study, on the memorizing of the one particular meaning that happens to be given in the text-book. This memorizing of one meaning is, in fact, what many teachers mean by "mastering" a vocabulary.

4. SYNTAX. The study of syntax may well, in university work, be dealt with as a matter of special interest to the advanced student, and be offered in courses by itself. But for the student who is preparing for college it is merely an indispensable means to an end, namely, the power to read. This statement by no means implies that it is to be treated carelessly and superficially by the teacher (for, if that be done, no real power to read can possibly be gained), but only that it will be taught by him in the most helpful manner, if he will do the greater part of his syntactical questioning in connection with exercises in which the student is trying to get at the meaning of a new sentence (i. e., in translation at sight or at hearing) and in connection with the writing of Latin (see 5 and 6 below). No attempt should be made, however, to master the entire apparatus at the outset. A further suggestion of considerable importance may be offered. Where, as is constantly happening, a mistake in translation is due to a mistake in

syntax, the teacher should not be content with giving a correct translation himself, or with asking some pupil to do it, but should always
himself state, or ask some one in the class to state, what the Latin
would be for the English actually given. If this is done, syntax is
seen in its true light, as one of the means by which the writer expresses his thought: if it is not done, the syntax of a given passage
seems a matter of indifference.

5. ORDER. The importance of a genuine familiarity with Latin
order can hardly be over-estimated. No one can really *read* Latin
unless, whether consciously or instinctively, he is so familiar with the
way in which the Roman arranged his sentences that it seems as
natural to him as the English order. It will be a help if the teacher
will frequently point out whatever in this respect is noteworthy, and
particularly if he will always, in working with his classes at the exercise of translation at sight, hold to the Latin order until he thinks
that the thought has been grasped, — not pass from one part of the
sentence to another, to make out an English order. Much help will
also be found in the exercise described under C below (at the end of
the section), and in the exercise of listening, without looking at the
book, to the reading of a prepared text by the teacher or fellow-pupil.
And students should also be encouraged to read over and over by
themselves, without translating, Latin with which they have become
familiar in the class-room.

It is obvious that a proper Latin order should be insisted upon
from the outset in all Latin written by the student. "English-Latin"
should be as carefully avoided as the hybrid "Latin-English" too
often accepted as translation. Equally important is it that the editors
of elementary text-books should put before the student no Latin
arranged in any other than a Latin order.

6. LEARNING TO UNDERSTAND THE LATIN. The success of the
student in one of the points most essential to the attainment of
power to read, namely, in learning to understand his author in his
author's tongue, will depend in a large degree upon the attitude of
mind of his teacher. The latter should, from the very beginning,
hold up the idea that the highest aim of Latin scholarship, on the
literary side, is to be able to read Latin, as every competent scholar
learns to read French and German. with a direct comprehension and
enjoyment of the very words written by the author, not of an English
substitute made by the reader. The student should be taught to regard translation, not as a means of finding out what his author has
said, but as, on the one hand, a way of making it clear to his instructor
that he has understood, and, on the other, an exercise in expression,
— a literary exercise, — in his own tongue. And finally, it should be

shown him that, even on the most practical grounds, to attempt to find out the meaning of a Latin sentence through translating it (as the common way is) is an operation almost sure to miscarry; that the Latin, as in the case of a *qui*-clause, an *ut*-clause, a *cum*-clause, etc., often uses a single word as connective, where the English would employ one or another out of a large group (*e. g.*, for the *ut*-clause, "when," "just as," "although," "in order to," "so that"), and that to translate by anything whatsoever, before the complete evidence of the entire sentence has been had and the relation of part to part seen, is to run a very large risk of going astray at this point, and of being led still further afield in other points in the unconscious attempt to make them consistent with the first mistake. But the student, dealing with a language in which the form of the sentence is entirely new to him, is naturally prone to go astray in precisely this way. He should therefore constantly receive practical help. Practice in translating at sight, or more exactly, in *understanding* at sight, under the instructor's eye *and then* translating, ought to be given daily, or at least very frequently. In general, the best passage for the purpose will be the passage immediately following the lesson of the day, for the double reason that the student is familiar with the context, and that, when the additional exercise carries him straight on to his end, he feels the reality of his progress. The Latin should always be read aloud, sometimes by a student, sometimes by the master, before any translation is ventured upon. The master should stop the student here and there, if his way of reading shows that his grouping is wrong, or if any other indication proves that he has not understood; and other pupils should be asked to correct him. Where a word is employed to give notice in advance that something is coming, this should be made clear by the way of reading. Where a Latin word calls for some construction yet to come, to complete its meaning, and either of several constructions may be employed according to the exact shade of the author's thought (as, *e. g.*, *dico* may be followed by the interrogative subjunctive clause, or by the infinitive, or by an *ut-* or *ne*-clause, according as the idea is of asking a question, or stating a fact, or giving a direction), this range of possibilities should be pointed out (unless it has already been pointed out so frequently that the class has become familiar with it); after which nothing further need be said when the completing construction, thus already foreseen as a possibility or certainty, is actually reached. Where there is danger of going astray through misapprehension of the syntax of a word, the construction (*i. e.*, the force of the case, the mode, or the tense) should be asked for. No question upon construction should be put except as a means of guiding the class to an understanding of the meaning of the Latin; and consequently every question of this sort should precede the translation.

When a sentence is manifestly easy, and has probably been understood by the class, it is well to pass straight on without translating it. The greater part of what is read will, however, require translation.

The habit of trying to understand a sentence in the original, *before translating*, will be more easily acquired, if the teacher will from time to time put a new passage upon the board, a word or phrase at a time, or, better yet, read it aloud, calling attention as he goes along, by comment or question, to indications of meaning which would have guided a Roman, but asking for no translation until the whole passage has been written or read.

In the preparation of his daily lesson by himself, the student should be urged to study the Latin, in entire faithfulness to the aims stated above, in the order in which it is written, without any skipping about. The sentence should be read through once, twice, or, if necessary, three times *in the Latin*, with no reference to the making of a translation, but with the mind fixed upon grasping the meaning directly. If the effort has in part failed, the student may then help himself by making a rough rendering of the sentence, word for word, *still in the Latin order*, and with great suspense of mind in the case of words that are capable of corresponding to a variety of phrases in English. This rough rendering, however, must be regarded as a mere temporary expedient, at the last resort, for getting at the meaning, not, of course, as translation into English. The preparation for the translation to be given in the class-room is an entirely different exercise, and should be the last act of the preparation of the lesson.

7. LEARNING TO TRANSLATE INTO ENGLISH. There is probably no better exercise in English expression than the rendering of the thought of a Greek or Roman author into English idiom. The very difference of the two idioms increases the value of the exercise. But great loss is sustained by the student when, as is much too frequently the case, he is allowed to translate into a diction and idiom which have no existence in actual English speech or English literature. Such phrases, *e. g,* as "this one, that one" (*hic, ille*), which are never heard outside the class-room, ought not be tolerated in it. For the sake of the clearer exhibition of the grammatical manner of expression in the Latin, it is well that the translation should correspond to the original where the two idoms are identical, but no farther. Especial care should be taken to render the order of development of the thought in the Latin, as shown by the order of the original, and the student should unhesitatingly, where English idiom demands it, change the

active voice to the passive, and break a Latin sentence into as many English sentences as may be desirable.

A higher ideal of translation than it is easy to attain by oral work alone may be set up in the minds of students, if a passage is occasionally assigned for carefully studied written translation, and if a number of the compositions thus produced are then read aloud, criticisms of style being asked for from the class, and special excellencies pointed out by the teacher. It is also a great help, if the teacher makes a practice of giving the best version of which he is capable, after the lesson has been translated by the class, not allowing himself to interpose remarks, but translating fluently from the beginning to the end.

In what has been said thus far, stress has been laid upon the mastery of the mechanism of expression in Latin, — the words, their forms and syntactical constructions, and the order in which they stand in the sentence. But, at the very outset, the student should be made to understand that these things are not ends but tools, and that the end is to gain, through the reading of Latin, an insight into the thought and feeling of a people who have contributed very largely to make the life of the civilized world of to-day what it is. The Commentaries of Cæsar, the Epic of Virgil, and the Orations of Cicero, — commonly spoken of as subjects required for admission to college, — are in reality masterpieces of literary style, and historical documents of first-rate importance. The teacher, from whose attitude of mind his pupils are likely to take their own attitude, will do well not to allow the burden of daily work and yearly repetition to lead him to set up a mechanical conception of Latin as a field for intellectual gymnastics, in place of the true conception of a vital literature, capable of exerting a strong attraction upon the young student (for the most part possessed as yet of but a very slight vision of any world except that which is immediately about him), and of becoming a powerful influence for the training of his taste and the awakening of his intellectual ambitions. As a help to this true conception, it is recommended that a few books, dealing with the authors studied solely from the point of view of their human and literary interest, be, if possible, made accessible to the student, — such books, for example, as Froude's Cæsar (Harper & Brothers), a book of perverted eloquence, but helpful if corrected by the next to be mentioned, Forsyth's Cicero (Charles Scribner's Sons), Trollope's Cicero (Macmillan), and Sellar's Virgil (Macmillan) ; to which should be added the articles on Cæsar, Cicero, and Virgil in the Encyclopædia Britannica, together with Sellar's article on Roman Literature in the same place, and Wilkins's Primer of Roman Literature (Macmillan).

The text of the formal expressions of opinion of the Conference follows : —

Recommendations of the Conference upon the subject of Latin.

(1) The formal requirements in Latin at present prevailing for admission to representative colleges ought not, so far as quantity is concerned, to be increased.

(2) Education below the high school course should be so organized that students may be prepared to enter upon that course at least a year earlier than, in most places, they now do.

(3) The study of Latin should be begun, in a four-year course, not later than at the age of fourteen years, and at a correspondingly earlier age when the course is of five or six years' duration.

(4) At least four years of study, with five recitation periods a week, of not less than forty-five minutes each, should be given to the study of Latin.

(5) In case the course extends through five or six years, there should, in the interests of more thorough work, be no diminution of the time which has been suggested as a proper weekly allotment for a four-year course.

(6) While the Conference does not find itself yet prepared to declare that translation at sight from Latin into English, and from English into Latin, without examination upon the ground previously gone over, constitutes a complete and satisfactory test of the student's knowledge, as well as of the power he has gained, it strongly recommends that such twofold translation at sight form a constant and increasing part of the examination for admission *and of the work of preparation.*

(7) The Bucolics of Virgil ought henceforth to form no part of the requirements for admission.

(8) In a four-year course, four books of Caesar's Gallic War, *or an equivalent,* should be completed by the end of the second year, and six orations of Cicero and six books of the Aeneid during the third and fourth years. The Conference makes no recommendation upon the question whether Cicero should precede Virgil, or Virgil Cicero; but suggests that, if Cicero precede, four orations be read, then six books of Virgil, followed by the remaining two orations.

(9) A portion of the Lives of Cornelius Nepos should be substituted for a part or the whole of Caesar's Gallic War, and, as an introduction to the reading of these authors, such books as the Breviary of Eutropius, Gradatim, and Viri Romae, are strongly recommended.

(10) The subject of Latin should be treated in the same way, whether students intend to go to college, to a scientific school, or to neither.

↗(11) The writing of Latin should be carried on, throughout the preparatory course, concurrently with the reading of prose. The main training in syntax should be given in connection with work in writing Latin ; and, during the reading of the text, questions upon syntax should generally be confined to points in which a clear recognition of the nature of the construction is essential to the understanding of the passage. The basis of the exercises in Latin composition should be limited portions of the text of authors read, — perhaps not more than forty or fifty pages. And, finally, the tests in writing Latin at admission examinations should be limited to the subject-matter of the authors studied in the preparatory course.

(12) Elementary books for the study of Latin should contain no sentences written in an un-Latin order.

(13) Except in unusually skilful hands, the so-called Inductive Method of teaching Latin should be used with extreme caution.[1]

✗ (14) The importance of the elementary instruction in Latin should be emphasized, and the necessity of a high grade of scholarship in teachers of the lower classes should be strongly insisted upon.

[1] NOTE. — On the general question here involved the chairman reserves his opinion, waiting for fuller experimental evidence from the schools, and from examinations for admission.

WM. GARDNER HALE, *Professor of Latin in the University of Chicago*, Chairman.

WM. C. COLLAR, *Head-Master of the Roxbury Latin School*, Secretary.

CHARLES E. BENNETT, *Professor of Latin in Cornell University.*

FREDERICK L. BLISS, *Principal of the Detroit High School.*

JNO. T. BUCHANAN, *Principal of the Kansas City High School.*

*JOHN S. CROMBIE, *Principal of the Adelphi Academy.*

JAMES H. DILLARD, *Professor of Latin in Tulane University.*

WM. GALLAGHER, *Principal of the Williston Seminary.*

JOHN C. ROLFE, *Acting Professor of Latin in the University of Michigan.*

JULIUS SACHS, *Principal of the Collegiate Institute for Boys, New York City.*

* Mr. Crombie took an active part in the deliberations of the Conference, and later gave his assent to the Report as it here stands. His official connection with it was therefore concluded. His associates, however, desire to append a record of his untimely death on the 16th of April, 1893; and to express their deep regret at the loss of a colleague of singular thoughtfulness, tact, and charm.

GREEK.

omit

To the Committee of Ten : —

The Conference on Greek met with every member present at Ann Arbor, Michigan, December 28th, 29th, and 30th, 1892.

In its discussions and recommendations the Conference has been guided by the existing conditions of the study of Greek in the schools and by the admission requirements of colleges, as well as by its desire to recommend some ideal plan of study. It is well known that the time and attention given to Greek vary greatly in different sections of the country, so that a recommendation that is simply a statement of the existing conditions for schools in some sections may be for a school in a less favored community — for the time — an unattainable ideal.

However unfortunate it may be thought, the fact remains that few schools will do more for their pupils in preparation for college than the college requirements for admission demand, so that the college determines in large measure the amount of work done in the school, as well as controls to some extent by the rigor or laxity of its entrance examinations the quality of the preparatory instruction.

Influenced then by these considerations, the Conference has aimed to make recommendations that may tend to unify methods of the study of Greek in the different sections of the country. The Conference would not have its recommendations regarded as restrictive in any sense ; it believes that under favorable conditions more can be accomplished than the amount proposed below (secs. II., III.) — many schools are doing more to-day ; but the Conference recommends an amount of work that every school can do in the time proposed. Schools that are favored in the early training of their pupils and in other ways, can accomplish more.[1]

The following votes and recommendations were made by the Conference : —

Voted : That in making the following recommendations this Conference desires that the average age at which pupils now enter college be lowered rather than raised, and the Conference urges that no addition be made to the more advanced requirements in Greek now prescribed for admission to college.

[1] The statement of a headmaster of long experience will not be without interest, as showing the possibilities of increase in the amount of work done, without extra time or a sacrifice of thorough teaching. He says that some years ago his classes read three books of Homer in the senior year ; as he received pupils better trained and secured better instruction, the amount read was increased to five books ; then to eight ; and he hopes in the same way to increase the amount read still further.

I. Period of Study.

The Conference recommends that the study of Greek be begun at least three years before the close of the course preparatory to college, and that to the subject be given five recitations per week, of at least forty-five minutes each, the first year, four recitations per week the second year, and four recitations per week the third year.

It will be seen that the Conference recommends as a minimum school course in Greek about 490 recitation periods. Most schools in which Greek is studied during two years only, give 360–400 recitation periods to the study, so that for such schools the time recommended amounts to an increase of little more than a half-year's work. It is believed by the Conference that this increase can be made in many cases without serious difficulty. On the other hand this amount of time recommended as a minimum is less than the time already given in most schools where Greek is studied three years. Of twenty-five representative schools having three-year courses in Greek, two only give less than the minimum number of hours proposed (490), while twelve devote to Greek 550 hours or more, one school giving 658 hours in three years.

While the Conference recommends three years as the minimum time for the study of Greek in schools, it would not have a pupil begin to study the language without a knowledge of the elements of Latin; so that the Conference would limit the study of Greek to two years in a school in which Latin is studied but three.

.

II. Course in Attic Greek.

The Conference recommends that the course in Attic Greek consist of four books of the Anabasis, or of two books of the Anabasis and an amount of the Hellenica, or of other Attic Greek, equivalent to two other books of the Anabasis.

The members of the Conference urge that the Anabasis be no longer retained in our schools as the only text-book in Attic Greek; they feel that as the events chronicled in the Anabasis had little effect on subsequent history, it is well for pupils to read more important works. The Hellenica, especially Books I. and II., has more historic value than the Anabasis, and the narrative portions of Thucydides may well be read in schools. The Conference believes that by such substitution of portions of the Hellenica and of Thucydides the pupil's interest in his work will be increased, and that better results can be obtained.

III. Homer.

The Conference recommends that three books of the Iliad, or its equivalent, four books of the Odyssey, be the prescribed work in Homer, suggesting that the Odyssey be preferred.

The demand is being made in some quarters that Homer be no longer studied in schools, thus limiting the study of Greek to the Attic dialect. While the Conference cannot favor this plan for schools in which Greek is studied during three years, and believes that the withdrawal of Homer from such schools would be a misfortune, it advises that schools which limit their courses in Greek to two years, make no attempt to teach Homer.

The charge that Homer is poorly taught in the schools seems to the Conference an argument against poor teaching, not against the subject taught. No one proposes to remove English Composition from the list of school studies, — and yet, if we can judge from current educational literature, men have great differences of opinion as to the best methods of teaching English Composition, as well as believe that there is much poor teaching of this subject. Poor instruction should be made the basis of attack upon the individual teacher who is at fault, or upon the wrong methods employed, not against the subject in which poor instruction is given. The Conference does recognize, however, that as a result of poor teaching a pupil may leave the preparatory school with neither the definite knowledge of Attic Greek that he can be expected to have, nor a clear understanding of the relation of the Epic to the later Classical language. This may come from an attempt to teach the pupil two dialects, whereas all instruction in Greek grammar and language should aim to fix in the pupil's mind by repetition and comparison some fundamental knowledge of Attic Greek. Homeric grammar, in the opinion of the Conference, is a subject for study in the College or University, not in the Preparatory School; the Iliad and Odyssey of all books must be studied as literature; sufficient instruction in the grammatical peculiarities of their language, however, should be given to insure a correct understanding of the text. (By continuing composition and the reading of Attic texts throughout the course the Conference seeks to avoid neglect of the Attic dialect during the study of Homer. — Sections IV. and VII.)

It appears from the experience of members of the Conference, and of others, that the prospect of reading Homer is no small inducement to pupils to study Greek; in schools where children have been encouraged to read translations of Homer, the number beginning Greek has been considerably increased. The Homeric poems appeal to the pupil's imagination and arouse his interest in the life and thought of the Greeks. It does not seem wise to the Conference to remove these works from the schools and thereby delay the time when pupils can begin their real acquaintance with the two greatest poems the Greeks have left us. If the study of Homer is relegated to the college, many graduates of our schools, both those who do not go to college and those who fail to continue their Greek after entrance, will know nothing of Homer in the original — and probably little through translation.

The Conference holds that the Odyssey is much to be preferred to the Iliad for school boys and girls. The Odyssey deals with fairy land, enchantment, and human effort: it is a story of the same class with, and can be compared to, the Arabian Nights and Robinson Crusoe. The Iliad, on the other hand, treats of deeds that belong to Gods and heroes, the conflicts seem far from us, and lack the human interest that Odysseus' adventures have. Young children read translations of the whole Odyssey eagerly, but are interested in scattered episodes only of the Iliad.

IV. Translation into Greek.

The Conference recommends that instruction in the translation of English into Greek be based upon the Attic prose Greek read, and that simple exercises of this nature, both oral and written, based upon the lesson of the day, be frequently given; that some manual of "Greek Composition," in which connected discourse is employed and the subject of syntax is topically treated, be used; and the Conference urges that the exercises in translation into Greek be continuous throughout the preparatory course.

It is well agreed, in theory, that Greek Composition is valuable as a means to secure the better understanding of the texts read, and there is no wide difference of opinion as to the desirability of basing exercises for translation on the Attic prose read, and of holding frequent exercises in re-translation. There is, however, great variety of practice: in some schools no exercises in re-translation are given after the first book; in many schools pupils are required to use text books in which the sentences and longer exercises are based solely on the author's ingenuity and fancy; and, furthermore, exercises in Greek Composition are neither taught by the instructor nor regarded by the pupil as a regular part of the school work but as an unfortunate and useless task devised by college teachers and inflicted by college entrance requirements. The Conference, therefore, wishes to emphasise the importance of Greek Composition, and urges that it be a part of each week's work. Each teacher must decide whether a portion of each recitation hour, or a separate hour each week, shall be given to such exercises.

V. Geography, History, Etc.

The Conference recommends that in the reading of the classical texts. the Geography, History, Mythology, and Antiquities connected with the subject matter read, receive proper attention.

VI. Sight Examinations.

The Conference recommends that pupils be prepared for an entrance examination in reading simple Attic prose at sight, and the Conference suggests that as a substitute for an examination on a prescribed portion of Homer, an examination in Homer at sight, with questions on the passage set for examination, may be given.

The Conference regrets that so few colleges through their entrance examinations encourage "reading at sight" in schools. Twenty-nine colleges only offer or require sight examinations for entrance; but nine have sight examinations in Homer; in two sight tests are the only ones required. As school work is little better than college requirements compel, the amount of sight reading done in schools can be readily estimated. In most schools, it is true, spasmodic exercises are held, but comparatively few schools seem to regard "sight work" as an exercise to be constantly practised.

It is quite evident that pupils who have read only 1500 verses of Homer are not prepared for examination in Homer at sight; but those who have studied 2500 or 3000 verses, and have been steadily trained in sight reading, should be allowed to take a sight examination in place of an examination on a prescribed portion of the text, or as a supplement to it.

(In recommending entrance examinations at sight and thereby the practice of sight reading in schools, the Conference wishes to avoid an overestimate of the value of such exercise, and does not urge its practice to the exclusion of carefully prepared work. A fuller statement of the views of the Conference on this subject will be found under section X.)

VII. Division of Entrance Examinations.

The Conference recommends that the preliminary examination for college be upon the essentials of grammar (forms and syntax) and four books of the Anabasis or its equivalent; the final examination to be upon Attic prose at sight, Homer, and Greek Composition.

The Conference does not favor any examination upon grammar apart from questions suggested by the text set for translation, and urges that the questions asked aim to determine the applicant's knowledge of the regular and more common inflections and constructions.

It is recommended that the examination in Greek Composition form part of the final examination, as the Conference believes that practice in translation into Greek should be continued throughout the school course. Since Attic Greek must be the basis of all grammatical study of Greek in schools, it follows that the reading of Attic prose ought to be continued parallel with the work in Homer and in connection with the composition exercises. By this means a model for composition is secured by the pupil, and his knowledge of Attic Greek is increased both by the reading and by the comparisons drawn between the Homeric and Attic dialects.

VIII. DIFFERENT CLASSES OF STUDENTS.

The Conference recommends that no difference be made in the treatment of Greek for the three classes of students named in the seventh question suggested by the Committee of Ten.

––––––––

Before making any recommendations as to methods of teaching Greek in the preparatory course, the Conference adopted the following statement as a definition of its conception of the purpose of the study of Greek in that course :

The suggestions which the Conference has to make concerning methods of instruction in the preparatory course are primarily determined by its conception of what constitutes the distinctive work of this course. This work it conceives to be the teaching of the language of standard Attic prose through instruction in Attic grammar and reading of Attic texts, and the awakening of interest in the literature and thought of the Greeks through the reading of Homer.

IX. INTRODUCTORY WORK.

The Conference recommends that the work in Greek, preceding the reading of connected discourse, aim to secure for the student a mastery of the common forms of the language, facility in the use of as full a vocabulary as possible, and an acquaintance with the simpler principles of syntax.

In the opinion of the Conference a thorough knowledge of the ordinary forms of Greek words can best be obtained by the use of some manual containing the more common paradigms, short and simple sentences for translation from Greek into English and from English into Greek, and also statements of the simpler principles of Greek syntax. The Conference urges that written as well as oral work be constantly required in the class room that both the eye and the ear may be appealed to in fixing firmly in the pupil's mind the forms of the language ; and that in all exercises special attention be paid to correct pronunciation of the Greek. This Conference cannot give its approval to any scheme for imparting a knowledge of Greek inflections which contemplates the learning of them from isolated examples as they chance to occur in the connected text of a classical author. It believes that any such attempt involves unnecessary difficulties that can be easily avoided by requiring pupils to memorise together those forms that are closely connected in form and meaning, as exhibited in the paradigms usually given in text books. The Conference feels that as the time for fixing forms by repetition is limited, a logical and systematic order should be followed in their acquisition ; and while the Conference believes in the use of the reasoning powers and of inductive methods in teaching language, it cannot view with favor any effort to introduce into our schools Greek text books based exclusively on the so-called " Inductive Method."

The Conference cannot urge too strongly that special attention be given to the acquisition of a vocabulary, and suggests that this may best be accomplished by a careful memorising of the vocabularies connected with the exercises and by a systematic study of groups of allied words. By a judicious selection of " root-words " and the mastery of the meaning of terminations, a vocabulary, adequate to the student's needs at this stage, may be acquired without much difficulty. Thus a necessary foundation for easy and rapid translation will be laid, and the habit — in the opinion of the Conference a very important habit — will be established of associating related words in groups, instead of regarding them as isolated and disconnected elements of the language.

This introductory work in Greek should include also a study of the simpler and more common usages of syntax. While the Conference would not have grammatical knowledge considered in any sense as an end in the study of Greek, yet it does regard such knowledge as an essential means to an end, and therefore urges that it be not neglected during the introductory period of the study. The simpler constructions of the cases of nouns and of the moods and tenses of verbs should be stated in the manual placed in the hands of the pupil. These constructions should be made familiar by repeated reference to them ; but whatever is unusual, exceptional, or abstruse may well be postponed to a later period of the study. In all this work the pupil should be encouraged to draw upon his knowledge of Latin syntax for illustration and comparison.

The Conference recommends that intelligent reading of the Greek text in class be regarded as an indispensable part of the work, and that for this careful preparation on the part of the student be required; that reading aloud in the class by the teacher, as well as by the pupil, be employed as a means of training the ear, and of gaining ability to grasp readily the thought of a passage; that from the outset sight translation go hand in hand with the prepared translation, and that for this purpose the text of the succeeding lesson or lessons be preferred to that of a separate work; that there be also some translation from hearing, of both prepared and unprepared work; that there be frequent practice in the reading at sight of easy passages of Greek without translation, and that, in order to be sure that the meaning of the passage is grasped, the pupil be required to state the substance of the passage read; that translation of the Anabasis, or its equivalent, be begun, at latest, in the last half of the first year, idiomatic English being demanded, and the questions on the text being asked before or after the connected translation of the whole passage, preferably before.

Reading of the Greek text is too often neglected in schools with the result that the average student on entering college cannot read a half-page of text intelligently. The reader's attention is so fully absorbed in his effort to pronounce the separate words that he gives little or no thought to the relation of the words in a sentence, or of the sentences in a paragraph. Indeed, it is not too strong a statement to say that the average pupil does not associate the reading of a sentence in Greek with the determination of the meaning of the same sentence; to his mind these are two separate processes, whereas he should regard the reading of the text as a necessary means to the understanding of the passage read. Therefore .the Conference urges that reading of the text be constantly practiced by both teacher and pupil; that no attempt to translate any Greek "in advance" be made until the passage has been carefully read; and that teachers require from their pupils no less intelligent reading of the text than accurate translation of the same.

Without underestimating the discipline which is gained from the study of Greek, or disregarding the training in English obtained by careful and studied translation, the Conference conceives that one of the chief objects in the study of any language is to secure for the student the power to appreciate the form and substance of that language. The facts of a literature can be translated, but the form, the something that makes every translation of Homer or Dante inadequate, cannot be alienated from its proper language. In the opinion of the Conference, therefore, the teaching of Greek from the first should aim to give the pupil, so far as possible, the ability to read and understand simple Greek as he reads. To obtain this power the student must, first of all, be supplied with a thorough knowledge of the common inflections and syntactical constructions of the language, and, secondly, he must gain skill in using this knowledge by reading as large amounts of text as possible. Two exercises should be constantly employed : careful preparation of text by the pupil outside the class-room and reading and translation at sight in the class. The first increases the pupil's knowledge of the language and secures to him independence in working, while " sight work" in the class gives him a free opportunity to use the knowledge he has gained, stimulates his interest, and quickens his perceptive faculties, at the same time allowing the instructor to teach the best methods of approach and imparting to the learner a sense of increasing power, — which last seems to the Conference a most important result.

As stated above, the Conference believes that reading of the text should precede any attempt at translation, and it would have a clear distinction made between the determination of the meaning of a passage and its translation. If from repeated readings of the text the meaning of the passage in hand is not clear, the pupil should be taught to approach the passage *in the order of the original*, and to determine its meaning word by word by noticing the inflectional endings, the force of compounds, and the relation of ideas implied in the position of words and phrases. Only when the meaning of a passage has been fully grasped, should the pupil be allowed to attempt a translation, and then idiomatic English should be required. The Conference believes that if translation be kept distinct from the earlier process of ascertaining the meaning of a passage, and if in translation only the best English of which the pupil is capable is accepted, the translation dialect, with its injury to the mother-tongue, can be made to disappear.

While reading at sight may fix knowledge already gained and gives skill in using such knowledge, it adds few new facts to the pupil's fund of knowledge. The meanings of words, new constructions and forms must be dwelt upon to be fixed in his memory. Therefore it is recommended that this sight practice be given on the passages which follow the day's lesson, and that the text read thus hastily form part of the succeeding day's work ; by this method the new facts presented during the sight reading can be fixed in the pupil's mind by his own study.

As the teacher's main purpose in asking questions on the text is to obtain proof that the pupil understands the passage in hand and is prepared to translate it intelligently, the Conference advises that such questions be asked before translation is begun, and, since nothing can be devised to destroy all interest in the subject matter read more thoroughly than the habit of having a lesson translated in small portions of a few lines each, the translations interrupted with questions, with no uninterrupted translation of the whole, the Conference urges that during some part of each recitation hour a connected translation of the whole lesson be made.

XI. PROSODY.

The Conference recommends that in the study of Homer attention be given from the beginning to the rhythmical reading of the text; that the teaching of prosody be limited to instruction in the most essential elements in the structure of the verse; and that the pupil be taught to use the knowledge already gained from the metrical reading of Virgil.

To get an adequate appreciation of any kind of Greek poetry, it must be read rhythmically. This is especially true of the Homeric poetry, which was originally composed to be heard rather than read. The practice of translating Homer without reading the text in its metrical form ought not to be tolerated. The teacher of Homer should at the outset read the text to his pupils and enable them to appreciate the effect of a rhythmical recitation. The details of the structure of the verse will best be learned and remembered from constant practice in metrical reading.

Voted: To concur with the Latin Conference in its recommendations as to the age at which the study of Latin should be begun.

The above is respectfully submitted as the report of the Conference on Greek.

(Signed.) MARTIN L. D'OOGE, *Professor, University of Michigan, Ann Arbor, Mich.*, Chairman.

CLIFFORD H. MOORE, *Phillips Academy, Andover, Mass.*, Secretary.

E. W. COY, *Principal of the Hughes High School, Cincinnati, O.*

A. F. FLEET, *Superintendent of the Missouri Military Academy, Mexico, Mo.*

ASHLEY D. HURT, *Head Master of the High School, Tulane University, New Orleans, La.*

ROBERT P. KEEP, *Principal of the Free Academy, Norwich, Conn.*

ABBY LEACH, *Professor, Vassar College, Poughkeepsie, N. Y.*

WILLIAM H. SMILEY, *Principal of the High School, Denver, Colo.*

CHARLES FORSTER SMITH, *Professor, Vanderbilt University, Nashville, Tenn.*

BENJ. IDE WHEELER, *Professor, Cornell University, Ithaca, N. Y.*

ENGLISH.

To the Committee of Ten : —

The Conference on the Study of English has the honor to submit the following Report : —

The Conference was called to order on Wednesday, December 28th, 1892, at quarter of eleven A.M., by Professor Allen. Principal Thurber was elected Chairman and Professor Kittredge, Secretary. The Conference remained in session till half past three o'clock Friday, December 30th, when it adjourned *sine die*. Every member was present at the deliberations and took part in debate. The results embodied in the present Report were arrived at after much discussion, and represent in all but a few points of minor importance the unanimous opinion of the Conference. The subjects which the Conference thought were included in its commission are those usually taught in schools under the names of English Language, English Grammar, Composition, Rhetoric, and English Literature. Elocution appeared to lie outside of the subjects which the meeting was convened to discuss.

The main direct objects of the teaching of English in schools seem to be two : (1) to enable the pupil to understand the expressed thoughts of others and to give expression to thoughts of his own ; and (2) to cultivate a taste for reading, to give the pupil some acquaintance with good literature, and to furnish him with the means of extending that acquaintance. Incidentally, no doubt, a variety of other ends may be subserved by English study, but such subsidiary interests should never be allowed to encroach on the two main purposes just indicated. Further, though it may be necessary to consider these main purposes separately in the Report or even to separate them formally in the statement of a programme, yet in practice they should never be dissociated in the mind of the teacher and their mutual dependence should be kept constantly present to the mind of the pupils. The recommendations of the Conference should all be interpreted in accordance with these general principles, which were never lost sight of in its debates.

The recommendations of the Conference fall naturally into two divisions : (1) English in schools below the high-school grade, and (2) English in the high-school.

I. The Study of English in Schools below the High-School Grade.

If the pupil is to secure control of the language as an instrument for the expression of his thoughts, it is necessary (1) that, during the period of life when imitation is the chief motive principle in education, he should be kept so far as possible away from the influence of bad models and under the influence of good models, and (2) that every thought which he expresses, whether orally or on paper, should be regarded as a proper subject for criticism as to language. Thus every lesson in geography or physics or mathematics may and should become a part of the pupil's training in English. There can be no more appropriate moment for a brief lesson in expression than the moment when the pupil has something which he is trying to express. If this principle is not regarded, a recitation in history or in botany, for example, may easily undo all that a set exercise in English has accomplished. In order that both teacher and pupil may attach due importance to this incidental instruction in English, the pupil's standing in any subject should depend in part on his use of clear and correct English.

In addition to this incidental training, appropriate special instruction in English should form a part of the curriculum from the beginning. For convenience this special instruction may be considered under three heads: (*a*) "language" and composition, (*b*) formal or systematic grammar, (*c*) reading, or lessons in literature.

A. "Language" and composition. — During the *first two years* at school, children may acquire some fluency of expression by reproducing orally in their own words stories told them by their teachers and by inventing stories about objects and pictures.

Not later than the first term of the *third school-year* children should begin to compose in writing. To assist them in overcoming mechanical difficulties (as of punctuation, the use of capitals, etc.), they should be required to copy and to write from dictation and from memory short and easy passages of prose and verse.

From the beginning of the *third* to the end of the *sixth* school-year, "language-work" should be of three kinds:

1. Oral and written exercises in the correct employment of the forms of the so-called "irregular" verbs, of pronominal forms, and of words and phrases frequently misused.

2. Oral and written exercises in the most elementary form of composition, that is, in the construction of sentences of various kinds. The matter out of which the sentences are to be constructed may, if necessary, be supplied by the teacher; but the pupil should, from his

earliest years, be encouraged to furnish his own material, expressing his own thoughts in a natural way. The greatest care should be taken to make these exercises practical rather than technical and to avoid the errors of the old-fashioned routine method of instruction in grammar.

3. The writing of narratives and descriptions. — These exercises should begin with the *third school-year* and should be continued throughout the course. The subjects assigned should gradually increase in difficulty: in the *seventh and eighth school-years*, if not earlier, they may often be suggested by the pupil's observation or personal experience. The paraphrasing of poetry is not to be commended as an exercise in prose composition: it is often of value to require the pupil to tell or write, in his own words, the story of some narrative poem ; but the reducing of lyric poetry to prose is hardly to be defended. Pains should be taken, from the outset, to enlarge and improve the child's vocabulary by suggesting to him, for the expression of his thoughts, better words than those he may himself have chosen. He should be trained to recognize when a sentence naturally closes, and should be warned against running distinct sentences together. He should also be trained to perceive the larger divisions of thought which are conventionally indicated by paragraphs. The teacher should bear in mind that the necessity of correctness in the formation of sentences and paragraphs is like the necessity of accurate addition, subtraction, multiplication, and division in mathematical work, and that composition proper, — the grouping of sentences and paragraphs, — as well as development of a central idea, should never be taught until this basis of correct sentences is attained.

Spelling should be learned incidentally, in connection with every subject studied, and not from a spelling-book.

Compositions and all other written exercises should receive careful and appropriate criticism, and the staff of instructors should be large enough to protect every teacher from an excess of this peculiarly exacting and fatiguing work.

B. *Formal or systematic grammar.* — Not earlier than the thirteenth year of the pupil's age the study of formal grammar, with drill in fundamental analysis, may be taken up. It should not be pursued as a separate study longer than is necessary to familiarize the pupil with the main principles. Probably a single year (not more than three hours a week) will be sufficient. Subsequently, although grammatical analysis (as an instrument of interpretation and of criticism) may properly accompany reading and the study of composition, it should not be regarded as a separate subject in the curriculum.

The teaching of formal grammar should aim principally to enable the pupil (1) to recognize the parts of speech, and (2) to analyze sentences both as to structure and as to syntax. Routine parsing should be avoided, and exercises in the correction of false syntax should be sparingly resorted to.

The study of word-analysis (etymology), — including the subjects of root-words, prefixes, and terminations — should not form a separate subject in the grammar-school course. All instruction in these matters should be incidental.

With regard to the study of formal grammar the Conference wishes to lay stress on three points : (1) a student may be taught to speak and write good English without receiving any special instruction in formal grammar ; (2) the study of formal grammar is valuable as training in thought, but has only an indirect bearing on the art of writing and speaking ; and (3) the teaching of formal grammar should be as far as possible incidental and should be brought into close connection with the pupil's work in reading and composition. These principles explain the considerable reduction recommended by the Conference in the amount of time allowed to this study.

C. Reading, or Lessons in Literature. — Reading-books should be of a literary character and should not attempt to teach physical science or natural history. They should make very sparing use of sentimental poetry.

From the beginning of the *third year* at school, the pupil should be required to supplement his regular reading-book with other reading-matter of a distinctly literary kind. At the beginning of the *seventh school-year* the reading-book may be discarded, and the pupil should henceforth read literature, — prose and narrative poetry in about equal parts. Complete works should usually be studied. When extracts must be resorted to, these should be long enough to possess a unity of their own and to serve as a fair specimen of an author's style and method. Children should be taught to read distinctly and with expression, but without exaggeration or mannerisms. They should be taught to comprehend the subject-matter as a whole and to grasp the significance of parts, as well as to discover and appreciate beauties of thought and expression. Due attention should be paid to what are sometimes thoughtlessly regarded as points of pedantic detail, such as the elucidation of involved sentences, the expansion of metaphors into similes and the compression of similes into metaphors, the tracing of historical and other references, and a study of the denotation and connotation of single words. Such details are necessary if the pupil is to be brought to anything but the vaguest understanding of what he reads, and there is no danger that an intelligent teacher will allow himself to be dominated by them. It should not be forgotten that in these early years of his training the pupil is forming habits of reading and of thought which will either aid him for the rest of his life, or of which he will by-and-by have to cure himself with painful effort.

In the opinion of the Conference it is expedient that the English work during the last two years of the grammar-school course (including formal grammar, reading, and composition) should be in the hands of a special teacher or teachers. But the appointment of such teacher or teachers should not be held to excuse the instructors in other subjects from the oversight of the English of their pupils. It is only by cordial coöperation in all departments that satisfactory results in this direction can be obtained. To the lack of such joint effort the present unsatisfactory condition of English study in the schools and colleges may be in great part ascribed.

II. The Study of English in the High–School.

The Conference is of opinion that the study of English should be pursued in the high-school for five hours a week during the entire course of four years. This would make the total amount of available time not far from eight hundred hours (or periods).

The study of literature and training in the expression of thought, taken together, are the fundamental elements in any proper high-school course in English, and demand not merely the largest share of time and attention but continuous and concurrent treatment throughout the four years. The Conference therefore recommends the assignment of three hours a week for four years (or 480 hours in the total) to the study of literature, and the assignment of two hours a week for the first two years, and one hour a week for the last two years (or 240 hours in the total) to training in composition. By the study of literature the Conference means the study of the works of good authors, not the study of a manual of literary history.

Rhetoric, during the earlier part of the high-school course, connects itself directly, on the one hand, with the study of literature, furnishing the student with apparatus for analysis and criticism, and, on the other hand, with practice in composition, acquainting the student with principles and maxims relating to effective discourse. For this earlier stage, therefore, extending through the first two years, no assignment of hours to rhetoric has been deemed advisable, and an assignment of one hour a week in the third year (a total of 40 hours), is thought sufficient for any systematic view of rhetoric that should be attempted in the high school. It will be observed, however, that if the teacher has borne in mind the practical uses of rhetoric in the first two years, he will have conveyed the essentials of the art (with or without references to a text-book) before the systematic view begins, so that this view will be a kind of codification of prinicples already applied in practice.

The history of English literature should be taught incidentally, in connection with the pupil's study of particular authors and works; the mechanical use of "manuals of literature" should be avoided, and the committing to memory of names and dates should not be mistaken for culture. In the fourth year, however, an attempt may be made, by means of lectures or otherwise, to give the pupil a view of our literature as a whole and to acquaint him with the relations between periods. This instruction should accompany, — not supersede, — a chronologically arranged sequence of authors. In connection with it a syllabus or brief primer may be used.

To the subject of Historical and Systematic (or Formal) Grammar, one hour a week in the fourth year (a total of 40 hours) may be assigned.

In the present state of text-books and teachers, the study of the History of English Language cannot, perhaps, be generally or even extensively introduced into the high schools. It is the opinion of the Conference, however, that certain parts of that study may be profitably undertaken during the last year of the high-school course, and that some systematic knowledge of the history of the language is of value to the student who goes no farther than the high school, as well as to the student preparing for college.

It is obvious that without a knowledge of Anglo-Saxon and Middle-English nothing can be accomplished by a study of the history of sound change as exemplified in derivation, word-composition, and inflections, nor can any great good come from an illustration of modern syntax through the syntax of stages of the language with which the student is unfamiliar; but, although these important branches of the subject must necessarily be reserved to a later period, it appears evident that certain other branches of the study might be pursued to advantage even by pupils who have no knowledge either of the earlier stages of English or of any foreign tongue. The Conference has in mind the following topics : —

1. *The History and Geography* of the English speaking people, so far as these illustrate the development of the English language.

2. *Phonetics.* — Though we do not recommend any study of details in the historical development of English spelling, we think it essential that every high school scholar should possess a clear idea of the general causes which have given English the peculiar value of its vowel symbols, and made them essentially different from the system

of other languages. Such study would prevent, for example, acquiescence in the common error of regarding the vowels in *rid* and *ride* as the short and the long of the same sound.

3. *Word-Composition.* — The historical study of inflections and of word-composition should not be included in this scheme. But some elementary treatment of prefixes and suffixes and of word-composition may come in incidentally. The purpose of including it, however, is rather to illustrate principles of historical development than to acquaint the pupil with a body of details.

4. *Elements of the English Vocabulary.* — This branch of English study is already pursued in some secondary schools as an independent subject, with the aid, perhaps, of such a book as Trench's "On the Study of Words"; but the view of the Conference is that it would be better to include it as a part of a systematic treatment of the history of the language. The extent to which the study of the sources of English words can be carried in any school or class will depend on the acquaintance the pupils possess with Latin, French, and German. This subject should be so pursued as to illustrate the political, social, intellectual, and religious development of the English race; and the knowledge thus obtained will be profitable to youth only in proportion as it links itself with other knowledge derived from their general reading or from their other school work.

5. *Changes in the meaning of words.* — A systematic study of development in the meaning of words should not come in as a distinct part of this plan. Such study should however, of course, be included incidentally in the interpretation of literature.

The teacher must of course be familiar with the more important facts of historical English grammar, and be able to use them in connection with the study of any branch of English, whenever they serve to explain difficulties or to fix grammatical principles. In addition to those parts of historical grammar that have been more specifically mentioned above, the following may be noted, as illustrations of the topics of this subject that may receive attention in high schools, so far as the advancement of the pupils in general linguistic study renders it advisable, and so far as time and opportunity can be found for such work: — dialects and literary language, authority and usage, decay of inflections.

It is the opinion of the Conference that the best results in the teaching of English in high schools cannot be secured without the aid given by the study of some other language, and that Latin—and German, by reason of their fuller inflectional system are especially suited to this end.

The Conference wishes also to emphasize in the case of high-schools what has been already said with regard to schools of lower grade : that every teacher, whatever his department, should feel responsible for the use of good English on the part of his pupils.

The question of requirements for admission to college was carefully considered by the Conference and a definite scheme of examinations devised for recommendation to American colleges. These recommendations concern all scholars in high-schools, for the Conference is of opinion that the high-school course in English should be identical for students who intend to go to college or to a scientific school, and for those who do not, and that the requirements in English for admission to college or to a scientific school should be so adjusted as not to contravene this principle. The practice now too prevalent of maintaining one course in English for pupils who intend to go to college, another for candidates for admission to a scientific or technical school, and a third for pupils whose schooling ends with their graduation from the high-school, cannot be defended on any reasonable grounds. There is no good reason why one of these three classes of students should receive a training in their mother tongue different either in kind or in amount from that received by either of the other two classes.

The Conference is also convinced that the cause of secondary education would be materially helped if the requirements for admission to college, in English as in other subjects, were to be made uniform in kind throughout the country. Uniformity in amount is certainly not practicable and probably not desirable.

The specific recommendations of the Conference as to English requirements for admission to colleges and scientific schools are the following : —

1. That the reading of certain masterpieces of English literature, not fewer in number than those at present assigned by the Commission of New England Colleges, should be required.

2. Each of these should be so far as possible representative of some period, tendency, or type of literature, in order that alternative questions like those suggested in § 5 (below) may be provided. The whole number of these works selected for any year should represent with as few gaps as possible the course of English literature from the Elizabethan period to the present time.

3. Of these books a considerable number should be of a kind to be read by the student cursorily and by himself. A limited number, however, may be read in the class-room under the immediate direction of the teacher.

4. In connection with the reading of all these required books the teacher should encourage parallel or subsidiary reading and the

investigation of pertinent questions in literary history and criticism. The faithfulness with which such auxiliary work is carried on should be constantly tested by means of written and oral reports and class-room discussion, and the same tests should be applied to the required books read cursorily (see § 3).

5. The Conference doubts the wisdom of requiring, for admission to college, set essays (e. g., on the books prescribed, as above, §1), — essays whose chief purpose is to test the pupil's ability to write English. It believes that there are serious theoretical and practical objections to estimating a student's power to write a language on the basis of a theme composed not for the sake of expounding something that he knows or thinks, but merely for the sake of *showing his ability to write.*

Therefore, so long as the formal essay remains a part of the admission examination, it is recommended that questions on topics of literary history or criticism, or on passages cited from prescribed works, be set as an alternative. These topics and passages should be such as (1) to bring out the knowledge of the pupil with regard to the subjects suggested in § 4, and (2) to test his ability to methodize his knowledge and to write clearly and concisely. The questions set should be so framed as to require answers of some length.[1]

6. The Conference is of opinion that in the hands of any but a highly intelligent teacher exercises in the correction of bad English may do more harm than good. And therefore the Conference believes that the correction of specimens of bad English should not form a considerable part of the admission examination,[2] though it is not prepared to recommend the exclusion of such specimens. Care should be taken that those selected are really offences against good English (not merely against good style) and, further, that they are such offences as experience has shown young writers are prone to commit. Obscure sentences and nonsensical or puzzling combinations of words should be avoided.

7. The admission of a student to college so far as English is concerned, should be made to depend largely on his ability to write English as shown in his examination-books on other subjects (such as history). If the candidate's translations from foreign languages are used for this purpose, the examiner should remember that vagueness and absurdity in such translations often result from ignorance of the foreign language rather than from incompetent knowledge of one's mother tongue, and that, further, the art of translation is a very difficult art even to a writer who is at home in both the languages

[1] Not less than a page of the examination-book.
[2] Say not more than one-fifth.

concerned. A student who in general writes well enough may, from either or both of these causes, appear to very poor advantage in an exercise in translation.

8. Though it is clear that the power to write a language can be obtained only by unremitting practice, yet, in the opinion of the Conference, such practice may properly be accompanied and illustrated by a course in elementary rhetoric. This course should include not only the principles of clearness, force, and good taste, but the principles of the arrangement of clauses in the sentence and of sentences in the paragraph. The teacher should bear in mind that any body of written English, of whatever length, is an organic unit, with principles that apply as well to the arrangement of the minor elements as to the grouping of the larger divisions of essay or book. Especial care should be taken that rhetoric is not studied by itself or for its own sake. Its connection with the pupil's actual written or spoken exercises should be kept constantly in view. The Conference therefore does not contemplate an examination in formal rhetoric as a requirement for admission to college.

9. There should be no division of the admission examination in English. When a college or scientific school allows a division of admission requirements into "preliminary" and "final," English should be a "final" subject.

10. The relative importance of the English language and literature as a subject among other requirements for admission to college is about one in six; but the Conference feels strongly that no student should be admitted to college who shows in his English examination and in his other examinations (as in § 7) that he is very deficient in ability to write good English.

May 13th, 1893.

SAMUEL THURBER, *Master of the Girls' High School, Boston, Mass.*, Chairman.

GEORGE LYMAN KITTREDGE, *Professor, Harvard University, Cambridge, Mass.*, Secretary.

EDW. A. ALLEN, *Professor, University of Missouri, Columbia, Mo.*

F. A. BARBOUR, *Principal Michigan State Normal School, Ypsilanti, Mich.*

F. A. BLACKBURN, *Professor, University of Chicago, Chicago, Ill.*

C. B. BRADLEY, *Professor, University of California, Berkeley, Cal.*

FRANCIS B. GUMMERE, *Professor, Haverford College, Pa.*

EDWARD E. HALE, JR., *Professor, University of Iowa, Iowa City, Ia.*

CHARLES L. LOOS, JR., *High School, Dayton, O.*

WM. H. MAXWELL, *Superintendent of Schools, Brooklyn, N. Y.*

OTHER MODERN LANGUAGES.

CAMRIDGE, March 11, 1893.

TO THE COMMITTEE OF TEN :

Gentlemen, — The Conference on Modern Languages, which met
in Washington on the 28th, 29th, and 30t' of December, 1892,
submits the following report.

C. H. GRANDGENT, *Chairman.*

A. TIME OF INTRODUCTION.

1. Wherever thoroughly competent teachers can be secured, we
are of the opinion that there should be introduced into the grammar
schools an elective course in German or French, open to all pupils
who have arrived at the fourth year from the end. It is supposed
that the average boy or girl will reach this stage at the age of ten.
We make the above recommendation, not with a view to separating,
at such an early period, the scholars who are likely to enter a high
school or college from those who are to receive only elementary instruction, but in the firm belief that the educational effects of modern
language study will be of immense benefit to all who are able to
pursue it under proper guidance. It will train their memory and
develop their sense of accuracy ; it will quicken and strengthen their
reasoning powers by offering them, at every step, problems that must
be immediately solved by the correct application of the results of
their own observation ; it will help them to understand the structure
of the English sentence and the real meaning of English words ; it
will broaden their minds by revealing to them modes of thought and
expression different from those to which they have been accustomed.
The study of Latin appears, it is true, to present these same advantages ; but living languages seem to us better adapted to grammar
school work, both on account of the greater ease with which they can
be taught and learned, and because of their closer relation to the
interests and ideas of to-day.

2. We believe that children should, if possible, begin their study
of German or French by the time they are ten years old. At that
age their perceptions are acute, their vocal organs are still flexible,
and they are comparatively free from the morbid fear of ridicule
which impedes their progress in later years: consequently they are
able to acquire a tolerably correct pronunciation and make some
headway in the practical use of the language. Moreover, their
interest is easily kindled, and they are eager to imbibe the life and

spirit of a foreign tongue. We do not on the other hand, recommend the introduction of German or French earlier than the fifth school year, because we fear that if it were begun sooner, it would necessarily be broken off before the end of the grammar school course; and any interruption of the modern language study should, in our opinion, be carefully avoided.

3. In places where it is as yet impossible, through lack of teachers or of money, to include a modern language in the grammar school curriculum, we believe that French or German should form, from the very first, a part of the high school course; it is essential that pupils should study at least one language long enough to reach some degree of maturity in it. If, however, classes are obliged, for any reason, to begin Latin or Greek on entering the secondary school, we recommend that the study of French or German be postponed a twelvemonth; for we regard as entirely inexpedient the introduction of two foreign languages in the same year. When a minimum of French or German is offered as a supplement to a curriculum comprising two other foreign languages, the last language should be taken up in the third year.

B. Number of Lessons per Week.

4. In the grammar grade we recommend that during the first year five recitation periods per week be given to the modern language; during the second, at least four; and during each of the other two years, at least three. To be successful, the study of a new language should present a sufficient number of weekly exercises to enlist and hold the full interest of the pupils. In the case of young children, especially, it is found that more is accomplished by short but frequent lessons than by longer ones at greater intervals.

5. For the high school we make the following recommendations, which refer, of course, only to modern languages: (a) the first foreign language studied should be taken up at once and carried on, with four recitations a week, through all four years; (b) the second foreign language studied — whether the first be ancient or modern — should be begun the second year and continued, with four exercises per week, through the rest of the course; (c) the third foreign language studied — whatever be the nature of the other two — should be introduced in the third year and pursued, with three lessons weekly, during the last two years. In the third case the suggestion of three hours a week for two years, rather than five recitations weekly for one year, is made with a view to avoiding too much pressure during the last year, when the pupil is most likely to be overworked, and a new subject is in greatest danger of being slighted; under

7

different circumstances five exercises per week for one year might, in our opinion, give somewhat better results than three hours weekly for two.

6. It will be seen that we take for granted a high school course of four years and a primary and grammar school course extending over at least eight years. The following table shows at a glance the proposed number of modern language recitations per week during the different years mentioned in the preceding paragraphs : —

	SCHOOL YEAR:	*1st.*	*2d.*	*3d.*	*4th.*	*5th.*	*6th.*	*7th.*	*8th.*
ELEMENTARY SCHOOLS — First Language :						5	4	3	3

			SCHOOL YEAR:	*1st.*	*2d.*	*3d.*	*4th.*
SECONDARY SCHOOLS	Maximum	First Language :		4	4	4	4
		Second Language :		4	4	4	
	Minimum, —	Third Language :			3	3	

In general the two maximum courses in secondary schools are supposed to cover the same ground : it is thought that the facility gained by the previous study of another language will compensate for the loss of one year. But where the elementary schools offer a German or a French course, we intend that the first language studied in the high school shall be the same one that was begun in the grammar grade ; and in this case the first maximum will comprise more than the second.

C. COURSE OF STUDY.

7. According to our best judgment, all pupils of the same intelligence and the same degree of maturity should be instructed alike, no matter whether they are subsequently to enter a college or scientific school, or intend to pursue their studies no further.

I. Grammar Schools.

8. It is expected that during the first two years the lessons will consist of interesting but systematic oral exercises, combined with the use of pictures and the reading of very elementary texts. The mass of knowledge thus acquired will, in the other two years, be classified, extended, and fixed in the memory by means of a larger amount of reading and a more formal study of grammatical principles. It is hoped, however, that oral work will not be neglected during any part of the course. The objects to be attained in these four years are : (*a*) a good pronunciation ; (*b*) ability to understand very easy German or French when it is spoken ; (*c*) ability to read, without painful effort, simple stories in the foreign language ; (*d*) ability to construct short German or French sentences, applying the elementary

rules of grammar. It is the opinion of the Conference that such a course as we have outlined would, in the hands of a competent teacher, produce results of permanent value, whether the study be considered as a means of mental training or as a foundation for further work in the same line.

II. High Schools.

9. In the following paragraphs the term " elementary " will be applied to the first half of the maximum courses and to the entire minimum course (sec § 6) ; the second half of the maximum courses will be called " advanced." The numbers of pages specified below are intended to include not only prepared work but all sight reading done in the class. Our recommendations are practically the same as those of the Commission of Colleges in New England on Admission Examinations. We are in favor of a course of study that will produce the following results : —

10. *In Elementary German.* — (a) Familiarity with the rudiments of grammar, and especially with these topics : the declension of articles, adjectives, pronouns, and such nouns as are readily classified ; the conjugation of weak and of the more usual strong verbs ; the commoner prepositions ; the simpler uses of the modal auxiliaries ; the elementary rules of syntax and word order. (b) Ability to translate at sight a passage of easy prose containing no rare words. It is believed that the requisite facility can be acquired by reading not less than two hundred duodecimo pages of simple German. (c) Ability to pronounce German and to recognize German words and easy sentences when they are uttered.

11. *In Advanced German.* — (a) Proficiency in more advanced grammar. In addition to a thorough knowledge of accidence, of the elements of word-formation, and of the principal values of prepositions and conjunctions, the scholars must be familiar with the essentials of German syntax, and particularly with the uses of modal auxiliaries and the subjunctive and infinitive modes. (b) Ability to translate ordinary German. It is thought that pupils can acquire this ability by reading, in all, not less than seven hundred duodecimo pages. (c) Ability to write in German a paragraph upon an assigned subject chosen from the works studied in class. (d) Ability to follow a recitation conducted in German and to answer in that language questions asked by the instructor.

12. *In Elementary French.* — (a) Familiarity with the rudiments of grammar, and especially with these topics : the conjugation of regular and the more usual irregular verbs, such as *dire, faire,* and the classes represented by *ouvrir, dormir, connaître, conduire,* and

craindre; the forms and positions of personal pronouns; the use of other pronouns and pronominal adjectives; the inflection of nouns and adjectives for gender and number, excepting rare cases; the partitive constructions.   (*b*) Ability to translate simple prose at sight.   It is believed that the requisite facility can be acquired by reading not less than four hundred duodecimo pages from at least three dissimilar works.   (*c*) Ability to pronounce French and to recognize French words and easy sentences when they are uttered.

13. *In Advanced French.* — (*a*) Proficiency in more, advanced grammar.   In addition to a thorough knowledge of accidence and of the values of prepositions and conjunctions, the scholars must be familiar with the essentials of French syntax — especially the use of modes and tenses — and with the more frequently recurring idiomatic phrases. (*b*) Ability to translate standard French. It is thought that pupils can acquire this ability by reading, in all, not less than one thousand duodecimo pages.   (*c*) Ability to write in French a paragraph upon an assigned subject chosen from the works studied in class.   (*d*) Ability to follow a recitation conducted in French and to answer in that language questions asked by the instructor.

14. The ability to translate at sight expected in each grade of French is greater than that required in the corresponding grade of German.   The texts used in the elementary courses should consist of ordinary nineteenth century prose, judiciously varied with such short pieces of poetry as the teacher may select.   In the advanced courses all the reading matter should be of high literary value.   The study of classical works should be reserved until the pupil can read with ease every-day modern prose.   If, however, the language has been taken up in the grammar school, the high school standard can be considerably raised, and some classical authors should be introduced at an early stage.

D. Method of Instruction.

15. The following recommendations are borrowed, in the main, from the *Synopsis of French and German Instruction* for 1890 in the high schools of Boston, Mass. : —

16. In modern language courses the efforts of teachers are naturally directed mainly toward enabling pupils to translate French and German at sight, and, ultimately, to read these languages without the interposition of English.   In order to gain the necessary vocabulary, a great deal of ground must be covered : reading must, therefore, be rapid.   A mistaken idea of " thoroughness " may cause the waste of much valuable time.   Sight translation should begin at the very out-

set of the first year's course, and should always form an important part of the work; it should proceed as briskly as possible, the teacher lifting beginners over hard places, and showing them how to find their own way through the rest. All passages of an abstruse or technical nature should be skipped, or translated by the instructor: not a moment should be lost in contending with difficulties that have no necessary connection with the language. Frequent reviews of reading-matter are not to be recommended: the students' time can nearly always be spent much more profitably on new texts, which have the advantage of stimulating fresh interest and of enlarging the vocabulary. As long as English versions are made, teachers should insist upon idiomatic English. Pupils often think that their foreign author is " silly : " this opinion is generally due to the fact that they see him only through the medium of their own stilted or meaningless prose. Every endeavor should be made to interest scholars in the subject-matter, to make them regard their text-books as literature, not as language-mills; if a story or play moves in an unfamiliar sphere, the surroundings (including the influence of foreign customs and ideas) should be briefly but intelligibly explained beforehand; references to things unknown to the class should be made clear; the beginnings and ends of lessons should coincide with natural breaks in the narrative.

17. The chief object of our modern language courses is, as has been said, the ability to read French and German; but to do this reading intelligently, the student must know more than the definitions of the words he sees; he must be able to imagine the phrases coming from the lips of a Frenchman or a German — he must know how they sound to a native hearer, and how they put themselves together in the mind of a native speaker. Something that approaches this knowledge can be acquired by practice in pronunciation, conversation, and composition. The translation into the foreign language of carefully graded sentences, based on the texts read, should be carried on from the very beginning; and as early as possible connected passages should be used, in order to cultivate good habits in the choice of connectives and the construction of sentences. Aside from set conversational exercises, the foreign language should be used as much as possible in the class-room. In the first year the pupil can catch by ear the names of familiar things and many common phrases; during the second he ought to form sentences himself; and in the third the recitations should, if the instructor has a practical command of French or German, be conducted mainly in that language. In teaching foreign sounds great care must be taken lest the scholar confirm himself in bad habits: uncorrected pronouncing is as bad as none. As

often as may be, the beginners should speak the sentences immediately after the teacher; a very little careful practice of this kind will do more good than any amount of original pronunciation by the pupil. The reading aloud of the French or German text should, in the lower classes, follow rather than precede the translation; otherwise it will be done blindly.

18. A thorough acquaintance with the leading facts of grammar is, of course, a necessary element in the acquisition of a foreign tongue. Grammatical abstractions should, however, not be forced upon the pupil too early. Difficulties can best be overcome by taking them one at a time. In studying language the three enemies that the novice must encounter are pronunciation and spelling, vocabulary, and grammar: singly they can be mastered; united they are likely to prove too strong. High school teachers are, therefore, advised, during the first third of the beginners' year, to devote the recitation hour mainly to sight reading, calling attention to the most important points of grammar as they occur. For his prepared lessons the scholar would meanwhile be learning by heart the inflections of the language, and repeating the translations made in the class. The rules of grammar and the exercises illustrating them should not be formally studied until the pupil has, by some three months' reading, gained a little insight into his French or German. Grammar exercises consisting of German or French sentences to be translated into English are to be done with the books closed, the scholar repeating the original sentence after the teacher, and then turning it into English.

19. In recommending the above course, we do not wish to be understood as implying disapproval of the so-called "natural method," which has, under favorable conditions, been pursued with marked success by teachers peculiarly adapted to that kind of instruction. We do not believe, however, that such methods can be generally applied.

E. College Requirements.

20. It is our opinion that college requirements for admission should coincide with the high school requirements for graduation, as described in §§ 10–13. If the college examination is divided, we recommend that the preliminary test cover our elementary, and the final our advanced course.

21. An examination in elementary French or German ought, in our judgment, to consist of: (a) the translation at sight of a passage of ordinary difficulty from the foreign language into English; and (b) the turning into French or German of simple English sentences immediately illustrative of the first principles of grammar, the vocab-

ulary of these sentences to be taken, as far as possible, from the foreign text set for translation.

22. As a test in advanced French or German we suggest: (a) the translation at sight of a passage of high literary quality from the foreign language into English; and (b) the turning into French or German of a connected passage of simple English prose.

F. SPANISH.

23. The recommendations we have made for French and German apply also to Spanish and to any other modern language that may be introduced into high or grammar schools.

G. PREPARATION OF TEACHERS.

24. The worst obstacle to the progress of modern language study is the lack of properly equipped instructors. There seems to be at present no institution where persons intending to teach German, French, or Spanish in our elementary or secondary schools can receive the special preparation they need. It is the sense of the Conference that universities, states, or cities should provide opportunities for such training.

CHARLES H. GRANDGENT, *Director of Modern Language Instruction in the Public Schools, Boston, Mass.*, Chairman.

WILLIAM T. PECK, *Principal of Latin School, Providence, R. I.*, Secretary.

JOSEPH L. ARMSTRONG, *Professor, Trinity College, Durham, N. C.*

T. B. BRONSON, *Lawrenceville School, Lawrenceville, N. J.*

ALPHONSE N. VAN DAELL, *Professor, Massachusetts Institute of Technology, Boston, Mass.*

CHARLES HARRIS, *Professor, Oberlin College, Oberlin, Ohio.*

SYLVESTER PRIMER, *Professor, University of Texas, Austin, Texas.*

JOHN J. SCHOBINGER, *Principal of Harvard School, 2101 Indiana Avenue, Chicago, Ill.*

I. H. B. SPIERS, *William Penn Charter School, 8 South 12th Street, Philadelphia, Pa.*

WALTER D. TOY, *Professor, University of North Carolina, Chapel Hill, N. C.*

MATHEMATICS.

March, 1893.

To President Charles W. Eliot, Chairman Committee of Ten, National Council of Education : —

Sir, — The undersigned, having been appointed by your Committee to hold a Conference on the subject of secondary instruction in Mathematics, have the honor to report that such Conference was held on the 28th, 29th, and 30th of December, 1892, in Cambridge, Mass.

On mapping out its work, the Conference found that the general subject of secondary mathematics might be conveniently considered under four different heads. It is deemed advisable to preface the separate reports on each of these heads with a general statement of the conclusions reached by the Conference. The following five reports are therefore submitted :

I. General statement of conclusions.
II. Special report on the teaching of arithmetic.
III. Special report on the teaching of concrete geometry.
IV. Special report on the teaching of algebra.
V. Special report on the teaching of formal geometry.

Very respectfully,

SIMON NEWCOMB, *Professor, Johns Hopkins University, Baltimore, Md.*, Chairman.

WILLIAM E. BYERLY, *Professor, Harvard University, Cambridge, Mass.*, Vice Chairman.

ARTHUR H. CUTLER, *Principal of a Private School for Boys, 20 East 50th Street, New York City*, Secretary.

FLORIAN CAJORI, *Professor, Colorado College, Colorado Springs, Colo.*

HENRY B. FINE, *Professor, College of New Jersey, Princeton, N. J.*

W. A. GREESON, *Principal of the High School, Grand Rapids, Mich.*

ANDREW INGRAHAM, *Swain Free School, New Bedford, Mass.*

GEORGE D. OLDS, *Professor, Amherst College, Amherst, Mass.*

JAMES L. PATTERSON, *Lawrenceville School, Lawrenceville, N. J.*

T. H. SAFFORD, *Professor, Williams College, Williamstown, Mass.*

I. General Statement of Conclusions.

The Conference was, from the beginning of its deliberations, unanimously of opinion that a radical change in the teaching of arithmetic was necessary. Referring to the special report on that subject for a statement of the reasons on which its conclusion is based, the conference recommends that the course in arithmetic be at the same time abridged and enriched; abridged by omitting entirely those subjects which perplex and exhaust the pupil without affording any really valuable mental discipline, and enriched by a greater number of exercises in simple calculation and in the solution of concrete problems.

Among the subjects which should be curtailed, or entirely omitted, are compound proportion, cube root, abstract mensuration, obsolete denominate quantities, and the greater part of commercial arithmetic. Percentage should be rigidly reduced to the needs of actual life. In such subjects as profit and loss, bank discount, and simple and compound interest, examples not easily made intelligible to the pupil should be omitted. Such complications as result from fractional periods of time in compound interest are useless and undesirable. The metric system should be taught in applications to actual measurements to be executed by the pupil himself; the measures and weights being actually shown to, and handled by, the pupil. This system finds its proper application in the course which the Conference recommends in concrete geometry.

The method of teaching should be throughout objective, and such as to call into exercise the pupil's mental activity. The text-books should be subordinate to the living teacher. The illustrations and problems should, so far as possible, be drawn from familiar objects; and the scholar himself should be encouraged to devise as many as he can. So far as possible, rules should be derived inductively, instead of being stated dogmatically. On this system the rules will come at the end, rather than at the beginning, of a subject.

The Conference at the same time insists upon the importance of practice in quick and accurate reckoning. The scholar should be thoroughly trained in performing correctly and rapidly the four fundamental operations with integers, vulgar fractions and decimals.

The course in arithmetic thus mapped out should begin about the age of six years, and be completed at the end of the grammar school course, say about the thirteenth year of age. The conference does not feel competent to decide how many hours a week should be devoted to it, and therefore leaves this question to teachers and other school authorities.

The second recommendation of the Conference is that a course of instruction in concrete geometry, with numerous exercises, be introduced into the grammar school. The object of this course would be to familiarize the pupil with the facts of plane and solid geometry, and with those geometrical conceptions to be subsequently employed in abstract reasoning. During the early years the instruction might be given informally, in connection with drawing, and without a separate appointment in the school calendar; after the age of ten years, one hour per week should be devoted to it.

While the systematic study of algebra should not begin until the completion of the course in arithmetic, the Conference deems it necessary that some familiarity with algebraic expressions and symbols, including the methods of solving simple equations, should be acquired in connection with the course in arithmetic. From the age of fourteen, systematic algebra should be commenced, and should be studied for five hours a week during the first year, and for about two hours and a half a week during the two years next succeeding.

The Conference is of opinion that the subject of reckoning in algebra should receive more attention than it actually does, and that the same skill and accuracy should be required in dealing with literal as with numerical coefficients and exponents. It strongly urges that when, as must sometimes be the case, the scholar has occasion to learn and use propositions before he is prepared to understand their rigorous demonstration, he should be convinced of their truth by abundant concrete illustrations and examples, instead of being allowed to accept them as empirical conclusions, or to found them on demonstrations that lack rigor.

The Conference believes that the study of demonstrative geometry should begin at the end of the first year's study of algebra, and be carried on by the side of algebra for the next two years, occupying about two hours and a half a week. It believes that if the introductory course in geometry has been well taught, both plane and solid geometry can be mastered at this time.

Exercises in constructing demonstrations of theorems in plane geometry will naturally occupy much of the attention of teacher and pupil. The Conference deems it very important that great stress be laid by the teacher upon accuracy of statement and elegance of form in such demonstrations, as well as on clear and rigorous reasoning. Special attention should be given to the oral statement of demonstrations.

It is very desirable that colleges should supplement their written admission examinations in geometry by oral ones; and a substantial part of the examination, whether written or oral, should be devoted to testing the ability of the candidate to construct original demonstrations.

Finally, the Conference is of opinion that up to the completion of the first year's work in algebra, the course should be the same, whether the pupils are preparing for college, for scientific schools, or intend their systematic education to end with the high school. In the case of those who do not intend to go to college, but to pursue a business career, the remainder of the term which has been allotted to algebra might well be devoted to book-keeping, and the technical parts of commercial arithmetic. Boys going to a scientific school might profitably spend a year on trigonometry and some of the higher parts of algebra, after completing the regular course in algebra and geometry.

II. Special Report on Arithmetic.

Among the branches of this subject which it is proposed to omit, are some which have survived from an epoch when more advanced mathematics was scarcely known in our schools, so that the course in arithmetic was expected to include all that the pupil would ever know of mathematics. Examples of these subjects are cube root, duo decimals, and compound proportion. Their teaching serves no useful purpose at the present time. So far as any useful principles are embodied in them, they belong to algebra, and can be taught by algebraic methods with such facility that there is no longer any sound reason for their retention in the arithmetical course.

The case is different with commercial arithmetic. The subjects taught under this head have been greatly multiplied and enlarged in recent years, in consequence of the popular demand for a system of education which should be more practical and better suited to the demands of modern commercial and business life, than the old one was supposed to be. It may be well that those pupils of our business colleges who are mature enough to understand such subjects as banking, insurance, discount, partial payments, equation of payments, and the other branches commonly included under the term commercial arithmetic, and who have no expectation of taking any other mathematical course than this, should study these subjects exhaustively. But the case is different with pupils who are going through the courses of our regular graded schools. For them the subjects in question have no practical value, for the reason that they are too young and inexperienced to understand the principles on which business is conducted, and therefore waste valuable mental energy in fruitless struggles with problems which they cannot comprehend. In the text-books we find the subjects in question prefaced by very excellent definitions. The pupil who masters them will be able to state on examination that " the market value of stock is what the stock brings per share when sold for cash " ; that " stock is at a discount when its market value is less than its par value " ; that " its par value is that named in the certificate " ; that " the payee of a bill of exchange is the person to whom the money is ordered to be paid " ; in fine, to state in brief sentences the first principles of commercial law. He may also, after much conjecturing, be able to solve many questions in banking, exchange, insurance, and custom-house business. But until he is brought into actual contact with the business itself, he can form no clear conception of what it all means, or what are the uses or applications of the problems he is solving. On the other hand, when he is once brought face to face with business as an actuality ; when for the first time he becomes a depositor in a savings bank, or a purchaser of shares in a corporation, he will find all the arithmetic necessary for his purposes to be interest, discount, and percentage. The conceptions which he vainly endeavored to master by recitations from a text-book take their places in his mind with hardly the necessity of an effort on his part.

The opinion is widely prevalent that even if the subjects are totally forgotten, a valuable mental discipline is acquired by the efforts made to master them. While the Conference admits that, considered in itself, this discipline has a certain value, it feels that such a discipline is greatly inferior to that which may be gained by a different class of exercises, and bears the same relation to a really improving discipline that lifting exercises in an ill-ventilated room bear to games in the open air. The movements of a race horse afford a better model of improving exercise than those of the ox in a tread-mill. The pupil who solves a difficult problem in brokerage may have the pleasant consciousness of having overcome a difficulty, but he cannot feel that he is mentally improved by the efforts he has made. To attain this end he must feel at every step that he has a new command of principles to be applied to future problems. This end can be best gained by comparatively easy problems, involving interesting combinations of ideas.

Most of the improvements which the Conference has to suggest in teaching can be summed up under the two heads of giving the teaching a more concrete form, and paying more attention to facility and correctness in work. The relations of magnitudes should, so far as possible, be represented to the eye. The fundamental operations of arithmetic should not only be performed symbolically by numbers, but practically, by joining lines together, dividing them into parts, and combining the parts in such a way as to illustrate the fundamental rules for multiplication and division of fractions. A pupil can learn to divide a line into parts more easily than he can master definitions; and when this is done he has a conception of fractions which he cannot gain in any other way. The visible figures by which principles are illustrated should, so far as possible, have no accessories. They should be magnitudes pure and simple, so that the thought of the pupil may not be distracted and that he may know what feature of the thing represented he is to pay attention to. The elementary theorems of arithmetic should be enforced and illustrated in the same way, without an attempt at formal demonstration, the generalization being reached inductively. Thus, when the pupil comprehends clearly, by means of dots arranged in a rectangle, that three fives contain the same number of units as five threes, that is, when he sees that the commutative law is true, then it may be expressed to him in the general form, $a \times b = b \times a$.

The concrete system should not be confined to principles, but be extended to practical applications in mensuration and physics. Measurements of the room, the house, and the yard; the calculation of the weights of visible objects, or of the number of articles that a given receptacle will hold; the computation of distances and areas in the town, by measures on a map of known scale, of the number of cubic feet in a room, and of the weight of the air which fills the room, are examples of problems which can be extended by the teacher indefinitely. The simple operations of arithmetic can be better exemplified by problems set on the spur of the moment, and springing naturally from the environment of teacher and pupil, than by those given in a printed book; and have the inestimable advantage of exciting the interest of the pupil.

When such a system of teaching is once introduced, the teacher will probably be surprised to find to what seemingly abstruse problems the simplest principles of arithmetic can be applied. The problem of computing the quantity of coal which would have to be burned in order to heat the air of a room from the freezing point to 70° would probably be beyond the powers of all our college graduates, except those who have made physics one of their specialties. Yet there is nothing in its elements above the powers of a boy of twelve. At this age the child could, by a few very simple experiments, gain the idea of a quantity of heat much more easily than the idea of stock in a corporation. Having gained this, the elements which enter into the problem in question could be measured one by one.

III. Special Report on Concrete Geometry.

The Conference recommends that the child's geometrical education should begin as early as possible; in the kindergarten, if he attends a kindergarten, or if not, in the primary school. He should at first gain familiarity through the senses with simple geometrical figures and forms, plane and solid; should handle, draw, measure, and model them; and should gradually learn some of their simpler properties and relations. It is the opinion of the Conference that in the early years of the primary school this work could be done in connection with the regular courses in drawing and modelling without requiring any important modification of the school curriculum.

At about the age of ten for the average child, systematic instruction in concrete or experimental geometry should begin, and should occupy about one school hour per week for at least three years. During this period the main facts of plane and solid geometry should be taught, not as an exercise in logical deduction and exact demonstration, but in as concrete and objective a form as possible. For example, the simple properties of similar plane figures and similar solids should not be proved, but should be illustrated and confirmed by cutting up and re-arranging drawings or models.

This course should include among other things the careful construction of plane figures, both by the unaided eye and by the aid of ruler, compasses and protractor; the indirect measurement of heights and distances by the aid of figures carefully drawn to scale; and elementary mensuration, plane and solid.

The child should learn to estimate by the eye and to measure with some degree of accuracy the lengths of lines, the magnitudes of angles, and the areas of simple plane figures; to make accurate plans and maps from his own actual measurements and estimates; and to make models of simple geometrical solids in pasteboard and in clay.

Of course, while no attempt should be made to build up a complete logical system of geometry, the child should be thoroughly convinced of the correctness of his constructions and the truth of his propositions by abundant concrete illustrations and by frequent experimental tests; and from the beginning of the systematic work he should be encouraged to draw easy inferences, and to follow short chains of reasoning.

From the outset the pupil should be required to express himself verbally as well as by drawing and modelling, and the language employed should be, as far as possible, the language of the science, and not a temporary phraseology to be unlearned later.

It is the belief of the Conference that the course here suggested, if skilfully taught, will not only be of great educational value to all children, but will also be a most desirable preparation for later mathematical work.

Then, too, while it will on one side supplement and aid the work in arithmetic, it will on the other side fit in with and help the elementary instruction in physics, if such instruction is to be given.

IV. Special Report on Algebra.

It is desirable, during the study of arithmetic, to familiarize the pupil with the use of literal expressions and of algebraic language in general. The teacher may advantageously introduce the simple equation in the study of proportion, of the more difficult problems in analysis, and of percentage and its applications. The designation of positive integral powers by exponents may also be taught.

Avoiding the introduction of negative numbers, the pupil should be drilled in easy problems like the following :

If one stone weighs p pounds and another weighs q pounds, what is the weight of both together?

If a square table is a feet long, what is its area?

If a yards of cloth cost b dollars, what will c yards cost?

Such exercises should grow out of similar ones involving numerical data.

The average pupil should be prepared to undertake the study of formal algebra at the beginning of the fourteenth year. For students preparing to enter college, the time assigned to this study in the high school should be about the equivalent of five hours per week during the first year, and an average of two hours and a half per week during the two following years. This affords ample time for the thorough mastery of algebra through quadratic equations and equations of quadratic form. The course should include radicals, but exclude the progressions, series, and logarithms, although a familiarity with logarithmic tables is desirable for those who expect to take a technical course in any department.

There are certain propositions in algebra the rigorous demonstration of which is unintelligible to pupils at the time when these propositions are first encountered. Such is usually the case with the rule of signs in multiplication and with the binomial formula. In cases of this kind the proof should be at first omitted, but always introduced at a later period in school or college. When such omissions are made, the pupil must be convinced of the truth of the propositions by illustration or induction. In many of our text-books the proofs of the theorems above referred to are not rigorous. The truth of the binomial formula for fractional or negative exponents had best be reserved for the more advanced courses in college or the scientific school. In case of positive integral exponents the pupil should arrive at the mode of expansion through the examination of products obtained by actual multiplication.

Oral exercises in algebra, similar to those in what is called "mental arithmetic," are recommended. Such exercises are particularly helpful in conducting brief and rapid reviews. Quickness and accuracy in both oral and written work should be rigidly enforced. The same facility should be attained in dealing with expressions containing coefficients and exponents that are literal as with expressions in which they are numerical. Radicals and fractional and negative exponents need more attention than they commonly receive. Especial emphasis should be laid upon the fundamental nature of the equation. The distinction should be clearly and repeatedly drawn between the ordinary algebraic equation and the identities with which the pupil has grown familiar in his study of arithmetic. He should also be given drill in the solution of an ordinary equation with reference to any letter that it may contain.

V. Special Report on Demonstrative Geometry.

In regard to the teaching of formal geometry the Conference invites attention to the following considerations:

1. A course of study in demonstrative geometry properly begins with a careful and exhaustive enumeration of those properties of space which do not admit of being deduced from still simpler properties; that space is continuous and of three dimensions; that figures may be moved about in it without change of size or shape; that straight lines and planes may exist in space, determined by two and three points respectively; that of two intersecting straight lines but one can be parallel to a given straight line — the so-called geometric axioms.

It is of the first importance that the role which these axioms — or better, postulates — play in the demonstrative geometry be correctly understood: together they constitute a *definition of space*, from which — with certain formal definitions of figures — it is the business of demonstrative geometry to deduce all other facts regarding space with which it may concern itself.

2. The function of the construction postulates also, by which the elementary geometry is restricted in its constructions to the use of

the compasses and ungraduated straight-edge, merits careful exposition, inasmuch as these postulates define the province of the elementary as distinguished from higher geometry. That it is not always understood is obvious from conceptions which are current as to what is and what is not allowable in the elementary geometry.

3. There are two methods employed in geometry for dealing with size-relations among the geometric magnitudes, the methods of immediate comparison of the magnitudes, and of comparison by means of their numerical measure. Thus the theorem, "the square on the sum of two lines is equal to the sum of the squares on those lines plus twice their rectangle," is demonstrated after the first method by showing that the square on the sum may be actually divided into these four parts; after the second, by deducing it from the algebraic theorem that the square of the sum of two quantities is equal to the sum of the squares of those quantities plus twice their product.

The first method is purely geometrical. None of its notions are arithmetical. Magnitudes are defined as equal when they can be made to coincide, they are added and substracted geometrically — by juxtaposition and separation — and their ratios are not expressed numerically but, like the magnitudes themselves, compared directly. The second method, on the other hand, is essentially arithmetical. Replacing the magnitudes by their measures, it at the same time replaces geometric equality, addition and substraction by the equality, addition and substraction of irrational numbers.

Opinions differ as to what the relative prominence of these two methods should be in elementary geometry. But, the first method being pure and thoroughly elementary and involving no abstraction, is surely better suited to the beginner. Indeed the student is most likely to become a sound geometer who is not introduced to the notion of numerical measures until he has learned that geometry can be developed independently of it altogether. For this notion is subtle, and highly artificial from a purely geometrical point of view and its rigorous treatment is difficult. The student generally only half comprehends it, so that for him demonstrations lose more in rigor as well as in vividness and objectivity by its use than they gain in apparent simplicity. Moreover the constant association of number with the geometric magnitudes as one of their properties tends to obscure the fundamental characteristic of these magnitudes — their continuity.

The numerical method is of course to be taught — with due attention to its rigorous presentation — for its own sake and for the sake of the mensuration to which it leads; but serious harm is done by allowing it to entirely supplant the pure method at as early a period as is customary.

4. Many students who can reason logically cannot present a geometrical demonstration orally with due elegance of form. Their statement of the argument is incomplete or illogical, or they express themselves in an awkward and inexact manner. This is a fault which may render the recitation of the proofs of geometry practically valueless, inasmuch as it prevents the discipline for which this exercise is chiefly prized, and cultivates instead the vicious habit of slovenly expression. It is due in part to the willingness of certain teachers to accept in lieu of the demonstration of a proposition any kind of evidence that the pupil understands it, in part to the widespread practice of substituting written for oral demonstration. The remedy is obvious: abundance of oral recitation — for which there is no proper substitute — and the rejection of all proofs which are not formally perfect.

5. The elementary ideas of logic may be introduced early in the course in demonstrative geometry with great advantage. One need only explain that if a class of things be represented by a symbol, say *A*, all things not belonging to this class may also be thought of as constituting a class, represented by the symbol *not A;* and that the proposition *A is B* is not a declaration of the equivalence of *A* and *B*, but that every individual of the class *A* belongs to the class *B* — to make it easily understood why the converse proposition *B is A* is not a necessary consequence of *A is B* and under what conditions it becomes such a consequence; and why, on the other hand, the "contrapositive" *not B is not A* is the logical equivalent of *A is B* and the "obverse" *not A is not B* of *B is A.*

Yet this little knowledge would add materially to the student's equipment for geometry. The contrapositive of a proposition is oftentimes more readily demonstrated than the proposition itself, its obverse than its converse; and when it has been proven that *A is B* it is often easier to show that there is but one *B* (when such is the case) than to show directly that *B is A.*

This knowledge, furthermore, is seriously needed to dispel existing confusion. For many students have a strong, though of course unformulated conviction — with apparently a good deal to justify it — that the logic of algebra is quite distinct from the logic of geometry, and both from the logic of ordinary correct thinking. Without a knowledge of the conditions under which the truth of the converse of a demonstrated proposition may be immediately inferred, for instance, it is difficult to see how the student is to reconcile the need of demonstrating converses in geometry with the practice which is common in algebra of establishing a proposition by proving its converse — as in proving the truth of an algebraic relation by showing that it leads to an identity.

Finally the very fact that demonstrative geometry is the most elaborate illustration of the mechanism of formal logic in the entire curriculum of the student, makes the consideration of these elementary principles of logic more interesting and profitable in this connection than in any other.

6. As soon as the student has acquired the art of rigorous demonstration, his work should cease to be merely receptive. He should begin to devise constructions and demonstrations for himself.

Geometry cannot be mastered by reading the demonstrations of a text book; and while there is no branch of the elementary mathematics in which purely receptive work, if continued too long, may lose its interest more completely, there is also none in which independent work can be made more attractive and stimulating. It possesses remarkable qualifications for quickening and developing creative talent. Its materials are a few simple, concrete, and easily apprehended notions which admit of numberless interesting and valuable combinations, some very simple, some very complex. The lack of general methods is the weakness of elementary geometry as a science. Each theorem must be demonstrated for itself by a process differing in some respect from that followed in the case of every other. But the invention of these processes — unimportant as they may be individually — is an intellectual exercise as much higher than the mechanical illustration of some powerful and general method — which is all that the ordinary exercises of elementary algebra involve — as it is lower than the discovery of a new truth by aid of such a method.

At the same time this characteristic of the elementary geometry makes the acquisition of any considerable degree of skill in independent geometrical work difficult. It requires abundant practice in exercises which have been carefully graduated and adapted to the abilities of the individual student. In particular it is important that the student should comprehend that, notwithstanding the rigorously synthetic form of its demonstrations, the method of investigation in elementary geometry, as in all science, is essentially analytic — that the clue to a demonstration or construction is most likely to be found by assuming it accomplished and tracing its consequences until results previously established have been deduced from it.

By wise instruction after this method, the inferior student can at least be freed from slavish dependence on his text book, while the able student will gain power enough in large part to construct his own geometry. But whatever the training may accomplish for him geometrically, there is no student whom it will not brighten and strengthen intellectually as few other exercises can.

7. It is desirable, if feasible, that solid as well as plane geometry be studied in preparation for college.

A place should also be found either in the school or college course for at least the elements of the modern synthetic or projective geometry. It is astonishing that this subject should be so generally ignored, for mathematics offers nothing more attractive. It possesses the concreteness of the ancient geometry without the tedious particularity, and the power of analytical geometry without the reckoning, and by the beauty of its ideas and methods illustrates the esthetic quality which is the charm of the higher mathematics, but which the elementary mathematics in general lacks.

PHYSICS, CHEMISTRY, AND ASTRONOMY.

To the Committee of Ten:

The Conference on Physics, Chemistry, and Astronomy, met on December 28, 1892, in Chicago. Its first session was held at 10 A.M. in a room of the University of Chicago provided for the purpose. Shortly after the appointed hour all the ten members were present, — Mr. George W. Krall, of St. Louis, presenting himself as the accredited substitute for Mr. W. C. Peckham, of Brooklyn.

The Conference organized at once by the election of Professor Ira Remsen as Chairman, and Mr. I. W. Fay as Secretary.

Morning and afternoon sessions were held for three days. At the end of the second day two members, Professor Payne, of Minnesota, and Mr. Gage, of Boston, were obliged to leave, and those remaining continued the work to the end.

The results of the deliberations of this Conference will be found embodied in the following resolutions, which have been arranged as far as possible in the order corresponding to the list of questions suggested by your committee.

This Conference recommends : —

1. That the study of simple natural phenomena be introduced into the elementary schools and that this study, so far as practicable, be pursued by means of experiments carried on by the pupil; also that in connection therewith, in the upper grades of these schools, practice be given in the use of simple instruments for making physical measurements.

2. That, wherever this is possible, special science-teachers or superintendents be appointed to instruct the teachers of elementary schools in methods of teaching natural phenomena.

[While no resolution was passed in regard to the amount of time to be devoted to the study of natural phenomena in the elementary schools, it was the sense of the Conference that at least one period per day be given to such study.]

3. That the study of Chemistry should precede that of Physics in high-school work.

4. That the study of Physics be pursued the last year of the high school course.

5. That the study of Chemistry be introduced into the secondary schools in the year preceding that in which Physics is taken up.

6. That at least 200 hours be devoted to the study of Physics in the high school.

7. That at least 200 hours be given to the study of Chemistry in the high school.

8. That both Physics and Chemistry be required for admission to college.

9. That Astronomy be not required for admission to college.

10. That when the high school course is four years, an elective in Astronomy be offered. Time — five recitations per week during a period of twelve weeks.

11. That there should be no difference in the treatment of Physics, Chemistry, and Astronomy, for those going to college or scientific school, and those going to neither.

12. That the study of Astronomy should be by observation as well as by class-room instruction.

13. That in secondary schools Physics and Chemistry be taught by a combination of laboratory work, text-book, and thorough didactic instruction carried on conjointly, and that at least one-half of the time devoted to these subjects be given to laboratory work.

14. That laboratory work in Physics should be largely of a quantitative character.

15. That careful note-book records of the laboratory work in both Physics and Chemistry should be kept by the student at the time of the experiment.

16. That the laboratory work should have the personal supervision of the teacher at the laboratory desk.

17. That the laboratory record should form part of the test for admission to college, and that the examination for admission should be both experimental and either oral or written.

18. That in the subjects dealt with by this Conference there be no separation of the examinations into preliminary and final.

19. It was further resolved that it is the opinion of this Conference that the admission to college by means of certificates from approved schools is the ideal method.

20. That in the opinion of this Conference it is better to study one subject as well as possible during the whole year than to study two or more superficially during the same time.

21. That in the instruction in Physics and Chemistry it should not be the aim of the student to make a so-called rediscovery of the laws of these sciences.

22. That a committee to consist of Mr. Fay and Mr. Krall have charge of making out a list of 50 experiments in Physics, and 100 experiments in Chemistry, to be subject to the approval of the Conference.

The above resolutions were carried unanimously, with one exception, and in this case with but one dissenting vote.

Each one of the resolutions was fully discussed and the discussions showed clearly that the members of the Conference were, in the main, in hearty accord. Every member evidently felt strongly that the ordinary method of secondary education that ignores the study of nature is highly objectionable. The study of books is well enough and undoubtedly important, but the study of things and of phenomena by direct contact must not be neglected. If it is conceded that the study of scientific methods is important, then it appears evident that in the early stages of education the mind should be prepared for this kind of study, and not rendered unfit for it. Therefore the Conference passed the first resolution.

But it would be impossible at present to provide a sufficient number of properly qualified teachers for elementary work in science, and for a time, at least. it would be necessary to instruct the teachers. To this end, Resolution 2 provides for the appointment of special science superintendents, who should have supervision over the elementary work in science, somewhat as the superintendents of drawing have over their branch of work.

As regards Resolutions 3, 4, and 5, it should be said that the order recommended for the study of Chemistry and Physics is plainly not the logical one, but all the members with one exception voted for Resolution 3 because they felt that the pupils should have as much mathematical knowledge as possible to enable them to deal satisfactorily with Physics, while they could profitably take up elementary Chemistry at an earlier stage.

Resolution 13 is an important one. It requires no argument to show that the study of a text-book of Chemistry or of Physics without laboratory work cannot give a satisfactory knowledge of these subjects, and cannot furnish scientific training. Such study is of little, if any, value. On the other hand, the mere performing of experiments in a laboratory, however well equipped the laboratory may be, cannot accomplish what is desired. Further, a pupil may work conscientiously in the laboratory, and study his text-book thoroughly, and yet receive a very inadequate training. He needs an intelligent teacher to aid him in interpreting the statements of the book and the phenomena observed, as well as to show him how to work. Loose work in the laboratory is as harmful as loose work in the class-room, and much of the laboratory work done in schools, as well as in colleges, is loose work. The great majority of pupils are sure to do bad work unless carefully guided. In mathematics and the languages accuracy can be secured, and is secured, by thorough questioning. Similar thorough questioning by a good teacher at the laboratory desk can make an exercise of great value, that without it might be positively harmful. There is no doubt that lack of this coöperation on the part of the teacher is one of the reasons why courses in science often fail to give satisfactory results. Resolution 16 emphasizes the importance of this supervision.

While the good teacher will prevent the laboratory work from becoming mechanical, another instrument is of great value for this same purpose. This is the keeping of records. Resolution 15 directs attention to this. Without constant watching, this part of the work will degenerate and become harmful instead of helpful. There are at least three sources of danger in it:

1. The pupil, no matter what he may actually see, will tend not to record his own observations, but to transcribe statements found in his text-book.

2. If the facts observed point to a conclusion, the relation between the facts and the conclusion may not be stated logically.

3. The record and the reasoning may be expressed in faulty English.

It is the teacher's business to guard against these dangers, and the records, if properly treated by a conscientious teacher, furnish the means for most instructive talks between teacher and pupil.

To this it will no doubt be objected by some that the kind of instruction indicated requires much more time than can generally be given to the work. It is certainly true that to give good instruction in the sciences requires more work of the teacher than to give good instruction in mathematics, the languages, etc. The sooner this fact is recognized by those who have the management of schools, the better.

Resolution 17 was the result of a discussion upon a subject with which some members of the Conference had little familiarity. The unanimous opinion was, however, that by means of a laboratory examination alone it must be extremely difficult to form an opinion as to the attainments of a pupil; that the same is equally true of either an oral or a written examination; and that only by a combination of the two can the examiner convince himself that the pupil has been properly trained. The laboratory record may also furnish valuable evidence, and, further, if this be required as part of the test for admission to college, an incentive will be furnished to both teacher and pupil to see that the record is well kept.

Resolution 19 was not the result of much discussion, and is of importance simply because it is an expression of the unanimous opinion of the Conference. The arguments for and against the certificate-system are so familiar that they need not be mentioned here.

Resolution 21 is intended to counteract, as far as possible, the tendency to lead pupils to think that, in their work in the laboratory, they are engaged in rediscovering the laws of Nature. The pupils may, to be sure, become imperfectly acquainted with the methods of work that have led to the discovery of the laws, and they will, no doubt, come to see more and more clearly the relations between the facts and the laws, but the Conference is clearly of the opinion that it is wrong to speak of the work of the pupils as leading to the discovery of laws.

IRA REMSEN, *Professor, Johns Hopkins University, Baltimore, Md.*, Chairman.

IRVING W. FAY, *The Belmont School, Belmont, Calif.*, Secretary.

*W. J. WAGGENER, *Professor, University of Colorado, Boulder, Colo.*

JAMES H. SHEPARD, *Professor, South Dakota Agricultural College, Brookings, So. Dak.*

WILLIAM W. PAYNE, *Professor, Carleton College, Northfield, Minn.*

G. W. KRALL, *Manual Training School, Washington University, St. Louis, Mo.*

BROWN AYRES, *Professor, Tulane University, New Orleans, La.*

WILLIAM McPHERSON, Jr., *2901 Collinwood Avenue, Toledo, O.*

GEORGE RANTOUL WHITE, *Phillips Academy, Exeter, N. H.*

†ALFRED P. GAGE. *English High School, Boston, Mass.*

To the Committee of Ten:

I respectfully beg leave to submit the following minority report on the subjects of Resolutions 3 and 5 of the report of the Conference on Physics, Chemistry, and Astronomy; to-wit: that in the resolutions mentioned the words "Physics" and "Chemistry" be interchanged, so that Physics shall be studied before Chemistry.

* Submits a minority report against Resolutions 3 and 5.
† See two qualifications below.

In support of this dissenting opinion I submit the following reasons :

In training the faculties to make accurate observations and to draw safe inferences, the order of proceedings should be from the more simple subject-matter to the less simple and from that which is more obvious to the senses to that which is less so.

Also, other things equal, that should be first studied which has the more abundant material for illustration and application — which occurs the more frequently in the experiences of every-day life.

Admitting, of course, the deep mystery which underlies and limits all kinds of knowledge alike, it is still true that a great part of the body of knowledge called Physics relates to phenomena wherein the bodies concerned are distinctly perceptible, and their behavior is also directly perceptible to the senses at every stage of the phenomenon. The first results come thus from direct perception rather than by inference; but it is upon such phenomena that the power of making inferences should first be trained; for the inference based upon complete observation is more simple and more safe than that based on other inferences. It is in the light of and from analogy with the behavior of the visible bodies that we may later infer and at least partly understand the behavior of the invisible parts, as considered in both Physics and Chemistry.

The behavior of the parts of matter concerned in chemical changes is inferred — not observed : and the conceptions of it are less simple than those of even molecular physics ; as it involves a special distribution of more than one kind of matter ; and as chemical affinity is evidently more special and less simple than cohesion or adhesion.

The rational study of chemical phenomena is therefore of a higher order of difficulty than those of physics — certainly than those of molecular physics — the portion of the subject to which the work of the high school in this branch is largely directed.

If it be contended that chemistry may be studied without inquiring into the distribution and changes in the distribution of the small parts — seeking only to know the products of these changes ; it may be answered that few or none would seriously favor reducing the study of the science to the cataloguing of chemical products, or dispensing with the aid of the atomic theory and of chemical formulas and equations based thereon. So far as this method is applicable at all, it should go to the primary school — and a very little of it should suffice there.

To make the study of chemical theory as little artificial and as much rational as possible, and to secure intelligent conception of its many and close relations to physical laws, a previous training in the conceptions and measurements of such fundamental quantities as mass, density, specific gravity, heat, specific heat, and others, would seem practically indispensable. A knowledge of optics is necessary to an intelligent study of spectrum analysis, some treatment of which, at least, should be included in the high school course; likewise some treatment of the facts of electrolysis, better if preceded by some knowledge about electrical currents. In fact it seems not unreasonable to suggest that the whole subject of elementary physics forms a desirable basis for the study of the elements of chemistry.

On the other hand a knowledge of elementary chemistry is to but a small extent helpful in getting the knowledge of physics expected from a high school course.

W. J. WAGGENER.

To THE COMMITTEE OF TEN:

Resolutions 4 and 5, which give to Chemistry the priority of time in relation to Physics, received my approval, not that I deem that this is the natural or logical order of sequence, but because Physics requires the largest knowledge of mathematics that the secondary school affords, and because the difficulty of this study demands the greatest maturity of mind.

My approval of Resolution 7 is recorded, but on further and more careful consideration, I am constrained to state that it is my opinion that 150 hours may suffice for Chemistry.

ALFRED P. GAGE.

JOINT SESSION OF THE CONFERENCES ON PHYSICS, CHEMISTRY, AND ASTRONOMY, ON NATURAL HISTORY, AND ON GEOGRAPHY.

This joint session was held in the main building of the University of Chicago, with the purpose of considering the amount of time which should be devoted to the work represented by these three Conferences during the high school course. The result of their deliberations will be found in the following resolution which was carried with but one dissenting vote : —

Resolved, That it is the opinion of this joint Conference that at least one-quarter of the time of the high-school course should be devoted to nature-studies and that this amount of work should be required for admission to college.

IRA REMSEN, *Secretary of the Joint Session.*

REPORT OF THE COMMITTEE ON EXPERIMENTS TO THE CONFERENCE ON PHYSICS, CHEMISTRY, AND ASTRONOMY.[1]

GENTLEMEN: — In accordance with your resolution appointing a committee to select a list of fifty experiments in Physics and one hundred in Chemistry, the Committee hereby submit the following Report:

The task of selecting these lists has been a difficult one as it must necessarily have been from the great variety in kind and difficulty of the same experiments described by different authors.

It has been the aim of the Committee to select experiments that by common consent are used by several authors. Where experiments have been taken that are not found widely used, it has been on account of their quantitative character, suitable experiments of this kind being the most difficult to find.

We fully realize that these lists have only a suggestive force and are not to be regarded as a prescribed list by those into whose hands they will fall. It has been our purpose to make our work of such character as shall be most helpful to any teacher wishing to know the kind and degree of difficulty of experiments suitable for preparation for admission to college in Physics and Chemistry.

In Physics the titles of the experiments indicate more completely the nature of the work than those in Chemistry.

In order that any teacher wishing to make the difficult change from text-book to laboratory work may have as tangible and helpful sugges-

---

[1] Resolution 22 was agreed to with some hesitation, as it was thought that any list might be misleading and would be sure to be imperfect. No committee could hope in a short time to work out courses of experiments differing materially from those found in the commonly used text-books, and the authors of text-books who were members of the Conference felt strongly that it would be in exceedingly bad taste, to say the least, to send out a report referring to their books as containing the proper kinds of experiments. The arguments for the appointment of the committee prevailed, and their report is submitted herewith. The chairman of the Conference has heard from all of the members in regard to the report. All but one approve the list of experiments in Physics. Seven approve the list of experiments in Chemistry in which reference is made to books. Two approve the list without references, but one of these nevertheless thinks that the other list would be likely to prove the more helpful. One (the same one who does not approve the list in Physics) does not approve either list. He writes: " I think it would be better for these lists to be submitted simply as a report from our sub-committee." Under these circumstances the chairman is not clear as to his duty, but, in view of the fact that seven of the ten members, not including himself, have expressed their approval of the list of chemical experiments with references to books, he has decided to submit that one, together with the list of physical experiments which, as already stated, has been approved by nine members of the Conference. It is, however, to be understood that the list is rather suggestive and tentative than final.

IRA REMSEN, *Chairman.*

11. Water of crystallization.
    Remsen, Exp. 28. (Alum.)

12. Water of crystallization. (Efflorescence.)
    Remsen, Exp. 32.

13. Water of crystallization. (Deliquescence.)
    Remsen, Exp. 31.

14. Decomposition of water by sodium.
    Remsen, Exp. 33.
    Shepard, p. 328, art. 363, Exp. 23.
    Eliot & Storer, p. 215, Exp. 176.
    Williams, Exp. 47.

15. Distillation of a solution of copper sulphate.

16. Preparation of hydrogen.
    Remsen, Exp. 35.
    Cooke, p. 59, Exp. 25.
    Shepard, p. 37, Art. 35, Exp. 24.
    Eliot & Storer, p. 23, Exp. 11.

17. Properties of hydrogen. (Extreme lightness — soap bubbles.)
    Eliot & Storer, p. 25, Art. 38.
    Shepard p. 38, Art. 36, Exp. 26.
    Remsen, Exp. 38.

18. Lightness of hydrogen (by decanting).
    Shepard, p. 38, Exp. 29.
    Remsen, Exp. 37.
    Eliot & Storer, p. 25, Exp. 12.

19. Properties of hydrogen. (Inflammability.)
    Eliot & Storer, p. 27, Exp. 14.
    Remsen, Exp. 39.
    Shepard, Art. 36.

20. Combustion of hydrogen, forming water.
    Cooke, p. 61, Exp. 27.
    Shepard, p. 40, Art. 40.
    Eliot & Storer, p. 28, Exp. 15.

21. Decomposition of water by the electric current. (Lecture Exp.)
    Eliot & Storer, p. 16.
    Remsen's Elements, p. 43, Exp. 34.
    Shepard, Exp. 22.

22. Preparation of nitric acid.
    Shepard, p. 67, Exp. 60.
    Eliot & Storer, p. 39, Exp. 22.
    Remsen, Exp. 42.
    Williams, Exp. 36.
    Cooke, p. 81, Exp. 43 (a).

23. Action of nitric acid on tin.
    Remsen, Exp. 43.

24. Action of nitric acid on copper.
    Shepard, p. 69, Exp. 66.
    Remsen, Exp. 44.

25. Preparation of nitric oxide.
    Eliot & Storer, p. 33, Exp. 19.
    Remsen, Exp. 46.
    Williams, Exp. 51.
    Cooke, p. 85, Exp. 44 (a)
    Shepard, p. 61, Exp. 56.

26. Properties of nitric oxide.
    Cooke, p. 85, Exp. 44 (b).
    Remsen, Exp. 47.
    Eliot & Storer, p. 33, Exp. 19 (b).
    Shepard, Exp. 56, Art. 62.

27. Preparation of nitrous oxide.
    Shepard, p. 59, Exp. 54.
    Eliot & Storer, p. 31, Exp. 17.
    Williams, Exp. 49.
    Cooke, p. 176, Exp. 77.
    Remsen, Exp. 45.

28. Action of lime, caustic soda, and caustic potash, on ammonium chloride.
    Shepard, p. 52, Exps. 45, 46.
    Remsen, Exp. 40.

29. Ammonia gas.
    Eliot & Storer, p. 48, Exp. 27.
    Remsen, Exp. 41.
    Williams, Exp. 45.
    Shepard, Exp. 48.

30. Preparation of chlorine.
    Cooke, p. 71, Exp. 36.
    Shepard, p. 93, Exp. 70.
    Williams, Exp. 60.
    Eliot & Storer, p. 56, Exp. 30.
    Remsen, Exp. 49.

31. Properties of chlorine.
    Remsen, Exp. 49.
    Shepard, p. 95, Exps. 71–73.
    Williams, Exp. 61.
    Cooke, p. 72, Exp. 36.
    Eliot & Storer, p. 57, Exp. 32.

32. Action of sulphuric acid on common salt.
    Remsen, Exp. 50.
    Shepard, Exp. 74.

33. Preparation of hydrochloric acid.
    Eliot & Storer, p. 51, Exp. 28.
    Williams, Exp. 33.
    Remsen, Exp. 51.
    Cooke, p. 70, Exp. 34.
    Shepard, p. 97, Exp. 74.

34. Properties of hydrochloric acid.
    Eliot & Storer, p. 50.
    Cooke, p. 70, Exp. 35.
    Remsen, Exp. 51.

35. Neutralization.
    Eliot & Storer, p. 42, Exp. 25.
    Williams, Exp. 28.
    Cooke, pp. 93, 94.
    Remsen, Exp. 52.
    Shepard, Exp. 52.

36. Mixture and chemical compound.
    Eliot & Storer, p. 75, Exp. 47.
    Remsen, Exps. 9–10.
    Cooke, p. 108, Exp. 60.
    Shepard, Exp. 4.
    Williams, Exp. 6.

37. Physical and chemical solution.
    Cooke, p. 109, Exp. 61.

38. Action of carbon on solutions.
    Eliot & Storer, p. 118, Exp. 72.
    Remsen, Exp. 33.
    Williams, Exp. 20.
    Shepard, Exp. 92.

39. Reducing action of carbon.
    Remsen, Exp. 54.
    Eliot & Storer, p. 119, Exp. 74.
    Williams, Exp. 22.
    Shepard, Exp. 152.

40. Carbon dioxide and lime-water.
    Eliot & Storer, p. 119, Exp. 73.
    Remsen, Exp. 57.
    Shepard, p. 138, Exp. 99

41. Preparation of carbon dioxide.
>   Shepard, p. 140, Exp. 102.
>   Remsen, Exp. 59.
>   Williams, Exp. 54.
>   Eliot & Storer, p. 120, Exp. 75.

42. Weight of carbon dioxide.
>   Eliot & Storer, p. 121, Exp. 77.
>   Shepard, Exps. 104, 105.

43. Effect of acids on carbonates.
>   Remsen, Exp. 58.
>   Shepard, Art. 152, 3.

44. Preparation of carbonates.
>   Remsen, Exps. 61, 62.
>   Shepard, Art. 152, 1.

45. Preparation of carbon monoxide.
>   Eliot & Storer, p. 123, Exp. 81.
>   Remsen, Exp. 63.
>   Shepard, p. 137, Exp. 98.
>   Cooke, p. 78, Exp. 40 (b).

46. Carbon monoxide as a reducing agent.
>   Remsen, Exp. 64.

47. Nature of flame.
>   Cooke, p. 62, Exp. 28.
>   Remsen, Exp. 65.
>   Shepard, p. 27, Exp. 17.
>   Williams, Exp. 56.

48. Preparation of bromine.
>   Shepard, p. 109, Exp. 82.
>   Remsen, Exp. 66.
>   Williams, Exp. 66.

49. Hydrobromic acid.
>   Remsen, Exp. 67.
>   Shepard, Art. 116.

50. Preparation of iodine.
>   Shepard, p. 116, Exp. 85.
>   Remsen, Exp. 68.
>   Williams, Exp. 67.

51. Preparation of hydriodic acid.
>   Remsen, Exp. 71.
>   Shepard, p. 117, Exp. 87.

52. Solvent for iodine.
    Shepard, p. 117.
    Remsen, Exp. 69.

53. Action of iodine on starch.
    Eliot & Storer, p. 63, Exp. 39
    Williams, Exp. 69.
    Remsen, Exp. 70.
    Shepard, Art. 125, 2.

54. Hydrofluoric-acid etching.
    Remsen, Exp. 72.
    Williams, Exp. 35.
    Eliot & Storer, p. 67, Exp. 41.
    Shepard, Exp. 91.

55. Crystallized sulphur.
    Cooke, p. 65, Exp. 31.
    Eliot & Storer, p. 73.
    Williams, Exp. 71.
    Remsen, Exp. 73.
    Shepard, pp. 158-9, Exps. 111, 113.

56. Amorphous sulphur.
    Eliot & Storer, p. 73, Exp. 44.
    Shepard, p. 158, Exp. 112.
    Cooke, p. 66, Exp. 31.
    Williams, Exp. 71.

57. Action of boiling sulphur upon metals.
    Remsen, Exp. 74.
    Eliot & Storer, p. 75, Ex. 47.
    Shepard, p. 159; p. 11, Exp. 4.

58. Preparation of hydrogen sulphide.
    Remsen, Exp. 75.
    Williams, Exp. 72.
    Eliot & Storer, p. 76, Exp. 48.
    Shepard, p. 161, Exp. 115.
    Cooke, p. 105, Exp. 59 (b).

59. Action of hydrogen sulphide upon salts.
    Shepard, p. 162, Exp. 116.
    Eliot & Storer, Exp. 51.
    Cooke, p. 120.
    Remsen, Exp. 76.
    Williams, Exp. 73.

60. Preparation of sulphur dioxide.
    Eliot & Storer, p. 78, Exp. 52.
    Remsen, Exp. 77.
    Shepard, p. 164, Exp. 118.

61. Bleaching by sulphur dioxide.
    Shepard, p. 166, Exp. 119.
    Eliot & Storer, p. 80, Exp. 53.
    Remsen, Exp. 78.

62. Preparation of sulphuric acid.   (Lecture Exp.)

63. Burning of phosphorus.
    Eliot & Storer, p. 93, Exp. 57.
    Williams, Exp. 74.
    Remsen, Exp. 80.
    Shepard, Exp. 11.

64. Arsenic, Marsh's test.
    Remsen, Exps. 82, 83.
    Shepard, Art. 254, 2.

65. Reduction of arsenic oxide.
    Shepard, p. 242, Exp. 152.
    Eliot & Storer, p. 104, Exp. 62.
    Remsen, Exp. 84.

66. Preparation of stibine.
    Remsen, Exp. 85.
    Shepard, Art. 258, 2.

67. Potash from wood ashes.
    Eliot & Storer, p. 220, Exp. 179.
    Remsen, Exp. 86.
    Shepard, p. 325.

68. Potassium on water.
    Eliot & Storer, p. 222, Exp. 181.
    Remsen, Exp. 87.
    Williams, Exp. 46.
    Shepard, Art. 359.

69. Preparation of potassium carbonate.
    Eliot & Storer, p. 226, Exp. 184.
    Shepard, p. 325.

70. Potassium nitrate and charcoal.
    Remsen, Exp. 88.
    Williams, Exp. 78.
    Eliot & Storer, p. 226, Exp. 184.
    Shepard, Exp. 64.

71. Flame tests for potassium and sodium.
    Shepard, p. 326, Art. 360; p. 333, Art. 364.
    Remsen, Exp. 91.

72. Volatility of ammonium chloride.
    Remsen, Exp. 95.

73. Examination of lime-water.
    Remsen, Exp. 97.
    Eliot & Storer, p. 243, Exp. 195.
    Shepard, p. 314.

74. Plaster of Paris from gypsum.
    Remsen, Exp. 98.
    Eliot & Storer, p. 245, Art. 423.
    Shepard, p. 315, Art. 349 (b).

75. Action of zinc and iron on copper sulphate.
    Shepard, p. 259, Exp. 161.
    Remsen, Exp. 99.

76. Burning magnesium.
    Eliot & Storer, p. 252, Exp. 201.
    Shepard, Exp. 107 and Art. 353.

77. Caustic soda on copper sulphate.
    Eliot & Storer, p. 276, Exps. 220, 221.
    Remsen, Exp. 100.

78 and 79. Analysis of coin silver.
    Cooke, p. 116, Exp. 65.
    Remsen, Exp. 98.
    Williams, Exp. 91.
    Eliot & Storer, p. 236, Exp. 192.
    Remsen, Exp. 102.

80. Preparation of silver chloride.
    Eliot & Storer, p. 236, Exp. 192.
    Remsen, Exp. 103.
    Shepard, Arts. 241 and 242.

81. Action of lead acetate on zinc.
    Remsen, Exp. 109.
    Eliot & Storer, p. 255, Exp. 204.
    Shepard, Exp. 136.

82. Potassium chromate and dichromate.
    Remsen, Exp. 101.
    Shepard, Art. 297 (c) and (d).

83. Preparation of barium and lead chromates.
    Remsen, Exp. 107.
    Shepard, Art. 297 (e), and 342 (a).

84. Action of water upon lead.
    Remsen, Exp. 110.
    Shepard, Art. 237.

85. Copper and mercury.
    Shepard, Art. 246, 4.
    Eliot & Storer, p. 280, Exp. 224.

86. Aluminum and caustic soda.
    Eliot & Storer, p. 259, Exp. 206.
    Shepard, Art. 301.

87. Alum and potassium carbonate (dissolved separately and poured
    together).
    Shepard, Art. 301.

88. Aluminum in hydrochloric acid and caustic soda.

89. (Quantitative) Solvent power of water.
    Cooke, p. 36, Exp. 11.

90. Composition of hydrochloric acid gas.
    Cooke, p. 70, Exp. 35.

91. Illustration of law of definite proportions.
    Cooke, p. 111, Exp. 63.

92. Composition of nitric oxide.
    Cooke, p. 85, Exp. 44 (b).

93. Density of hydrogen.
    Cooke, p. 60, Exp. 26; p. 128, Exp. 69.

94. Specific gravity of carbon dioxide.
    Cooke, p. 130, Exp. 70.

95. Specific gravity of vapor of alcohol.
    Cooke, p. 132, No. 71.

96. Atomic weight of zinc.
    Cooke, p. 144, Exp. 74.

97. Heat of hydration and solution.
    Cooke, p. 179, Exp. 79.·

98. Identification of substances by the characteristic properties.

99. Five unknown substances, e. g., salt, potassium chloride, calcium
    chloride, ammonium chloride, barium chloride, given out for
    identification.

100. To solutions of sulphuric acid, sodium sulphate, potassium sulphate, ammonium sulphate, zinc sulphate, calcium sulphate, add a little hydrochloric acid and then a solution of barium chloride. To the chlorides of the same metals add the same reagents.

NOTE. — The books referred to in the preceding list are :
1. "Elements of Inorganic Chemistry," by James H. Shephard.   Publishers, D. C. Heath & Co. Boston. 1892.
2. "An Elementary Manual of Chemistry," abridged from Eliot & Storer's Manual, by Wm. Ripley Nichols. Publishers, American Book Company. New York, Cincinnati, Chicago.
3. "A Laboratory Manual," by Ira Remsen. Publisher, Henry Holt & Co. 1890. New York.
4. "Laboratory Practice," by Josiah Parsons Cooke. Publishers, D. Appleton & Co. 1891. New York.
5. "Laboratory Manual of General Chemistry," by R. P. Williams. Ginn & Co. Boston. 1892.

NATURAL HISTORY.

To the Committee of Ten : —

The Conference on the study of Natural History (biology, including botany, zoölogy and physiology) in elementary and secondary schools met, December 28, 1892, at the University of Chicago.

There were present at the first session, Prof. C. E. Bessey of the University of Nebraska; Prof. S. F. Clarke of Williams College; Prof. D. H. Campbell of Leland Standford, Jr. University; President J. M. Coulter of the Indiana University; Prof. C. B. Scott of the St. Paul High School; Dr. O. S. Westcott of the North Division High School, Chicago, and W. B. Powell of Washington, D. C.

W. B. Powell was made Chairman, and Prof. C. B. Scott, Secretary of the committee.

At subsequent sessions, Prof. A. H. Tuttle of the University of Virginia and Prof. A. C. Boyden of Bridgewater Normal School joined the committee.

Six sessions were held. At these sessions full discussion was had respecting the work in biology, adapted to primary schools, grammar schools and high schools.

Courses of study were discussed at length and compared, while methods of instruction received due consideration by the committee. After full and harmonious discussion, in whose conclusions there was finally perfect agreement, results were reached as set forth in the following : —

ANSWERS TO QUESTIONS SUGGESTED BY THE COMMITTEE OF TEN.

QUESTION 1. In the school course of study extending approximately from the ages of six years to eighteen years — a course including the periods of both elementary and secondary instruction — at what age should the study, which is the subject of the conference, be first introduced ?

Resolved, That it is the judgment of the Conference that, while the principles of hygiene should be included in the work of the lower grades, the study of physiology as a science may best be pursued in the later years of the high-school course. We recommend that in the high school a daily period, for one half year, be devoted to the study of anatomy, physiology and hygiene, with as large an amount of practical work as is possible.

Resolved, That the study of natural history (botany and zoölogy) should begin in the primary schools at the beginning of the school course.

NOTE. — The study of both plants and animals should begin in the lowest grades, or even in the Kindergarten. One object of such work is to train the children to get knowledge first hand. Experience shows that if these studies begin later in the course, after the habit of depending on authority — teachers and books — has been formed, the results are much less satisfactory. Experience shows also, that if from the beginning, "nature study" is closely correlated with or made the basis of language work, drawing, and other forms of expression, the best results are obtained in all.

QUESTION 2. After it is introduced, how many hours a week for how many years should be devoted to it?

Resolved, That no less than one hour per week, divided into at least two periods, should be devoted, throughout the whole course below the high school, to the study of plants and animals; that in this study no text book should be used, and that these observation lessons should, as far as possible, be made the basis of, or, correlated with, work in language, drawing and literature.

NOTE. — It is agreed that, by exercising forethought in collecting materials and judgment in planning the work, the study of natural history can be continued, to the best advantage, throughout the whole year, instead of being confined to the fall and spring, as is now the practice in most schools where the study is pursued. Much can be studied during the winter which is not accessible at any other time.

QUESTION 3. How many hours a week for how many years should be devoted to it during the last four years of the complete course; that is, during the ordinary high school period?

Resolved, That a minimum of one year's study of natural history should be required in every course in the high school, and that at least three fifths of the time should be employed in laboratory work.

NOTE. — It is agreed that the year of study in natural history, recommended as a minimum for the high school, should be a consecutive year of daily recitations or laboratory work, and that it is better to have the year's work devoted to one subject, either botany or zoölogy, than to have it divided between the two.

While the choice between botany and zoölogy should be made by the teachers or pupils, the members of the Conference, with one or two exceptions (the only point about which there has been any decided difference of opinion shown in their deliberations), believe that botany is better for the high school than zoölogy, because materials for the study of that subject are probably more easily obtained than those for the study of zoölogy; because the study of plants is more attractive to the average pupil; and because in the study of animals many prejudices or aversions have to be overcome.

The study, to be of much value, *must consist largely of laboratory work,* actual work, by the pupils, with the plants or animals. This cannot be too strongly emphasized.

The Conference also urges that, in addition to the year's study, recommended as a minimum requirement in every course in the high school, opportunity be given for additional work in these sciences.

QUESTION 4. What topics or parts of the subject may reasonably be covered during the whole course?

QUESTION 5. What topics, or parts, of the subject may best be reserved for the last four years?

Resolved, That the general comparative morphology of plants and animals be recommended as the part of natural history most suitable for study in the secondary and lower schools; that in the primary and grammar grades there should be a study of gross anatomy, and in the secondary schools a study of minute anatomy.

NOTE.—The study of botany and zoölogy should include a general view of the plant and animal kingdoms. Limiting the study of botany to flowering plants and of zoölogy to two or three sub-kingdoms of animals, gives the learner imperfect and distorted ideas. The plants and animals selected for study should be typical forms, or types, and at the same time, when possible, forms familiar to the students, or common in their vicinity. In the lower grades the work should be a study of living forms, of the plant growing and of the animal in action. Here the steps should be (1) life and function, (2) structure, (3) comparison. Mere analysis or identification is believed to be of very little value. Too many scientific or technical terms should be avoided. No text-book should be used below the high school.

The work in the high school should be a study of minute anatomy and classification.

Throughout all the work the aim should be to make the observations and notes of the pupils systematic, clear and exact. Careful drawings should be insisted on from the beginning. If effort is made to have the pupils obtain clear and exact ideas, and to express them clearly and exactly in words or by drawings, the study will be successful as a department of science, and, at the same time, valuable and efficient as an aid in training pupils in the arts of expression.

QUESTION 6. In what forms and to what extent should the subject enter into college requirements for admission? Such questions as the sufficiency of translation at sight as a test of knowledge of a language, or the superiority of a laboratory examination in a scientific subject to a written examination on a text-book, are intended to be suggested under this head by the phrase " in what form."

Resolved, That the year's work in natural history, as outlined for the high school, should be required for entrance to college in every course; that the examination should be both a written test and a laboratory test, and that the laboratory note books, covering the year's work, certified by the teacher as original, should be required at the examination.

NOTE.—The members of the Conference feel that, while an examination in science may be partly written, to test the pupil's general knowledge of the subject, it should be mainly a laboratory examination, to test his method of study and his ability in using it.

QUESTION 7. Should the subject be treated differently, for pupils who are going to college, for those who are going to a scientific school, and for those who, presumably, are going to neither?

QUESTION 8. At what stage should this differentiation begin, if any be recommended?

Resolved, That differentiation appears to be unwise and therefore not desirable.

QUESTION 9. Can any description be given of the best method of teaching this subject throughout the school course?

Resolved, That the study of natural history in both the elementary school and the high school should be by direct observational study with the specimens in the hands of each pupil, and that in the work below the high school no text-book should be used,

NOTE. — See notes on Questions 3, 4 and 5.

QUESTION 10. Can any description be given of the best modes of testing attainments in this subject at college admission examinations?

NOTE. — See answer to Question 6.

QUESTION 11. For those cases in which colleges and universities permit a division of the admission examination into a preliminary and a final examination, separated by at least a year, can the best limit between the preliminary and the final examinations be approximately defined?

Resolved, That the members of the Conference believe that a division of the admission examination is unwise, if the entrance requirement includes but one year of natural history study, but, that if the entrance requirement includes two years of such study, a division may be advisable; in which case the preliminary examination should cover a general outline of the plant or animal kingdom with laboratory tests; while the final examination should be a test for knowledge, and for skill in examining and showing some special phase of botany or zoölogy.

The following action was taken in a joint session of the three conferences held in Chicago :

Resolved, That it is the sense of the Joint Conference that at least one fourth of the time of the high-school course should be devoted to nature studies, and that this amount of preparation should be required for entrance to college.

WORK SUGGESTED.

Though a full exchange of opinion was had respecting courses of study in the different subjects under consideration for the different grades of school, yet no course of study was made at the conference.

It was agreed that Prof. Scott should outline a course of nature study, including both botany and zoölogy, for grades of school below the high school.

That President John M. Coulter should prepare an outline of work in botany to be recommended for high schools.

That Prof. O. S. Westcott should prepare an outline of work in zoölogy for high schools.

That Prof. Albert H. Tuttle should outline a course in physiology for primary and secondary schools.

That Prof. C. E. Bessey should report upon the best methods of teaching natural history throughout the schools, including recommendations for the use of instruments and note books.

That Prof. A. C. Boyden of Bridgewater Normal School should consider the form of examination to be adopted for admission to college.

The sub-reports of Messrs. Scott, Coulter, Westcott and Tuttle are appended. A subreport submitted by Prof. Bessey which covers the ground of that submitted by Prof. Scott is not given here. Prof. Boyden reports that the resolutions passed by the Conference cover adequately the subjects referred to him.

Respectfully submitted,

W. B. POWELL,
Chairman.

NATURE STUDY FOR GRADES OF SCHOOL BELOW THE HIGH SCHOOL.

GENERAL PRINCIPLES AND PLANS.

Objects.

1. It must be remembered that the primary object of nature study is not that the children may get a knowledge of plants and animals. The first purpose of the work is to interest them in nature. This must be done before other desirable results can be obtained. The second purpose is to train and develop the children; *i. e.*, to train them to observe, compare, and express (see, reason, and tell) ; to cause them to form the habit of investigating carefully and of making clear, truthful statements, and to develop in them a taste for original investigation. The third purpose is the acquisition of knowledge. This, however, must be " gained by actual experience," and it must be "knowledge classified," or science.

For the attainment of these objects, interest, power, knowledge, *the children must study the plant;* no book should be used by them. The effort of the teacher should be so to interest and guide them, that they will learn how to work profitably.

Materials.

2. The children should study the plant as a whole, not merely a part, as seeds, leaves, flowers ; it is a mistake to limit the work to one part to the exclusion of the others, and is as great a mistake to allow the children to study the parts without leading them to see the mutual relations and dependence of the parts.

3. The study should not be restricted to flowering plants, as trees and weeds, but should be extended as well to flowerless plants, such as ferns, horse-tails, mushrooms and toadstools, mosses, lichens, fungi, and fresh and salt-water algæ. Those children who carry the work through eight years should obtain a fair idea of the plant kingdom, including its principal divisions. Those who stop short of the eight years' work should have a general idea of the whole plant as a type of the plant kingdom, more or less detailed and generalized according to the amount of time spent in school.

Methods.

4. The plant should be studied as a living organism and not merely as a form or structure. The child should learn that each part has something to do, and he should discover that what it does, and the way in which it does it, determine its form and structure. The study of seeds, buds, or flowers should begin with growth and development or unfolding, which should lead to an investigation of use or function, and, finally, to an examination of structure. The comparison of the uses and structure of different plants results in classification.

The order of study is :

Life, growth, and development.

Use or function.

Structure.

Comparison.

Classification.

5. The plant should be studied in its relations to its environment,— light, air, water, soil, climate, and other plants,—and in its relations to the lower animals and to man. For the time being the plant is the centre of the world. The study furnishes many opportunities for coördinating science work with the other studies of the school, and at the same time for showing man's use of plants and his dependence on them.

6. As young children cannot generalize, it seems wise to limit the work during the first two years to the study of the germination, development, growth, and structure of three or four typical plants, like the bean, pea, and sunflower, studying, of course, only those features

that are easily understood. Gradually more details may be studied, and other kinds of plants, flowering and flowerless, examined, causing the pupils' ideas to be more and more complete and generalized.

7. Whatever is being studied, the questions to be answered are: What? Why? How?

First: What does it do, and what is it?

Second: Why does it do so, and why is it so?

Third: How does it do it, and how did it become so?

At first little can be done but answer the question "what"; gradually "what" includes so many particulars that an answer to "why" becomes possible; before the end of the course, "how" can and should be answered.

8. In the study, during the earlier years, of germination and of buds and flowers, that which appeals most to the children is the provision for the protection and care of certain parts; later the perfect order of nature will be seen, when the idea of system and plan may be developed. In time the highest function of the plant must be shown, that of reproduction, when the plant should be studied as an arrangement for producing seeds. While all these thoughts should be developed by slow degrees from the beginning, it seems wise to emphasize them in the order suggested. The central thoughts should be:

For the first and second years, care and protection.

For the third, fourth, and fifth years, order and system.

For the sixth, seventh, and eighth years, reproduction.

Expression.

9. Observation becomes more critical if its results are expressed by the observer. For the younger children, motion, stitching, modeling, drawing and painting, are more "expressive" than speech. Speech, as the most universal method of communicating ideas, should be emphasized in all but the earliest years of the course. A drawing gives better ideas of form and of relations of parts than can be given by verbal description. It will be found that often the simplest and quickest way for pupils to get clear, sharp ideas about the objects they are studying is to have them draw the objects.

Coördination with other Studies.

10. Nature study will not succeed unless it is coördinated with other studies. It should not be pushed into the course as an extra, but should be made the basis of much of the other work of the school. Experience has shown that when it is used as a basis for the early training in language and drawing, an interest in these studies is

easily secured and sustained. It is more pleasing to pupils to express ideas, resulting from their own observations, than to copy the expressions of others, or to put into somewhat different form expression obtained from teacher or book. The study of nature is a necessary preparation for a full understanding of much beautiful and valuable literature. Opportunities for connecting such work·with geography are almost numberless. By means of this work, even arithmetic may have reality, and thus new life, infused into it.

Time of Year for Studying.

11. It seems wise that the study of plants should begin in early spring time, from February to April, and that it should be particularly emphasized then, though not restricted to that season of the year. Much can be done in the fall and even in mid-winter. The Conference has urged that the study of plants be continued throughout the year, at least twice a week.

COURSE OF WORK.

Central thought : Care and protection.

Seeds and Germination.

Let the children :

1. Plant beans and watch their growth.

2. When the seedlings are two or three inches high, study the seed in its parts.

3. Study the pea in a corresponding way, and then compare it with the bean, noting first the differences and then the resemblances.

4. Study seed and plant, in each case, in relation to their surroundings, air, water, and sunlight. (Children should be led to discover the uses of the different parts, first to the plant and then to animals and man.)

5. Continue the observations on the bean and the pea during the remaining part of the school year, noting the development, use, and general structure of buds, stems, roots, leaves, and, if possible, of flowers and fruit.

Buds.

The study of buds should be carried on in connection with the work in germination suggested above.

Let the children :

1. Gather branches having large buds, such as the horse-chestnut, the elder, or the lilac ; put them in water ; watch them, and tell about their development and the gradual unfolding of their parts.

2. Study the stem and its parts, wood, bark, and pith, their uses and structure.

3. Later, study fresh buds and compare them with those which have unfolded.

4. Compare the first bud studied with some other large bud.

Reproduction and Flowers.

In connection with the study of buds, call the attention of the children to the catkins of the willow, the poplar, and the hazel, and then to the flowers of the elder, the lilac, and, if possible, of the bean and pea.

Let the children :

1. Find dust-bearing (staminate) and seed-bearing (pistillate) flowers and parts of flowers. (This will give opportunity to develop the idea that flowers are for the production and protection of seeds.)

2. Study the dissemination of seeds that fly, as those of the dandelion and the milkweed ; seeds that sail, as those of the maple and the basswood ; seeds that stick, as those of the burdock and the tick ; seeds that fall, as those of the bean and the pea.

3. Study fruits. (They should learn the use of fruit to the plant and to man.)

As early as may seem wise the teacher should develop, largely by stories and supplementary reading, the use of the other parts of the plant to the flowers and seeds.

Results of Two Years' Work.

At the close of the second year the children should have a fair idea of the plant as a whole, knowing something of all its parts, of their uses and relations, and particularly of the ways in which the plant and its parts are cared for and protected.

THIRD AND FOURTH YEARS.

Central thought : Care and protection leading to order and system, and plan.

Seeds and Germination.

Let the children :

1. Study the bean, the pea, the sunflower, and the pumpkin, as before, but more in detail, discovering something of the order or plan of growth, and searching for answers to the questions " why " and " how."

2. Study, more in detail, plants before studied, and examine other plants to learn the uses of the different parts of the seedling and the relation of the plant to its surroundings.

3. Discover where the seeds are formed, how they escape from the ovary, and how they are disseminated.

4. Compare the development and structure of the seeds suggested above with those of the morning glory and the four-o'clock, and learn the classification into albuminous and exalbuminous seeds.

Buds.

Let the pupils:

1. Study the same buds as before, but more in detail, to discover the order shown in the buds and their parts.

2. Compare these with several other buds, including some of the small ones, for the purpose of noticing their positions and arrangement, as well as their protection.

3. Study, as an introduction to leaves, the arrangement and.folding of leaves in the buds, and watch their unfolding, still noting the order and plan.

4. Study and watch in a similar way the development of flower buds.

Leaves.

Let the children:

1. Watch the unfolding of the leaves in the bud and notice their protection and arrangement as suggested before.

2. Note the uses of leaves and their parts, stipules, stalk, and blade, and of veins, epidermis, breathing pores, and pulp. (In connection with the uses of veins they should study venation.)

3. Study the positions, arrangement, and parts of leaves with reference to their uses; their relation to sunlight, air, rain, and the directing of water to the roots.

4. Study the positions of leaves with reference to buds, and note the order and plan shown in bud and leaf.

By means of charts or blackboard outlines, to which pupils may constantly refer, they should be familiarized with the more common forms of the leaf as a whole, and of base, apex, and margin, and should be trained to give orderly, exact, concise descriptions.

Reproduction and Flowers.

Develop by the study of the flowers themselves the fact that there are two kinds of flowers, those with seed boxes (pistillate) and those with boxes containing a .powder (staminate). By the study of the willow, maple, and early meadow-rue, develop the fact that these two kinds of boxes may be, and usually are, found, in the same flower.

Let the children:

1. Discover that both seed boxes (ovaries) and pollen boxes (anthers) are found in all kinds of flowering plants. (Both, then, must be very important.)

2. Note how well they are protected in bud and flower. (The floral envelope can be studied simply, at this stage, as a protection for stamens and pistils.)

3. Now study the use of the pollen and its function in the formation of seeds.

4. Note the order and plan of the flower and of its parts.

5. Learn now the fact that the main work of the plant is to produce seeds, and that root, stem, and leaf coöperate in this work.

Result of Four Years' Work.

At the close of the fourth year the pupils should be thinking about the "why" and the "how" of the world around them; they should have some knowledge of the order and system which prevails in nature, and should begin to comprehend something of the plan of common plants, of their reproduction and growth, and of the general uses and the gross structure of their parts.

FIFTH AND SIXTH YEARS.

Central thought: System, plan, and purpose.
The plant as an organism for producing seeds or new plants.

Seeds and Germination.

Let pupils:

1. Review at least two exalbumiuous and two albuminous seeds.

2. Plant corn, watch its development, and then study the seed and its parts, and afterwards study the pine seed in a corresponding way.

3. Review classification into exalbuminous and albuminous seeds for the purpose of classification into monocotyledons, dicotyledons, and polycotyledons, and learn that cotyledons are modified leaves.

4. Study the practical uses to man of the albumen stored in the seed.

Buds.

Let the children:

1. Review as much as may seem necessary.

2. Study buds with respect to their positions and arrangement.

3. Examine the rings left by the falling of the bud-scales, and learn the story the rings tell.

4. Examine the buds of underground stems and the characteristics of stems as distinguished from roots.

5. Study the relations of positions, arrangement and development of buds to the shape or character of trees. Learn by a study of the trees themselves, the causes of the development and non-development of buds.

Roots.

1. Study roots and root hairs and their uses to the plant, and the positions and kinds of roots, as well as their various uses to the plant and to man.

2. Examine the stem or a branch of an ordinary tree. Study the arrangement and character of its different parts, and their uses to the plant and to man; learn how such plants grow; compare these with a corn stalk; learn how this stalk grows; learn the classification of stems into exogenous and endogenous.

3. Study the relation of the structure of the stem to its method of growth; of the number of cotyledons to the character and venation of the leaves, and the plan of the flower.

Leaves.

Let the children:

1. Continue the study of function and arrangement, as suggested for third and fourth years.

2. Study the leaves as arrangements for directing water to the roots, and try to discover the relation between the arrangement of branches and that of the leaves; between the length of the leaf-stalk and the shape of the leaves.

3. Continue the examination of the forms of leaves. Study and describe compound leaves.

4. Study the changes of color and the falling of leaves, particularly in the autumn, and their causes.

Reproduction, Flowers and Seeds.

Let the children:

1. Review as much as may seem necessary.

2. Discover how the pollen escapes from the anther. Study dehiscence of anthers.

3. Discover how the pollen gets from anther to pistil. Study methods of and arrangements for fertilization; the relations of flowers and insects, and the use to the plant of color and odors.

4. Discover how the pollen gets into the ovary.

5. Study the flower as a whole, as an arrangement for producing, protecting, and disseminating seeds.

6. Study the provisions of nature for matured seeds. (Much of this can be done in the earlier years of the course; it should be emphasized now.)

Lead the children to discover:

1. How the seeds separate, often with the surrounding parts, from the plant.

2. How they are disseminated.

   3. How they escape from the ovary.

     a. By being enclosed in fleshy, edible parts.

     b. By having leaflike attachments, or wings, or hairy appendages.

     c. By bearing prickles, spines, hooks, etc.

     d. By being so light as to be carried by the wind.

     e. By having springs or elaters.

   4. How seeds are protected through the winter.

   5. How the embryo gets out of the enclosing coats.

   6. What provision is made for the little plant after it begins to develop.

   Let them:

   7. Study leaves, roots, and stems in their relations to the flower, as organs for taking in, conveying, assimilating, and storing up nourishment for the formation of flowers and seeds.

   8. Study ferns, mosses, liverworts, and horse-tails, and compare them with the plants before studied. Examine those as well as mushrooms, puff-balls, lichens, and fungi for spore cases and spores, and discover the fact that all are plants, and that all produce what correspond to seeds.

Result of Six Years' Work.

   Pupils are self-reliant and independent; they can observe, reason, and express; and they have a fair knowledge of the whole plant and its life history.

SEVENTH AND EIGHTH YEARS.

Germination.

   Lead pupils to note the germination of spores of mould; and study as carefully as possible the spore cases and spores of puff-balls, mushrooms, moulds, and other fungi, liverworts, mosses, ferns, horse-tails, lichens, lycopeds, stoneworts, and fresh and salt-water algæ.

Roots, Stems, and Leaves.

   Let pupils:

   1. Study the forms and modifications of roots (including aerial roots) and stems (including underground stems), to learn their uses to the plant and to man.

   2. Examine the forms of leaves (scales, cotyledons, prickles, tendrils, pitchers, etc.), to learn their uses to the plant and to man.

   3. Study the movements of leaves, tendrils, and rootlets, and examine or read about climbing plants.

   4. Study the parts and the plan of the flowerless plants suggested above, and compare them with the flowering plants that have been studied.

Reproduction, Flowers and Fruit.

Let pupils :

1. Review as much of the work of the previous years as may seem necessary.

2. Study flowers whose floral envelopes are more or less grown together and otherwise modified, and learn classification into apetalous, polypetalous, and gamopetalous.

3. Examine the clustered flowers, gradually leading to the study of compositæ.

4. Become familiar with the characters of several of our common, sharply-defined families of flowering plants.

5. Study the flowers of the cone-bearing trees, and learn the classification into angiosperms and gymnosperms.

6. Restudy the flowerless plants suggested above, and learn the classification into phenogams and cryptogams, and study the characteristics of the principal divisions of cryptogamous plants.

7. Investigate the movements of flowers and their parts.

BOTANY FOR COMMON SCHOOLS.

Laboratory work should be the chief feature of the year's course in botany recommended for secondary schools. No books should be put into the hands of the pupil, except such as are to be used as laboratory guides or as books of reference. Table-room, a good compound microscope magnifying from at least 50 to 300 diameters, and a few ordinary reagents in small quantities (including at least alcohol, potassic hydrate, glycerine, iodine and other staining fluids), should be furnished each pupil. The work should consist of the careful study of typical plants, each selected to represent a prominent group of plants or an important phase of plant development. This study of types should not become a study of isolated and hence barren facts. Frequent lectures or talks will be found valuable for broadening the outlook of pupils and for leading them to see the true significance of the work they are doing, while frequent examinations of work and of pupils will be indispensable. Experience has shown that a good allotment of the five weekly periods allowed for this work will be made by giving three of them to laboratory work, one to lecturing and one to quizzing.

The study of a plant should consist of an examination of all its essential features ; such as its cell structure ; its mode of development; its mode of reproduction; in short, as much of its life-history as is possible. Careful examination of specimens is secured best by careful sketching. Too much importance cannot be given to drawing, as it is not only an excellent device for securing close observation, but it is also a rapid method of making valuable notes. A very few verbal descriptions may accompany the sketches to make their meanings clear. These sketches and notes should be made in a permanent note-book, for future use.

Below is suggested a list of plants that will be serviceable in this proposed general survey of the plant kingdom. It must be remembered that many other plants will do as well as those named; for this reason the specimens to be studied in the various groups must be determined by the teacher, according to location or other conditions. All the principal groups of plants are well represented in the flora of any region, with the exception of the red and brown sea-weeds. These groups, however, should not be neglected. By forethought sea-weeds may be easily provided. Plants may be preserved in weak alcohol (35 to 50 %); dried specimens can be kept indefinitely and soaked when wanted for use.

It is much more satisfactory and scientific to begin with the study of the simplest forms than with complex forms, not only because they are more easily understood, but also because this order of study will give the learner some idea of the evolution of the plant kingdom from simple to complex forms. It is believed that the numerous advantages offered by this order of study, advantages which have been proved by much experience, outweigh the supposed advantages offered by beginning with the study of more complex forms.

COURSE OF WORK.

1. The simplest forms can be represented by the green-slimes, such as species of *Chroöcoccus* and *Oscillaria*, both to be found usually about springs and in shallow water. These could well be supplemented by Nostoc and other forms. It is not advisable to attempt any study of bacteria, yet they could be easily demonstrated at this point and their importance indicated.

2. The green algæ should be studied by means of such forms as *Protococcus*, *Cladophora*, *Œdogonium*, *Spirogyra*, *Desmids*, and *Vaucheria*. The doubtful but very interesting and common *Diatoms* might also be studied in this connection. It would be a very remarkable region in which all these forms could not be found abundant, since they constitute the most common green growths in water and damp places.

3. The brown algæ are well represented by the common *Fucus* or

"rock-weed," and the "kelps" (*Laminaria*, etc.) which can be obtained in abundance from the sea-shore.

4. The red algæ, also to be obtained from the sea-shore, can be studied in such common forms as *Callithamnion*, *Polysiphonia*, *Chondrus*, *Corallina*, or *Grinnellia*, etc.

5. *The fungi* should be represented by such plants as *Mucor*, *Cystopus*, some common powdery mildew (such as that found on lilac leaves), a cup fungus, a lichen, some rust (such as wheat-rust), a puff-ball and a toadstool.

6. Now the stone-worts (*Chara or Nitella*) should be studied if material is convenient.

7. The *Bryophytes* would be fairly represented by the study of a single liverwort and a moss.

8. The *Pteridophytes* could be studied in some ordinary fern; any greenhouse will furnish a supply of fern prothalli. If possible, the view of the group should be enlarged by the examination of an Equisetum or club-moss.

9. The *Gymnosperms* are well represented by the common *Pinus sylvestris*.

10. The *Phanerogams* should be represented by a monocotyledon (such as *Trillium* or *Erythronium*), and a dicotyledon (such as *Capsella*).

Such a list of forms will give the student a very intelligent idea of the plant kingdom. It is possible, in one year, to study thoroughly as many types as are here enumerated; thorough work, however, should be done even though the number of specimens examined should be reduced. It will undoubtedly be claimed that many of these forms are entirely unfamiliar to teachers. It can only be said in reply, that under such circumstances the teaching of any forms could hardly be profitable, and that study for a single season at any one of the numerous summer schools where botany is taught will enable such teachers not only to understand these forms, but also to collect materials with which to teach them, as well as to know how properly to direct their use.

As it is desirable that the year of work should be *continuous*, we recommend that it begin in September and continue uninterruptedly throughout the school year. Nearly all the plants suggested, or others that may be chosen, can be found in the autumn and early winter in sufficient numbers and in good condition for study. Many of these may be properly preserved for use, while a common greenhouse, or a tank, or a few jars of water, will yield a full supply of others needed during the winter months.

ZOÖLOGY FOR SECONDARY SCHOOLS.

Several considerations · have influenced the arrangement of the following scheme of work in zoölogy for secondary schools.

1. It is unfortunately true that many students at secondary schools will have had no instruction, or but desultory instruction, in any department of Natural History. In devising a plan of work for the secondary schools, such students must not be overlooked.

2. It is incontestable that neither an elaborate scheme of classifi‚ cation, nor the very fine points that enter into a discussion of the possible beginnings of things are easily comprehended by untrained minds. Hence, both ultimate classfication and primordial things must, at first, be left out of consideration.

3. Success in teaching is sometimes jeopardized by the early presentation of disagreeable features of the subject taught. It is desirable to postpone the consideration of these, if it can be done without essential loss, until the interest of the student has been so secured as to induce him to face the disagreeable for the sake of probable though distant advantage. Hence everything like dissection should be postponed until the eager curiosity of the tyro overcomes a possible nervous timidity incident to anatomical investigation.

4. In some sections of our country it is difficult to obtain materials which are wastefully common in other sections. It is believed, however, that, by the exercise of a little forethought and diligence on the part of the instructor, the materials here suggested can be obtained at slight expense in any part of the United States.

5. The contemplated work in zoölogy is intended to occupy the student's time five hours per week for one year of forty weeks. These two hundred hours work are to be employed, one hundred twenty in laboratory research, and eighty in reports on laboratory and text-book work.

The work may begin with a living fish for study. The ordinary carp (gold fish) will answer an admirable purpose. The fish should be studied in its entirety as a living organism ; its mode of locomotion, its body-covering and all other visible parts, thoroughly familiarized. Subsequently, the pupils should be provided with other fishes. As large a variety of fishes as possible should be studied for comparison. Perch are usually obtainable, as are also smelts in their season, and other common varieties of fishes, whether the school be located inland or on the seaboard.

Some general ideas of classification may be here introduced, but minutiae which are likely to produce weariness and consequent distaste should be avoided. Close anatomical investigation may well be left for future study. Concerning this the shrewd teacher will determine for himself. He will not lay down rules from which no circumstance may swerve him, but rather will be guided in some respects by the abilities of his class, irrespective of what has been done by previous classes. As this elementary work with fishes will furnish materials for subsequent constant reference it should not be hurried.

The microscope may well be employed in calling attention to the structure of the scales. No better subject will ever be found for exciting interest among young naturalists than these scales offer as exhibited by polarized light. Two or three weeks or more, of time here occupied will yield abundant fruitage in future study. Proper supervision of notes and drawings made by the pupils will lead them to appreciate and acquire the true method of making valuable descriptions, regarding and recording the essential while disregarding the non-essential.

It is believed that by means of the work suggested above there will be aroused in the pupils an interest which will render them enthusiastic in pursuing a course of lessons like the following. The preferences of the teacher, as well as the conditions offered by locality, will be factors in determining the individual species to be used for study and illustration. The text-book, which should be a brief one, should be supplemented by books of reference to be consulted when special organisms or other topics are under discussion.

COURSE OF WORK.

The Protozoa.

The study of these animals may well begin with the Amoeba. Specimens which by proper forethought may easily be secured should be before the class. All the conditions that enter into a full determination of the position of the Amoeba as belonging to the animal kingdom need not be sought by the class. Reference to the fish already made a subject of special study will aid greatly in determining some of the conditions that should be learned. Life, sensation, voluntary motion, use of oxygen, use of organic food, protoplasm are naturally some of the facts that must be seen and understood. The question of calcareous *vs.* siliceous frame-work will naturally be postponed. Following a discussion of the Amoeba, some rhizopod, as *Actinophrys*, which is sufficiently common, may well receive a little attention. Of the Infusoria, *Stentor*, *Vorticella*, *Paramoecium* which are always obtainable will excite great enthusiasm in pupils.

The Porifera.

Spongilla is accessible in almost every locality, while on the sea-coast marine sponges may be obtained.

The Coelenterata.

Hydroids may be procured on the sea-coast and kept dry in mass. Preserved in alcohol they make excellent class specimens. Specimens mounted on slides for the microscope will aid in giving pupils definite ideas of the appearance of the animals when alive. When possible, living specimens should be provided. The fresh-water hydra should not be overlooked; the work, at least, of polyps is always obtainable.

The Echinodermata.

A supply of starfishes, sea-urchins and crinoids is indispensable. The mode of growth of crinoids as indicated by fossil remains may be, in a certain sense, paralleled by the hydroids and *Vorticellae* already somewhat familiar.

The Vermes.

The earth worm furnishes cheap and abundant material for study. With a good microscope in use it will not be surprising if representatives of the *Gregarinidae* are discovered by the inquisitive student. The teacher may thus have an excellent opportunity to impress on the minds of the pupils the fact that school work is at best but a beginning, and that abundant opportunities are offered for further discovery.

The Mollusca.

The clam, whether marine or other, will here serve an excellent purpose. Univalves should receive a share of attention. Some ideas of classification may be developed in this branch with satisfactory results from the conchological side, even with malacology temporarily disregarded. The development of gasteropods, being a subject of absorbing interest, may well occupy a small share of attention.

The Arthropods.

Lobsters, edible crabs and crayfish, which are all easily obtained, may be dissected with little repugnance on the part of learners. For the study of minute crustacea, *Cyclops* and *Daphnia* are available everywhere. On a larger scale shrimps or sand fleas are abundant, and on the coast the different stages of growth of the common crab and living barnacles furnish abundant materials for study.

Insects.

A special and, so far as possible, thorough study of some common species of grass-hopper will prepare the pupils for the further investigation of Insects. The Cuverian rather than the modern and more accurate classification of insects will be found of great practical value. Representatives of the Diptera, the Neuroptera, the Coleoptera, the Hemiptera, the Lepidoptera, and the Hymenoptera may be made subjects of special study, possibly in the order named. The pupils themselves will easily arrange a crude classification of insects as follows :—

1. Mandibulata
{
Coleoptera,
Hymenoptera,
Orthoptera,
Neuroptera,
}

2. Haustellata
{
Lepidoptera,
Heteroptera,
Homoptera,
Diptera.
}

The Vertebrata.

1. *Fish.* In schools away from the coast the characteristic features of sharks and rays may well be enforced by the use of alcoholic specimens. Fossil fishes or fragments of the same, as teeth and cales, will be found useful here. The presence of scales, the classification of fishes as homocercal or heterocercal, and the question of edibility may well be discussed together. As many types of fishes as can easily be obtained should be studied for purposes of classification. The local markets may be drawn upon very advantageously.

2. *Batrachians.* Special studies of toads and frogs and such salamanders as are procurable will be of advantage. *Nocturus* should be made a subject of special investigation.

3. *Reptiles.* Lizards, snakes and turtles need attention. By this time a comparative examination of the circulatory apparatus of the classes of vertebrates will furnish opportunity for much study. The terms, *cold-blooded* and *warm-blooded* begin to have definite significance now, while the different types of heart suggest reasons for, or concomitants of, many other conditions of life, that have been noticed.

4. *Birds.* The comparison of vertebrate differences and resemblances should continue with the study of birds. The structure of the vertebræ themselves will demand considerable attention. The

close relationship of birds and reptiles despite their outward dissimilarity will at once suggest itself to the thoughtful observer.

5. *Mammals.* The teacher will be his own best judge as to the needs of his class in the broad field here before him. Physiological models, manikins, etc., subserve an excellent purpose, if the dissection of some mammal, as a rabbit or a cat, cannot conveniently be accomplished. The work can thus be made to furnish valuable human anatomical information if not to culminate in the study of human anatomy.

Ideas, before somewhat crude, in what has been called physiology, may now be crystallized into permanent and available shape.

It must not be forgotten that the plan here outlined is only suggestive. It is perhaps hardly necessary to repeat that drawings and written descriptions should be constantly required. Close observation and accurate expression are mutually helpful.

Withal it should be constantly borne in mind that the acquisition of facts is not the most important desideratum. Discipline, intellectual growth, and broad and varied culture should be the aims to which the acquisition of special information will be properly subsidiary.

PHYSIOLOGY IN PRIMARY AND SECONDARY SCHOOLS.

" It is the judgment of this Conference that, while the principles of hygiene should be included in the work of the lower grades, the study of physiology as a science may best be pursued in the later years of the high-school course. We recommend that a daily period for one half year be devoted in the high school to the study of anatomy, physiology and hygiene, with as large an amount of practical work as is possible."

The recommendations of the report upon this portion of the work of the Conference are based upon the following considerations :

The study of physiology is in a great measure the study of the mechanics, the physics, and the chemistry of the living body ; before it can be pursued profitably the student should have, at least, a fair elementary knowledge of these sciences as fundamental. It is not possible to teach it as a science to pupils devoid of such knowledge ; any effort to do so is apt to lead either to the bewilderment of the learner, or else to attempts at "simplification" on the part of the instructor which convey erroneous ideas unless the teacher has exceptional knowledge and skill.

The study of physiology demands as a prerequisite a certain amount of anatomical knowledge, and much of what is called physiology in elementary text-books on that science consists of statements concerning the anatomy of the human body that are of more or less importance as a basis for physiological knowledge. It is, in the judgment of this Conference, not desirable to teach a great deal of anatomy to young children. Such instruction is likely to lead, in some instances at least, to morbid if not prurient curiosity that is productive of far more evil than the instruction is likely to counterbalance with good.

Considerations such as these lead to the conviction expressed in the resolution of the Conference concerning the teaching of physiology in the lower grades. It is their belief, however, that simple and practical instruction upon the subject of personal health and its care may with advantage be given to young children. Such instruction, however, should rather be given and received (as many other things concerning conduct must be received by young children) upon authority, than as an appeal to the judgment of the pupil as based on his physiological knowledge.

Instruction in hygiene adapted to the capacity of young children may be profitably given on the subjects of personal cleanliness; pure air, and the relation of the carriage of the body to healthy respiration; wholesome foods, and moderateness and regularity in their use; regular and sufficient sleep; regularity in other bodily habits; care as to temperature, and prudence concerning exposure; and abstinence from narcotics and stimulants, and from drugs generally.

Where instruction in physiology and hygiene is required in the primary grades by the law of the state, it may be preceded by a simple account of the structure of the body. It should include brief and elementary discussions of the principal groups of functions; and should lay greatest stress, as is the intent of the law in most cases, upon such simple precepts of hygiene as may be clearly understood and practiced by the child.

What has already been said concerning the study of physiology as a science, will, if accepted, justify the opinion expressed by the Conference that such study may best be pursued in the later years of the high-school course. It should follow rather than precede the portion of the course devoted to physics and chemistry, as well as such other biological study as the course provides for.

While physiology is one of the biological sciences, it should be clearly recognized that it is not, like botany or zoölogy, a science of observation and description; but rather, like physics or chemistry, a science of experiment. While the amount of experimental instruction (not involving vivi-section or experiment otherwise unsuitable) that may with propriety be given in the high school is neither small nor unimportant, the limitations to such experimental teaching, both as to kind and as to amount, are plainly indicated. For this reason the study of physiology as a component of the high-school course should be regarded as of importance rather as an informational than as a disciplinary subject, and should be taught largely with reference to its practical relations to personal and public hygiene.

It should be preceded by a brief study of the general plan of the body. As each group of functions is taken up, the organs involved should be specially studied both as to their anatomy and their histology. Anatomical demonstrations should be made whenever possible upon fresh material from the bodies of domestic animals ; where fresh material cannot be obtained, permanent alcoholic preparations properly dissected may be shown ; models and engravings of the organs of the human body may, with advantage, be exhibited in connection with demonstrations of the same organs, from the bodies of the lower animals most available for comparison ; but dependence should never be placed entirely on such artificial representation, if original specimens can be obtained. All anatomical teaching in this connection should keep clearly in view the physiological knowledge to which it is subservient ; attention should be directed to the structural features of greatest importance in this respect ; and facts of purely morphological significance should be disregarded, whenever attention to them would distract the mind of the pupil from the study of the relation of structure to function.

Demonstrations of the histological structure of the various organs of the body require the use of a good microscope, with powers to four or five hundred diameters. A set of thirty or forty permanent preparations may be provided, which will suffice to show all that is most important, but it will add greatly to the interest of the student and to the reality of the knowledge obtained, if the teacher is able to make a portion, at least, of such preparations in the presence of the class. If the possession of a number of microscopes renders it possible, it is very desirable that an opportunity be afforded students for making for themselves preparations of, at least, the simple structural elements that may be dissociated by teasing or other methods, as well as of sections and other complex preparations which the school equipment will permit. Such practical exercises in histology may properly accompany the anatomical dissections that students should be, as far as possible, encouraged to make for themselves.

The obvious limitations to experimental work in physiology in the high school, already referred to, make it necessary for the student to acquire much of the desired knowledge from the text-book only.

Nevertheless, much may be done by a thoughtful and ingenious teacher to make such knowledge real, by the aid of suitable practical exercises and demonstrations. Space will not permit a detailed statement in this report, of the various ways in which this may be accomplished, but a few typical instances may be cited, such as artificial salivary and peptic digestion; the study of arterial circulation, as illustrated by the movement of a rhythmically impelled fluid in elastic tubing toward a variable resistance; the working of a model of the respiratory mechanism, and the illustration of the optics of normal (and abnormal) vision, by means of a properly constructed schematic eye. As excellent examples of direct physiological experiment, at once practicable and valuable, may be mentioned the experimental study of the sensations and their illusions, notably the tactile and the visual.

The instruction in hygiene for the high-school course may, in addition to a fuller discussion of the subjects cited in a previous portion of this report, discuss matters advantageously which concern the adult, though beyond the control of the child; as examples, may be mentioned the subjects of dietetics; of heating and ventilating; of water supply and drainage. Such instruction should now include a consideration of the reasons which underlie the rules of hygiene, and the student should be encouraged and guided in efforts to make practical application, in this respect, of the knowledge which he has acquired by the study of physiology.

Finally, attention should be called to the fact that, while it is true of the sciences generally, it is eminently true of physiology, that it is vain to expect good results in the classroom unless the subject is taught by well-trained teachers. No person should be regarded as qualified to teach physiology in a high school, whose preparation has not been at least as thorough as that of his fellow-teachers in mathematics or the languages.

11

HISTORY, CIVIL GOVERNMENT, AND POLITICAL ECONOMY.

To the Committee of Ten:

PRESIDENT CHARLES W. ELIOT, *Chairman:* —

Dear Sir, — Herewith we respectfully submit the resolutions reached by the Conference held at Madison, Wisconsin, Dec. 28–30, 1892, to consider the teaching of History, Civil Government, and Political Economy in the schools; together with an explanatory report. In an appendix will be found brief categorical answers to your specific questions.

I. RESOLUTIONS OF THE CONFERENCE.

Time to be occupied.

1. *Resolved*, That history and kindred subjects ought to be a substantial study in the schools in each of at least eight years. [*Report*, §§ 7–9, 16.]

Subjects.

2. *Resolved*, That American history be included in the program. [*Resolutions* 14, 16; *Report*, §§ 12–14, 16, 17.]

3. *Resolved*, That English history be included in the program. [*Resolutions* 14, 16; *Report*, §§ 12–14, 16, 17.]

4. *Resolved*, That Greek and Roman history, with their Oriental connections, be included in the program. [*Resolutions* 14, 16; *Report*, §§ 12–14, 16, 17.]

5. *Resolved*, That French history be included in the program. [*Resolution* 14; *Report*, §§ 12–14, 16.]

6. *Resolved*, That one year of the course be devoted to the intensive study of history. [*Resolution* 14; *Report*, §§ 15, 16.]

7. *Resolved*, That the year of intensive study be devoted to the careful study of some special period, as for example the struggle of France and England for North America, the Renaissance, etc. [*Report*, §§ 14–16, 33.]

8. *Resolved*, That a list of suitable topics for the special period be drawn up as a suggestion to teachers. [*Report*, §§ 14–16.]

9. *Resolved*, That formal instruction in political economy be omitted from the school program; but that economic subjects be treated in connection with other pertinent subjects. [*Resolution* 30; *Report*, § 19.]

10. *Resolved*, That to American history in the first group of studies be added the elements of civil government. [*Resolutions* 28, 29 ; *Report*, §§ 16, 18.]

Programs.

11. *Resolved*, That the eight-year course be consecutive. [*Resolution* 14 ; *Report*, §§ 10, 16.]

12. *Resolved*, That the first three years of study be devoted to mythology and biography based on general history and on American history. [*Resolution* 14 ; *Report*, §§ 16, 30.]

13. *Resolved*, That the point at which the program should be divided into two groups be fixed at the beginning of the high school course. [*Resolutions* 14, 16 ; *Report*, §§ 6, 10.]

14. *Resolved*, That the Conference adopt the following as the program for a proper historical course. [*Report*, §§ 10, 13, 14, 16.]

1st year.   Biography and mythology.

2d year.   Biography and mythology.

3d year.   American history ; and elements of civil government.

4th year.   Greek and Roman history, with their Oriental connections.

[At this point the pupil would naturally enter the high school.]

5th year.   French history.   (To be so taught as to elucidate the general movement of mediaeval and modern history.)

6th year.   English history.   (To be so taught as to elucidate the general movement of mediaeval and modern history.)

7th year.   American history.

8th year.   A special period, studied in an intensive manner ; and civil government.

15. *Resolved*, That the Conference frame an alternative six-year program. [*Report*, § 17.]

16. *Resolved*, That the following program be recommended for schools which are not able to adopt the longer program. [*Report*, § 17.]

1st year.   Biography and mythology.

2d year.   Biography and mythology.

[In the intervening year or years, if any, historical reading should be pursued as a part of language study.]

3d year.   American history, and civil government.

[At this point the pupil would naturally enter the high school.]

4th year.   Greek and Roman history, with their Oriental connections.

5th year. English history.   (To be so taught as to elucidate
the general movement of mediaeval and modern
history.)

6th year. American history and civil government.

17. *Resolved*, That in no year of either course ought the time
devoted to these subjects to be less than the equivalent of three
forty-minute periods per week throughout the year.   [*Report*,
§§ 7-9.]

Methods in History.

18. *Resolved*, That it is desirable that in all schools history should
be taught by teachers who not only have a fondness for historical
study but who also have paid special attention to effective methods
of imparting instruction.   [*Report*, §§ 25, 26.]

19. *Resolved*, That in the first two years oral instruction in biography and mythology should be supplemented by the reading of simple
biographies and mythological stories.   [*Report*, §§ 16, 17, 30.]

20. *Resolved*, That after the first two years a suitable text-book or
text-books should be used, but only as a basis of fact and sequence
of events, to be supplemented by other methods.   [*Report*, §§ 27-29.]

21. *Resolved*, That pupils should be required to read or learn one
other account besides that of the text-book, on each lesson.   [*Report*,
§§ 27-29.]

22. *Resolved*, That the method of study by topics be strongly
recommended, as tending to stimulate pupils and to encourage independence of judgment.   [*Report*, § 33.]

23. *Resolved*, That the teaching of history should be intimately
connected with the teaching of English : first, by using historical
works or extracts for reading in schools ; second, by the writing of
English compositions on subjects drawn from the historical lessons ;
third, by committing to memory historical poems and other short
pieces ; fourth, by reading historical sketches, biographies and
novels, outside of class work.   [*Report*, §§ 50-34.]

24. *Resolved*, That, so far as practicable, pupils should be encouraged to avail themselves of their knowledge of ancient and modern
languages, in their study of history.   [*Report*, §§ 30, 32, 34.]

25. *Resolved*, That the study of history should be constantly
associated with the study of topography and political geography, and
should be supplemented by the study of historical and commercial
geography, and the drawing of historical maps.   [*Report*, § 35.]

26. *Resolved*, That in all practicable ways an effort should be
made to teach the pupils in the later years to discriminate between
authorities, and especially between original. sources and secondary
works.   [*Report*, §§ 15, 33.]

27. *Resolved,* That a collection of reference books, as large as the means of the school allow, should be provided for every school, suitable for use in connection with all the historical work done in that school. [*Report,* §§ 23, 24, 30, 31.]

Civil Government and Political Economy.

28. *Resolved,* That civil government in the grammar schools should be taught by oral lessons, with the use of collateral text-books, and in connection with United States history and local geography. [*Report,* § 18.]

29. *Resolved,* That civil government in the high schools should be taught by using a text-book as a basis, with collateral reading and topical work, and observation and instruction in the government of the city, or town, and State in which the pupils live, and with comparisons between American and foreign systems of government. [*Report,* § 18.]

30. *Resolved,* That no formal instruction in political economy be given in the secondary schools, but that, in connection particularly with United States history, civil government, and commercial geography, instruction be given in those economic topics, a knowledge of which is essential to the understanding of our economic life and development. [*Resolution* 9 ; *Report,* § 19.]

Relations with Colleges.

31. *Resolved,* That the instruction in history and related subjects ought to be precisely the same for pupils on their way to college or the scientific school, as for those who expect to stop at the end of the grammar school, or at the end of the high school. [*Report,* §§ 2, 11.]

32. *Resolved,* That the examinations in history for entrance to college ought to be so framed as to require comparison and the use of judgment on the pupil's part, rather than the mere use of memory. [*Report,* §§ 20, 21.]

33. *Resolved,* That satisfactory written work done in the preparatory school ought to be accepted as a considerable part of the evidence of proficiency required by the college. [*Report,* § 21.]

34. *Resolved,* That, where a division is permitted, the entrance examinations in history ought usually to be a part of the final examinations for college rather than of the preliminary examination. [*Report,* § 22.]

Resolution of Thanks.

35. *Resolved,* That the Conference extend its thanks to the University of Wisconsin and citizens of Madison for their gracious hospitality. [*Report,* § 1.]

II. Preliminary.

1. Basis of the Discussion in the Conference.

By the politeness of the University of Wisconsin and of the citizens of Madison, your Conference was invited to hold its sessions in that city. The convenient rooms of the Seminary of Political Science were placed at our disposal, and the courtesy and hospitality of the people of the city did much to make our stay agreeable and to facilitate the work. We held two prolonged sessions on each of three days. At the first session steps were taken to prepare a program, and on the adjournment of the sixth session all the subjects of that program had been examined and our conclusions formulated in definite resolutions. It was our effort to examine the ground thoroughly, to find out what was being done by the schools on the subjects assigned, and to suggest an harmonious and comprehensive scheme of historical study.

Of the ten members one was a college president; one the principal of an academy including primary as well as secondary grades; two were high school principals; and six were college professors of history, civil government, or political economy. Several members had had experience in other grades of schools, as teachers, superintendents, or members of school governing boards. The Conference was further materially assisted by the advice of Professors Frederick J. Turner and Charles H. Haskins of the University of Wisconsin, and of Mr. Wells, State Superintendent of Education for Wisconsin. At least twelve states in the Union, extending from Maine to Virginia, and west as far as Iowa, were represented by men who had lived in them, and who knew something of their system of schools.

Without assuming to speak for the great body of teachers of history and kindred branches throughout the Union, we believe that we are acquainted with, and fully represent, the opinions of many thoughtful individuals in widely distributed parts of the country.

It may be further stated that upon each of the thirty-five resolutions which were framed, the Conference voted unanimously. This does not mean that, for the sake of harmony, members withdrew strongly-felt opposition to some of the resolutions; but that in each vote, as finally formulated, every member of the Conference heartily concurred.

Besides their natural desire to see the instruction in their favorite study improved, it is the mature conviction of the members of the Conference, as teachers, that the subjects in question, especially when taught by the newer methods herein advocated, serve to broaden and cultivate the mind; that they counteract a narrow and provincial spirit; that they prepare the pupil in an eminent degree for enlightened and intellectual enjoyment in after years; and that they assist him to exercise a salutary influence upon the affairs of his country. Hence it is the especial desire of the Conference to see these advantages as widely diffused as possible.

2. Fundamental Questions.

Four fundamental questions confronted the members of the Conference upon assembling. They were: how far they should make recommendations which could be applied only in favored parts of the country; whether they should recommend an ideal program, or a simpler program practicable in good schools with their present means and apparatus; how far they should insist on a uniform program; and what relations they should suggest between the schools and the colleges.

On the first point we agreed that the recommendations should be the same for all. (§ 10.) Upon the second point, the recommendation of an ideal program, the Conference was unanimously of the opinion that it would suggest nothing that was not already being done by some good schools, and that might not reasonably be attained wherever there is an efficient system of graded schools. (§ 9.)

Upon the third question we especially trust that we may not be misunderstood. It would not be our purpose, if we had the power, to reduce the teaching of history to one uniform program carried out on a uniform method. We believe that the time devoted to history and allied subjects should be increased; that the subjects treated should not be confined to our own country; and that the dry and lifeless system of instruction by text-book should give way to a more rational kind of work; but our recommendations will have little effect unless they are carried out in an intelligent and discriminating spirit, which will alter the details according to local necessities and difficulties.

As to the fourth question, we believe that the colleges can take care of themselves; our interest is in the school children who have no expectation of going to college, the larger number of whom will not enter even a high school. This feeling is strengthened by the consideration that proportionally a much smaller number of the girls go to college than of the boys, and it is important that both sexes shall be well grounded on these subjects. An additional responsibility is thrown upon the American system of education by the great number of children of foreigners, children who must depend on the schools for their notions of American institutions, or of anything outside their contracted circle. Hence our recommendations are in no way directed to building up the colleges, increasing the number of college students, or taking out of the hands of the colleges the historical work which they are especially fitted to do. (§§ 10, 11, 20–22.)

3. Usual Objects of Historical and kindred Studies.

At the outset a clear statement of the objects of historical training is necessary. The result which is popularly supposed to be gained from history, and which most teachers aim to reach, is the acquirement of a body of useful facts. In our judgment this is in itself the most difficult and the least important outcome of historical study. Facts of themselves are hard to learn, even when supported by artificial systems of memorizing, and the value of detached historical facts is small in proportion to the effort necessary to acquire and retain them. When the facts are chosen with as little discrimination as in many school text-books, when they are mere lists of lifeless dates, details of military movements, or unexplained genealogies, they are repellant. To know them is hardly better worth while than to remember, as a curious character in Ohio was able to do some years ago, what one has had for dinner every day for the last thirty years. It cannot be too strongly emphasized that facts in history are like digits in arithmetic; they are learned only as a means to an end.

4. Training of the Mind.

The principal end of all education is training. In this respect history has a value different from, but in no way inferior to, that of language, mathematics, and science. The mind is chiefly developed in three ways: by cultivating the powers of discriminating observation; by strengthening the logical faculty of following an argument from point to point; and by improving the process of comparison, that is, the judgment.

As studies in language and in the natural sciences are best adapted to cultivate the habits of observation; as mathematics are the traditional training of the reasoning faculties: so history and its allied branches are better adapted than any other studies to promote the invaluable mental power which we call the judgment. Hence statesmen have usually been careful students of history. History is a subject unequalled for its opportunities of comparison, for it is pre-eminently a study of the relation between cause and effect. History combines the advantages of a philosophical and a scientific subject: upon the one side, it is a study of the human mind, of character, and motives; upon the other hand, historical records form a body of material which, in the demand its analysis makes upon the mind, may be compared with that of chemistry or geology. Indeed it has some practical advantages over science; for the examples in a geological or mineralogical museum fill many shelves, while in history they may be brought within the covers of a few books. The value of history is increased if it is looked upon in part as a laboratory science, in which pupils learn to assemble material and from it to make generalizations. (§§ 31–33.)

" Since grappling with history is grappling with life," says an able teacher, " the main aim in teaching history is to develop those powers in the pupil which will best serve him in life." In almost every other subject taught in the grammar schools the basis of knowledge is fixed; the child meets axioms in mathematics, and takes in his reading and geography without reasoning upon them; history properly taught offers the first opportunity for a growth of discriminative judgment; it should train the pupil to throw away the unimportant or unessential, and to select the paramount and cogent. It may be so taught, also, as to lead him in some degree to compare and weigh evidence; that is, through history a child should be taught to exercise those qualities of common-sense comparison, and plain, everyday judgment which he needs for the conduct of his own life. Historical material is as abundant and familiar as geological; books, or at least newspapers, are to be found in every home; and the methods of historical criticism may be applied constantly to the news or gossip of the household.

5. Other Advantages.

History has long been commended as a part of the education of a good citizen. Locke said: " History is the great mistress of prudence and national knowledge." Milton said that children ought all to know the beginning, the end, and reasons of political societies. " History," says Bacon, " supplies examples." " History," says an English writer, " furnishes the best training in patriotism, and it enlarges the sympathies and interests." This is particularly the case with the history of one's own country, and America needs the training because we Americans know that our country is great, better than we know why it is great.

A significant advantage of history is that, intelligently taught, it may be a medium for the literary expression of the pupils (§ 32). Where but in a school in which history is well considered, could one hear a child sum up her judgment of the character of the English race in so cogent a phrase as this: " The English have such a sticking quality " ? History is the source of a great number of con-

'ventional metaphors and allusions.   Every intelligent child knows
what is meant by crossing the Rubicon, by meeting a Waterloo, by
ringing out like a liberty bell.   History abounds in literary material.

Another very important object of historical teaching is moral training.   History is the study of human character.   " Perhaps the most
valuable part of our work " says a teacher, " is that we are all made
— teacher as well as pupil — to learn personal lessons from history, to
watch the course of humanity as we would that of an individual, to
shun its errors, and make use of its excellencies "; and it is a study
in which the mistakes and failures of national life, like those of private life, become suggestive warnings.

To sum up, one object of historical study is the acquirement of
useful facts; but the chief object is the training of the judgment,
in selecting the grounds of an opinion, in accumulating materials for
an opinion, in putting things together, in generalizing upon facts,
in estimating character, in applying the lessons of history to current
events, and in accustoming children to state their conclusions in their
own words.

III. Arrangement of Studies.

6. Time to begin historical and kindred Studies.

With these general objects in view, your Conference has attempted
to settle how much time may reasonably be devoted to the subjects
which it has been asked to discuss.   First of all comes the preliminary question, at what time may children profitably begin to study
history?   Upon this subject there seems to be a general concurrence
of opinion among the persons whom we have consulted.   An interest
in the stories and adventures in which history abounds may be cultivated as soon as children begin to read at all.   On the question
where the formal and systematic study of history is to be begin, there
is more divergence ; two of the most eminent New England superintendents say, at ten years ; others would begin at about twelve.   In
the opinion of your Conference children from nine to eleven may well
begin by reading historical selections from standard authors, and the
careful study of history ought not to be delayed beyond the eleventh,
or at the latest, the twelfth year ; our recommendations (Resolutions
12, 14) provide for at least two years of methodical study of history
in the grammar school.

7. Question of consecutive Study.

Next comes the question, over how many years ought the study of
history to be distributed?   At present the average seems to be one
year in the grammar schools, and two years in the high schools.   A

few cases have been found in which history is systematically taught in each of four or five years of a high school course.

The inquiry involves the question of consecutive study. Shall we recommend a course in which the instruction shall be massed in a few years, a considerable number of recitation periods being appropriated in each; or shall we recommend that the study be pursued in a few exercises through a long succession of years? The German plan of education certainly turns out boys who are acquainted with details of history, and are able to make generalizations; that system calls for recitations in history and geography twice a week during the first two years, and three times a week during the following eight years of the course. The Germans believe, as the result of careful thought and observation, that the system of short courses with many exercises is pernicious; they find that the student educated in this way acquires a temporary interest only; and that the knowledge obtained, even though at the moment it may be more thoroughly comprehended, and may make a more vivid impression on the mind, is not so assimilated and made a part of the intellectual bone and sinew of the future man, as it is when, even once or twice a week, the subject is continued through a considerable number of years. In American schools the tendency is to compress the subject into a short period. The result is that history and kindred subjects assume an entirely different position in the minds of pupils, from that of studies continuously pursued. They get a notion that history ends and then begins again; the histories of different countries seem to them disconnected; and the value of historical training is almost lost by interruption and want of practice. We strenuously recommend, therefore, (Resolution 1) that "History and kindred subjects ought to be a substantial study in each of at least eight years"; and (Resolution 11) that "The eight-year course be consecutive."

8. Time now devoted to the Subjects.

In this, as in all these recommendations, it is not our purpose to lay down a hard and fast system for all schools under all conditions; but we do consider it essential that history be made a substantial subject for a fair number of hours during a considerable number of years. The actual time now devoted to these subjects is in most schools less than the importance of the subject demands. The smallest allowance observed in any school which pretends to teach history is twice a week for a term of twelve weeks. A very common allowance is once a week for a year in Ancient History, — manifestly a cram for entrance to college. A study of the reports of four hundred students, seems to show that two hundred recitation periods, or five periods a week for a year, is a little above the average in the grammar schools ; but in about three per cent of the cases as many as six hundred recitation periods are given in the grammar schools.

The secondary schools show a similar lack of uniformity. The smallest allowance observed is seventy-two exercises — apparently twice a week for a year — in two of the best known endowed academies of New England. In some cases history and kindred subjects reach seven hundred exercises in all ; the largest allowance seems to be about nine hundred and fifty exercises during the secondary course. Perhaps the most thorough course which has come under our observation is that of a New England academy : three hours a week throughout the four years, or about four hundred and eighty exercises ; but these are full hours with very thorough collateral work. The present average in high schools would seem to be two hundred to two hundred and forty periods in all.

Upon the question of the proper allowance for history, experienced persons differ ; but two of the best known school superintendents in the country agree that it should continue during eight or nine years. The head of an excellent normal school suggests three hours a week through the whole course of study.

9. Time recommended.

Your Conference has considered these fundamental questions with due seriousness, and recommends (Resolutions 14, 16, 17) that the actual time devoted to history be not less than three forty-minute periods per week throughout the course of eight years, — a total of about nine hundred exercises in all. This is no more than is being done by some favored schools, and it has the support of many practical educators acquainted with the details of schools. It is, in the judgment of the Conference, a reasonable time to be devoted to the group of subjects — history, civil government, and political economy. It is about one-eighth of the school time of the child during two-thirds of his whole course, extending to the end of the high school. Where is this time to be found? We respectfully ask you to consider whether there are not some subjects in the grammar school curriculum which may reasonably give up part of their time to history. We particularly suggest that, in accordance with Resolution 25, the time given to political geography be so applied as to connect that subject with the study of history. To history may be assigned part of the time saved by a rational rearrangement of arith- metic. Finally, in view of the probable improvement in the study of English through the proper teaching of history, (Report, §§ 5, 32 ;

Resolutions 22, 23) we ask for a share of the time now devoted to language study.

It is not our expectation that such radical changes can be brought about in a moment; nor would the recommendation be made, but for the belief that the community expects a new provision for those subjects. We believe that the program which we suggest might at once be put into operation in the whole system of schools in some large cities; and that once established, it would gradually extend to schools where the conditions are less favorable.

10. Distribution of Time.

How shall the time thus suggested be distributed among the years of the school course? It has seemed to us desirable to introduce about one-half of the consecutive study of history into the grammar schools.) The reasons for this arrangement hardly need be stated. The great majority of our children never pass beyond the grammar schools, and if these subjects are interesting, stimulating, and educating, they ought to be introduced early enough to accord their advantages to the child who does not enter the high school. (§ 2.) If the course is to be consecutive, distinct historical instruction would therefore begin four years before the pupil enters the high schools, and would end only with the high school course.

11. Question of Discrimination for those preparing for College.

The questions sent down by the Committee of Ten for our consideration include the following: "Should the subjects be treated differently for pupils who are going to college, for those who are going to a scientific school, and for those who, presumably, are going to neither?"

Several educational authorities advise such a separation. One New England superintendent thinks that a difference should be made "for the sake of its reflex effect on the secondary and primary schools"; others urge a more liberal provision for those who are not to go to college than for those who will have a later opportunity to study history; others think that the differentiation is made necessary by the preparation for college examinations; but no one seems to defend the system unhappily prevailing in some institutions, by which those who are to get most training hereafter are the only ones who have any training in history in the schools.

The Conference believes that such a distinction, especially in schools provided for the children by public taxation, is bad for all classes of pupils. It is the duty of the schools to furnish a well grounded and complete education for the child; it is the duty of higher institutions to accept a well grounded and complete education as a suitable preparation for entrance upon their courses. Whatever improves the schools must improve the colleges; but our function seems to be simply to recommend the best system which we can devise for the schools, without taking into account any subdivision of pupils. (Resolution 30.)

IV. SUBJECTS AND PROGRAMS.

12. Usual Subjects.

It appears from a comparison of the statements of college students that of one hundred and fifty-four who have studied history in the schools, seventeen have studied general history, twenty-two ancient history, and thirty-seven English history. In the high schools ancient history is far more common because many colleges require it as a subject for entrance. The next subject in favor is English history. American history is studied in only about one-third as many instances in high schools as ancient history, and in one-half as many schools as is English history. General history is about as common as American history. Our most enlightened advisers favor a considerable variety of subjects, and an enlargement of the historical curriculum of the grammar schools. Many of them urge the introduction of English history, European history, and, in a few cases, French history. In the state of Wisconsin a recent effort has been made to induce high schools to offer at least one half-year of ancient history and one-half year of English history.

A course in general history is frequently suggested "because the general outline is necessary to secure a true idea of historical perspective. . . . Get the outline at the very start, and then keep filling it in." The opinion of the Conference is decidedly against single courses in general history, because it is almost impossible to carry them on without the study degenerating into a mere assemblage of dates and names. Most text-books used in such courses are dry and lifeless; better books do not give a sufficiently clear and exact picture. We admit the advantage of a broad outlook, but contend that it is not to be had by gathering together a mass of details with no opportunity to show their relations.

The outlook can better be obtained by connecting the general course of events with the history of one or more countries. (§ 16; Resolution 14.) Fortunately the subject of history, like that of natural science, is one in which the educational advantages may be obtained without covering the whole field. It is important to look at the history of several countries side by side, and to notice the general movement of history, but that advantage may be gained indirectly in connection with specific subjects. (§§ 14, 15.)

13. Subjects recommended.

Out of the specific subjects we recommend Greek, Roman, English, American, and French history; and European history taught in connection with English and French history or in the year of intensive study. (Resolutions 2-7, 14, 16.) For the first three of these subjects the argument cannot be better stated than in the words of a practical teacher of history: "History is a unity. . . . The past lives in the present. I have no time for dry facts. I can give my children only life. Now what people of old times live most in the nineteenth century? . . . The tasks that press upon us to-day were first recognized in Greece. Here man put before himself in definite shape the specific problems that he wills to solve. Here he marked out the bounds of government, art, philosophy, literature, science; formulated and tested their principles; saw and stated clearly their problems. The work of the European world was mapped out in Greece, and here direction was given to human effort perhaps forever. So the study of history must begin with Greece, for in Greece all history is found in a nut-shell. . . .

"Roman history is the great central ganglion by which the history of the world is connected; Rome handed to us the civilization of Greece, gave us community of thought and ideals, rules us to-day in civil and ecclesiastical law. Hence Roman history lives in the present and must be taught. . . .

"English history has solved the problem of preserving local authority, selfish devotion to which wrecked Greece, and yet organizing it as efficiently as Rome did her empire. England teaches the world the secret of constitutional government and lives in every free state to-day. Hence English history must be taught."

American history needs no argument; it is already widely introduced; and the danger is not that it will be neglected, but that the schools may think it sufficient in itself. French history also commends itself to the Conference, because from the twelfth to the eighteenth centuries France was the leading nation of Europe, and her history is in a sense the history of civilization. General European history has the advantages of offering subjects capable of detailed and intensive study, and of furnishing a contrast to that development of the Anglo-Saxon race which is the main thought of English and American history. (§ 15.)

historical

14. Inter-relation of Subjects.

In arranging these various subjects we recognize the desirability of offering a small number of subjects thoroughly taught, rather than of breaking up the courses into many detached parts. (§ 7.) At the same time there should be a logical relation between the parts, and a use of the comparative method. As the teacher quoted above says: "To impress the unity of history upon my children . . . I must feel it myself in its every detail. . . . I must feel the points of similarity and difference between the Athenian dikasteries and the Anglican jury system. . . . Constant comparison, cross references, the showing of the past in the present is the very substance of my teaching."

Hence the importance of choosing a suggestive point of view from which comparison is easy. "The proper organization and government of a State is the highest task presented to man. Hence the greatest emphasis in class work should be placed on political and constitutional history. . . . I find that my pupils turn with the greatest interest to the constitutional problems of history; they feel their political importance as bearing upon the issues of to-day. One of my girls said to me not long ago: 'I am just as much interested in watching the growth of the House of Commons as in watching the plants in my window.'"

The opportunity for comparison and the training gained from a study of other systems are both lost if the study of history is confined to that of our own country. The details of that history are to a certain degree "absorbed through the pores"; for it is constantly discussed in periodicals and newspapers. On the other hand our own history is best understood in the light thrown upon it by other history. "We are all Americans; that is to say we have all been surrounded by a given political and social atmosphere from our birth. We are thus in no position to understand our institutions. The more vitally important these are, the more inherent the peculiarities of our civilization, the less apt we are to become conscious of them." While including American history as a considerable part of the work, we urge that in all schools the history of some other country in addition to that of the United States be pursued.

15. Intensive Study.

The history of any great country is so extensive that the schools can hardly expect to teach more than an outline. Another system which has in it many elements of highly valuable training is to select a brief period and put intensive study upon it. This is the practice in one of the best schools for girls to be found in New England: "The fourth year of the course is devoted to a special study of the period of American history extending from 1760 to 1790. The method is purely topical, no text-book being used." The importance of this intensive study was so strongly presented to the Conference that, after mature deliberation, it was voted that provision should be made for one year of such study. (Resolution 6.) This will offer an opportunity to apply, on a small scale, the kind of training furnished by the best colleges; it will teach careful, painstaking examination and comparison of sources; it will illuminate other broader fields of history; and it will give the pupil a practical power to collect and use historical material, which will serve him and the community throughout all his after life.

By vote of the Conference (Resolution 8) the following list of topics suitable for a year's intensive study is submitted, in accordance with Resolution 6:

1. The Struggle between France and England for North America.
2. Spain in the New World.
3. The French Revolution and the Napoleonic Period.
4. Some Phase of the Renaissance.
5. The Puritan Movement in the Seventeenth Century.
6. The Commerce of the American Colonies during the Seventeenth and Eighteenth Centuries.
7. American political Leaders from 1783 to 1830.
8. The Territorial Expansion of the United States.
9. American Politics from 1783 to 1830.
10. The Mohammedans in Europe.
11. The Influence of Greece upon modern Life.
12. Some Phase of the Reorganization of Europe since 1852.
13. Some Phase of the Reformation.
14. Some considerable Phase of local History.

It will be noticed that the list gives no preference to the history of one country over that of another. In any case, these subjects are only suggestive and many intelligent teachers will be able to find topics which the interest of their students and the resources of their libraries may make more suitable.

16. Distribution of Subjects and Eight-Year Program.

Perhaps the most difficult task of the Conference was to draw up a program in which a proper selection of subjects should be properly distributed. The result of our labors is set forth in Resolutions 12 and 14.

That the work of history should begin with elementary studies in biography and mythology, reënforced by good historical reading, needs no argument. The interest of the pupil is thus stimulated and he is

12

prepared to take up more serious study when the time comes. After two years of this kind of study in the grammar schools, a year of American history is next suggested because that is the subject in which local interest is most readily aroused, in which good parallel reading is easiest to find, and with which it is easiest to connect some study of civil government. For the fourth year we recommend "Greek and Roman history, with their Oriental connections." This order of subjects was strenuously urged in the Conference by professors and teachers of American history, upon the express ground that the large number of pupils who leave the schools at the end of the grammar school course should not be deprived of the opportunity of learning something of other civilizations. Classical history is now usually taught as a perfunctory subject in connection with studies in the Greek and Latin languages, and is rarely studied except by those who expect to go to college. This is an entirely wrong conception of the value of ancient history; it ought to be pursued for the sake of broadening the pupil's mind, widening his horizon, and bringing him into contact with a civilization so different from our own that it will suggest points of difference and comparison. No part of our recommendations seems to us more important than this, that something in addition to American history be taught in the grammar schools. It will be noticed, however, that in the six-year alternate course it has been found necessary to shift the Greek and Roman history to the first year in the high school (Resolution 16).

In the fifth and sixth years of historical study (the first and second years in the high school) we recommend French history and English history; here it is believed that the advantages of general history can be obtained without its drawbacks (§ 12). The intention of the recommendation is, that French history shall be considered as the central or leading history of Europe, about which shall be grouped the history of other countries. The subject, by its contrast, is an excellent means of bringing out the peculiarities of the following subject, English history, which the teacher should make the center of the great political and constitutional movement which England best exemplifies. In the seventh year it seems fitting that American history should again be taken up, this time with more reference to the development of the government and the character of statesmen. It seems particularly desirable to bring this phase of American history late in the course, when the students are more mature. Finally, in the eighth year, a subject is to be taken up for intensive or detailed study (§ 15). In this year we have desired to give the schools an opportunity to arrange a course each according to its own materials.

In this program we have not adopted either of two common ideas as to the proper arrangement and relation of courses. The subjects as recommended do not follow one another in chronological order, although from the fifth to the seventh year they form a logically connected series. Nor has it seemed desirable to recommend a method not uncommon in Germany, by which the student begins with the history of his own city and widens out to his nation, to Europe, and perhaps eventually to the rest of the world. The effect of this process in suggesting the relative importance of countries is perhaps shown by the name of a hotel in Paris : "Hôtel de l'Univers et des États Unis." What is most distant geographically is most distant also in thought; if this process is at any point interrupted the child is left with the feeling that the world stops where his study has ceased.

17. Alternative Six-Year Program.

Although strongly of the opinion that a minimum of three exercises a week during eight years is no more than good schools ought to provide, and that time may be found for it without sacrifice of other interests of the pupils (§ 9), we nevertheless recognize the practical difficulties which in many schools would prevent the introduction of so elaborate a system. We have therefore drawn up an alternative program for a six-year course (Resolution 16). The principal differences are the omission of French history as a separate subject, and the omission of the intensive study of a special period; there is the further defect of leaving the grammar schools with no other formal study than American history. Nevertheless the Conference believes this course to occupy no more time than is already given in a considerable number of schools, and to be an improvement upon most of the present programs, particularly if it is properly connected with the study of historical literature. (§§ 30–32.)

18. Civil Government.

Civil Government is pursued at present in very few grammar schools, — certainly in not more than one-sixth of those which have come under our observation. It is, however, rather a frequent subject in high schools, about one-third offering some sort of instruction in it. In actual teaching it seems little associated with history ; it is usually simply a text-book study during a part of one year ; and very few of the teachers seem to be familiar with the subject.

Among experienced teachers there seems to be a difference of opinion as to the proper place of the subject. Some would introduce it early in elementary form, on general topics ; others would make it an elaborate study late in the high school course. The Conference in

Resolutions 10, 14 and 16 has attempted to reconcile these two principles by introducing the study in two places, but always in connection with history, and as an adjunct to that subject.

While recognizing the importance of the study of government as a discipline and as an education for American citizens, we do not feel justified in recommending more time for the subject than is now employed by the best schools. We expect that it will occupy, including the elements of political economy (§ 19), about one-half the time devoted to the group of historical and kindred studies in each of the two years recommended; and we believe that this distribution is much better than the more common system of giving the subject a considerable number of hours during a few weeks only. But it is expected that good teachers in dealing with history throughout, and especially with American history, will constantly refer to the forms and functions of government with which the children are most familiar.

The question what subjects should be taught and what ground covered in the study of civil government is one which we have not thought it necessary precisely to determine. One system begins with the local government, as nearest to the child, and thence leads up through the State to the national government. Another method takes up first that which is most likely to attract the imagination of the child, the great machinery of the national government and its more striking functions, such as the postoffice, the army, the navy, and the collection of customs. Another principle is to associate with government practical ethics and rules of conduct. Each one of these systems, properly taught, has its value and may come within a program of history and kindred branches. Your Conference would, however, express the belief that the theoretical questions of government, such as the origin and nature of the state, the doctrine of sovereignty, the theory of the separation of powers, etc., are very difficult to teach to children ; and further, that a system of ethics can better be taught by example and by appealing to common sense and to accepted standards of conduct, than by formal lessons. On the other hand the simple principles underlying the laws which regulate the relations of individuals with the state, may be taught by specific instances and illustration ; and the machinery of government, such as systems of voting, may be constantly illustrated by the practice of the communities in which the children live (§ 34).

In Resolutions 28 and 29 the methods of study approved by the Conference are distinctly set forth. In the grammar schools the instruction ought to be simple and practical, using books and familiar institutions only as illustrations and collateral material; the study of civil government and that of history ought constantly to work into each other and to support each other. In the high schools civil government may be taught more elaborately; and here is an opportunity of which also some use may be made in the grammar schools: that of sending children to study their own local and state government in operation. A teacher of experience, a member of the Conference, has for years been in the habit of taking his high school class in civil government to the local courts, to the city councils in session, and to the capital of the state, fifty-six miles away, to see the legislature in session (§ 34). Other helpful methods are debates, mock town meetings, mock legislatures, reports of proceedings of legislatures and of Congress. At this stage the study lends itself to the topical method (§ 33), and pupils may be encouraged to prepare papers on the local institutions about them.

The subject of government is so difficult and requires so much practical illustration that the Conference would not recommend for schools an elaborate study of foreign systems. They believe, however, that constant reference to parallels or divergences in foreign politics will be interesting and helpful (Resolution 29). They commend, especially, reference to the German and Swiss governments, as suggesting different methods pursued by nations governing themselves under systems similar to ours; study of the English government, as presenting the contrast between the parliamentary and the committee systems, and study of the French government as a type of highly centralized systems, in which local government is entirely subordinated.

19. Political Economy.

The subject of political economy appears to be taught in only about one-twentieth of the high schools, and, in most cases, even there is confined to routine study and recitation from a text-book. Here, as in civil government, we believe that the essential principles are not above the reach of high school pupils; but that an attempt to master the whole subject will result in the understanding of only a small part. Few schools have teachers sufficiently trained to discuss and illustrate the general subject; nor are there proper text-books for high school use. It is believed that the subject is not attempted in schools of other countries corresponding in grade to our high school.

Upon no question which the Conference has considered is there greater difference of opinion among the persons consulted. Some eminent superintendents and principals would introduce or continue political economy in the last year of the high school course, or at least, in the last half-year. "Daily lessons for about twelve weeks

would be ample," says one. On the other hand several teachers
assert that political economy "has no place in secondary schools."
"It is not proved that the subject can be advantageously taught in
secondary schools, nor is the contrary proved." In this difference of
opinion it has seemed to the Conference wise, to recommend that there
be no formal instruction in political economy, but that the general
principles be taught "in connection particularly with United States
history, civil government, and commercial geography" (Resolutions
9, 30). The subject would, therefore, appear in its most elementary
form in the third year of the grammar school, and would be revived
in the last two years of the high school. In both places the subject
should not be introduced as a distinct and separate science; but as
illustrating government and political questions. In connection with
Resolution 30 the Conference adopted the following memorandum:

"It is suggested, for example, that when the tariff history of the
United States is being studied, the laws of value, the conditions of
production, and the principles of exchange, especially as relating to
international trade, be explained; that in connection with the study
of the development of means of transportation, such topics as the
concentration of population and of industry, the organic character of
society, the corporate organization of industry, the capitalistic mode
of production, the process of distribution, monopolies, labor organizations, etc., be discussed; that in connection with a study of Jack-
son's administration, the subjects of crises, banks and their functions,
the functions of money, the laws of its circulation, bimetallism, paper
money, and kindred topics be presented; that in connection with the
study of our great wars, certain topics in finance be introduced, as for
example, the principles of war finances, the history of our debt,
the process of debt conversion, and the methods of paying public
debts; that in connection with the study of civil government, such
topics as the assessment and collection of taxes, the principles of
taxation, the kinds of taxes, the functions of government, the formation and vote of the budget, the expenses of government, etc., be
studied.

"In making these recommendations the Conference does not intend
to suggest that less time than is customary be given to political
economy, or that less emphasis be given to its importance as a study
in the high schools; but rather that emphasis be laid on vital topics,
and that less time be devoted to controverted subjects and unsettled
questions."

It is desirable to avoid the impression that political economy is an
abstruse science of which no part can be understood without the
mastery of the system; teachers ought to set forth the principles of
finance, commerce, and business, as a part of the everyday life of the
community. The methods of teaching the economic principles thus
indicated must be left to the discretion of the teacher. It is a subject

in which text-book work is particularly inefficient, and no teacher ought to undertake the work who has not had some training in economic reasoning. The only methods which can possibly be successful are those which call upon the class for independent thought and suggestion.

V. College Examinations.

20. Present Requirements.

The usual requirement in history, where the subject appears at all in the conditions of entrance to college, is an elementary knowledge of the history of one country, or at most of two countries. The usual subjects are Greek and Roman history, — which are supposed to be taken up with classical study, — or American history ; in a few cases English history is also, or may be, a subject for examination. These requirements differ in amount and in application, and it would undoubtedly be a reform of much value if they could be made simpler and more uniform. The present subjects are very unsatisfactory, not because they are uninteresting in themselves, but because in many schools they are studied with a view only to the college examinations, and without reference to any preparation for life. In one of the schools in which preparation in history is best and most systematic for other pupils, boys and girls who are going to college are habitually deprived of that instruction, and are systematically crammed during a few weeks preceeding examinations. It is complained that " at present, examinations compel the teacher to accept bad methods for college preparation." We have not felt called upon to make any recommendations on the general subject of entrance to college ; but we desire to enter a protest against the present lax and inefficient system of historical examinations, and to urge a change by which schools which use proper methods shall have some advantage.

21. Suggestions of Improvement.

The dissatisfaction with the present system is shown by many protests from teachers. '' The requirements for college ought to be so framed," says a high school teacher, " that the methods of teaching best adapted to meet them will also be best for all pupils.'' Examinations " should be such as test the powers of the pupil and the methods of the teacher : analysis of subjects should be demanded ; . . . statements from analysis required. The pupil should be asked to state what books he has used in his course of study, and what service each book has done him; what methods are employed in his school; what work he has done in libraries. . . . In short, the mental training, alertness, and intelligence of the pupil should be tested rather than memory only."

A very ingenious suggestion, which deserves the attention of college authorities, is that the colleges accept any combination of two historical studies, — as Greek and American, French and English, — as a proper preparation for college, allowing additional historical subjects as advanced requirements. This method if adopted would go a long way to increase the number of historical subjects taught, and would facilitate the adoption of the reforms suggested by this report (§§ 13, 15).

Between the system of examinations and that of certificates the Conference has no recommendation to make, believing it to be a general subject which lies outside the present discussion. Where certificates are accepted, it is the duty of the colleges to take them only from schools which have suitable libraries and pursue intelligent methods. Where a college accepts no tests but its own, a proper written examination seems as fair a system as can be devised; but examinations may be so framed as to throw more weight upon general knowledge, and less on memory.

In Resolution 32 we have decidedly expressed the opinion that less attention be paid to detail and more to a power of comparison and judgment. Schools which adopt an improved general system of teaching history will give to their pupils a training in some respects of the same nature as that gained from science. Although it is impossible in history to simplify and vary the phenomena which are observed, it may nevertheless be made in part a laboratory subject. In some colleges the entrance requirements in physics call for an examination, but the pupils also submit note-books as evidence that they have pursued their previous work in a systematic and scientific fashion. We believe that a similar system may be applied with good effect to historical examinations. Besides the regular written tests, papers prepared in the schools may be submitted as a part of the evidence of preparation (Resolution 33). The effect would be that schools which had properly used collateral reading and other material would be more successful in getting their boys into college than those which depended solely on text-books; and that the colleges would be greatly improved by receiving into historical courses boys and girls who had had preliminary training of a proper kind. The time has come for the colleges to set their faces against perfunctory text-book methods in history, in the same manner as in classics and natural science.

22. Time of Examinations.

The question with reference to a division of examinations is answered in our Resolution 34, which agrees with the majority of the opinions collected from historical teachers upon this subject. With a proper system of examinations the eighth or intensive year would do most to prepare for entrance to college, and the examination would therefore naturally come at the end of the course. Hence history should be a "final" subject and not a "preliminary."

VI. METHODS OF HISTORICAL TEACHING.

23. Present Methods.

The last question submitted to the Conference is: "Can any description be given of the best method of teaching throughout the school course?" In our judgment the selection and arrangement of studies in the schools, imperfect as they now are, need reform less than the methods of teaching. In the grammar schools very few teachers know any other system than simple recitation by rote from text-books; and this is particularly the case in large city schools. The text-books are frequently poor and antiquated, and often have made so little impression upon the pupils' minds that their very names are forgotten. Outside reading and topical work does not appear in more than one fifth of the grammar schools, and is imperfect even in these. Not much better is the condition of the high schools and academies; in one hundred and thirty-five cases examined, all had recitations; sixty-nine used some kind of outside reference books; twenty-six used oral topics; forty-seven used written topics; in fifty-five there were written lessons; in eighty-two appears some kind of geographical instruction; but only in fifty-eight any form of map drawing. The apparatus for outside reading is usually small, although some high schools have large reference libraries. The present methods throw entirely too much stress on a few brief text-books; and comparatively few teachers have the spirit or the apparatus to carry their classes outside those narrow limits. Hence at least one experienced member of the Conference was at first inclined to think that possibly history should be omitted altogether from school programs, because, he said, teaching by rote from text-books made the subject disagreeable; and because it led to indefinite ideas, which were in many cases worse than none. The first necessity, he thought, was an improvement in the teachers.

24. Improved Methods.

Nevertheless the Conference had before it detailed accounts of at least three widely separated yet highly successful schools, in which history is taught in a common-sense and efficient manner; and they were greatly encouraged by the interest shown by pupils in those schools. The first is an academy in a State capital, in which history begins for very small children, with stories of heroic characters; then United States history and Cox's Mythology are taken up side by side; in the third year English history is begun; then American history, including the history of French and Spanish America as collateral with that of the English settlements. In the later years the pupils use the large and well appointed State Library. The master makes it his object to present history to them as a basis of enjoyment of art and literature; thus, he teaches American literature in connection with colonial history. There are constant references and comparisons from one field of history to another. Throughout the course he has in mind an ethical purpose — to suggest the causes of personal and national greatness and weakness; and his boys always elect history after they get into college (§ 34).

The second of these schools is a high school in a prosperous New England town; here note-books are used in the classes, and there are special topics for investigation, supplementary talks by the instructor and by members of the class, assignments and reports of collateral reading in history and literature, and debates on points upon which opinions or authorities differ. The third school, an endowed academy of a high grade, presents a systematic four-years program, covering successively Greek, Roman, English, and American history, with extensive parallel reading and much written work throughout.

These accounts, and those of similar schools, seem to show that good teaching of history is obtainable under present conditions, and that it is safe to recommend extended and systematic teaching of history with the expectation that some schools can at once adopt it in its entirety, and that it may gradually work its way into the system of American education.

25. Training of Teachers.

" Above all, the teacher must keep up with the times in books, methods, lines of thought, and interest . . . she must realize that the world is always passing on, and that, like Alice in Wonderland, she must run as fast as she can to keep where she is. . . . She must

keep herself in connection with the great teachers of her time."
That this ideal is not reached is shown by the lack of preparation on
the part of most teachers of history.

In Germany such teachers are almost invariably specialists. Such
subdivision is not uncommon in our large city high schools and
academies; but at present the work is very frequently divided up
among teachers of other subjects, none of whom has any real interest
in history. The opportunities of getting good historical training
both by men and women are now such that, in the judgment of the
Conference, all high schools and academies able to pay good salaries
ought to insist that the teacher of history should have " a knowledge
of illuminating methods of teaching history." Even under unfavora-
ble conditions we believe that too high a standard is not set up by
Resolution 19: "That in all schools it is desirable that history
should be taught by teachers who have not only a fondness for
historical study, but who also have paid special attention to effective
methods of imparting instruction." In other words it would be as
sensible for schools to employ a deaf and dumb person to teach reading, or to ask a Cherokee to teach Latin, as to depend for the
teaching of history on persons who have not had special training in
history. The supply of suitable candidates is now, or soon will be,
such that no School Board need put up with incompetent teachers
of history.

What is to be done with the teachers already in service who cannot
take even a year of special study? Some system of special teachers'
courses must be devised, with practical work going on during the
school year. When it is established there will doubtless still be
some bad teaching, but it will be without excuse. In the smaller
high schools the problem is more difficult, because the teachers are
fewer and must divide their time among several subjects; in such
cases the first step is to employ teachers with a good all-round training, with some preparation on each subject they undertake, in
preference to those who have a smattering of many subjects. In
the grammar schools the subjects are simpler, the collateral reading
and illustrations easy to apply, and the necessary training is correspondingly less. Perhaps the introduction of the " departmental
method" would improve the status of history in schools of that grade.
Here, also, fair dealing requires that the teachers now in service have
some opportunity to improve themselves. Is it not the duty of the
universities in or near large cities to coöperate with the schools in
establishing training courses?

26. Lectures.

What shall be the teacher's method of imparting his superior knowledge? Shall it be by lectures? It is the general opinion of experienced teachers that history should begin with simple stories told to the child; a little later they may read in books like Hawthorne's Wonder Book, or Bulfinch's Age of Fable, or from the collections of stories on American and English history. It is only in the later stages of the course, if at all, that formal lectures are applicable to school instruction.

One form of lecture is, however, both admissible and desirable; it is well in a brief talk to present the substance of the next or of approaching lessons, so as to suggest to the scholar the relations of the facts he is about to study. "In my presentation of a subject," writes a teacher, "I always work from circumference to center. I sketch, first, the barest outlines of the whole, so that the pupils may see the bearing and feel the relative importance of the subject in hand. For instance, if we are studying the Hannibalic Wars, the pupils know that this is one of the seven or eight great wars by which Rome conquered the world, that the period of conquest is one of the four periods of the Roman republic, and that the republic is one of the three forms of development which the government of Rome assumed."

Set lectures on the lesson, while very suitable for colleges, are not so well adapted to schools. To be useful they require elaborate note-taking, — a severe strain if well done, and if ill done productive of mental dissipation. We incline to recommend only informal talks which will explain the cause and effect of events, and which may add interesting illustrations and comparisons to the lesson of the day, as it appears in the text-book. In the advanced grades, an interesting and profitable exercise is to call upon pupils to prepare lectures under the direction of the teacher; on these, notes should be taken by the other pupils. If the subject is then reviewed at another exercise by the teacher, both the pupil, lecturer, and hearers will be quickened.

27. Text-Books.

In Resolution 20 we recommend: "That after the first two years a suitable text-book or text-books should be used, but only as a basis of fact and arrangement, to be supplemented by other methods." Since the text-book is, and ought to be, the center of the study of history in schools, a good text-book is essential. This simple and self-evident principle is not carefully observed. A rough analysis of the books used in one hundred and forty-nine high schools seems to show that seventy-six have poor books. The criteria of a good text-book are : first, that it should be written by an expert in the subject, who knows what to save and what to throw away ; second, that it should be arranged in a convenient form, with running headings, tables of contents, indexes, and other aids ; third, that it should deal with the essentials of history, avoiding accounts of military events, or the mere outline of political discussions ; fourth, that it should be embellished with numerous and correct maps to which repeated reference should be made in the text ; fifth, that it should be interesting to the average reader, and lightened by suitable illustrations and quotations from contemporary authorities. A few text-books possess most of these characteristics, but the present system of selecting or of placing text-books in the schools does not seem to give suitable preference to the better books. In the judgment of the Conference a text-book ought to be something more than the mere development of a " story," it ought to include something on the social and economic side, as well as on the political ; and it ought to refer to, and facilitate, outside reading and the preparation of topics.

We recommend further that a practice be established in the schools of using two, three, or four parallel text-books at a time. (Resolution 21). By preparing in different books, or, by using more than one book on a lesson, pupils will acquire the habit of comparison, and the no less important habit of doubting whether any one book covers the ground. The practical difficulties are few ; where school boards buy text-books four sets of ten books each cost no more than one set of forty books ; where pupils buy their own books classes may be divided into three or four groups, the members of each group providing themselves with the same book.

28. Recitations.

What is learned in the text-books ought in most cases to be brought home to the mind in recitations, which should be less a test of faithfulness than a supplement to the reading. It is better to omit history altogether than to teach it in the old-fashioned way, by setting pupils painfully to reproduce the words of a text-book, without comment or suggestion on the teacher's part. The first duty of the teacher is to emphasize the essential points in the book, to show, if possible, what is the main thing worth remembering in the lesson of the day. It is also a duty to point out things which the writer of the text-book has inserted, but which, in the teacher's judgment, may safely be neglected. Few teachers have the courage to do what a member of the Conference recently saw done in class : to tell the children to " pass over Appius Claudius and the sacred chickens because they were of little account." The teacher may have underestimated the historical value of legend ; but she sent home to the minds of her pupils the wholsomee thought that⟨not all is essential that appears in print.⟩

Again, the questions in a recitation ought not to demand from the pupils a bald repetition of the phrases or ideas of the book, but ought to call for comparison and comment. The questions ought constantly to go forward and backward, to bring up points of comparison from previous lessons, and to bring in illustrations from other parallel subjects. A course in American history may be made doubly interesting by frequent cross references to previously studied Greek and Roman history ; and a course in English history is enriched by illustrations from English literature. Here is the place where the teacher's superior knowledge and training tells ; here is the place also for stirring up the minds of the pupils.

How far should pupils be expected to memorize? " A few things should be learned by heart and, when forgotten, learned again, to serve as a firm ground work upon which to group one's knowledge : without knowing the⟨succession of dynasties, or of sovereigns, or of presidents, or the dates of the great constitutional events,⟩the pupil's stock of information will have no more form than a jelly-fish." But those few necessary facts ought to be clearly defined as only a framework to assist the memory. The pupil's stock of material is to be kept in mind not by calling for it in glib recitations devoid of thought, but by constantly framing questions which will require for an answer a knowledge of the necessary facts ; thus, a comparison between Henry VIII and Charles I requires a pupil to remember the essential dates and events of both reigns, and their relations of cause and effect.

29. Further Suggestions as to Recitations.

An excellent suggestion is that of " open text-book recitations," in which with their books before them, pupils are asked questions on cause and effect, on relations with previous lessons, etc. ; answers may, if necessary, be written out and corrected in class. Such an exercise trains pupils to take in the thought of a printed page, and to grasp the essential points.

Such a system tends to encourage the habit of applying what one knows to a new problem. Still more helpful in the same direction are the off-hand discussions and impromptu debates which spring up in an eager class and which should be encouraged by every good teacher.

In many schools there are systems of review, too often perfunctory repetitions of what was dull when first recited. Some system is perhaps necessary to recall the attention to the relations of the parts of the subject. Two helpful substitutes for the ordinary review may be mentioned. The first is that of "fluent recitations." "The pupil is given the entire subject, for instance the Homeric Age, the Conquest of Italy by Rome, the Early Norman Kings, the New England Colonies. To recite these 'fluents' are the special glory of the class; the brilliant recitation that holds the interest of all the pupils, although the subject is familiar, is one that is especially prized. After the 'fluent' is finished it is criticised as to matter and manner; the English, the attitude, and intonation of the reciter all coming under fire, as well as the historical matter."

The second device is thus described. "But a very important part of the work yet remains — the fixing of the whole indelibly on the mind. This is attempted by what . . . . are called 'cards' i. e. a raking fire of short, sharp questions every morning to which a prompt direct answer is required, or the dread 'next,' 'next,' 'next' is heard. To fail in cards is thought a great disgrace, for they are taken up only when the subject has been most carefully explained, and failure in them is an evidence of unfaithfulness on the part of the pupil." . . . : These systems are admirable if applied so as to teach pupils to combine what they know, and to bring their knowledge to bear on unforeseen problems.

Another form of recitation is the written exercise repeated at frequent intervals: a single, properly framed question given at the beginning or end of each recitation, with ten minutes to answer it in writing, will train pupils in the habit of combining and applying their own information. For such an exercise questions involving comparison are well adapted. A good question would be, to make up a list of the sovereigns of England who were born out of the realm; or, after a lesson on the English in India, might come the question whether the occupation of India had been a good thing for the English nation.

The blackboard is used in some schools; the recitation begins with an analysis of the subject for the day, prepared by the teacher, and written out beforehand, or written by a pupil in the presence of the class. This, of course, emphasizes the teacher's own subdivision of the subject, as contrasted with that of the text-book, and breaks up the feeling that facts in order to be accurate can be stated in only one order. A few text-books have been prepared with topical

analyses of this kind, and in a good school pupils are sometimes
called upon themselves to prepare a suitable analysis for the criticism
of the teacher and of the class (§ 32).

To sum up their recommendations on this point, the Conference
is of the opinion that text-books must continue to be used, but that
they should be carefully selected, and that the pupil should have the
constant use of at least two different books; that the recitations upon
them should not consist of an historical catechism, but should be
made up of suggestive questions requiring a comparison and combination of different parts of the pupil's material; and that the
proper relations and proportions of that material may be promoted
by some system of rapid recitation, with criticism by teacher and
class.

30. Reading.

Recitations alone, however, cannot possibly make up proper teaching of history. It is absolutely necessary, from the earliest to the
last grades, that there should be parallel reading of some kind. In
Resolution 19 we recommend: "That in the first two years oral
instruction in biography and mythology should be supplemented by
the reading of simple biographies and mythological stories." The
numerous historical readers and selections of stories and poems now
offer a large amount of suitable introductory matter; when regular
text-book work begins, this system of parallel reading should be continued. "The sooner we can get a boy into touch with something
else than a hand book, the better." This principle is expressed in
Resolution 21. "That pupils should be required to read or learn one
other account besides that of the text-book, on each lesson." Such
parallel reading must necessarily take two forms: in the first place,
the use of distinct historical literature bearing immediately on the
subject in hand; and, secondly, the use of miscellaneous literature,
poems, historical novels, and biographies.

The system of more elaborate reading is well described as follows:
"The class work should be as elastic as possible, that it may adapt
itself to the different kinds of minds. I must surely give my brightest
pupils food enough, for a teacher's greatest fault is starving her
children, yet I must not crowd the weaker ones. . . . Certain books
bearing upon the subject in hand are designated to the pupils; every
one is required to read something outside her daily work, and the
better scholars are expected to read more. A special report of the
work done is handed in Monday morning, with the private note-books
containing a topical analysis of what has been read and original
remarks upon it. The reports and note-books are examined and
commented upon by the teacher."

31. Material for Reading.

Such a system, of course, requires a considerable school library. Out of one hundred and fifty-one high schools whose methods have been examined, only about fifty appear to have a good library of ordinary reference books, and only about forty a general library of comparative historical literature. Yet to provide a collection of books suitable for school work is not an expensive process: one hundred dollars, or fifty dollars, or even twenty dollars properly applied, will furnish a reserve of historical literature for the use of the pupil.

In addition, of course, every special subject ought to have a little galaxy of standard books grouped about it. Resolution 27 reads: " That a collection of reference books, as large as the means of the school allow, should be provided for every school, suitable for use in connection with all the historical work done in that school." Wherever public libraries exist, it is almost always possible to arrange for their use by the pupils of the public schools; and in a few favored places like Albany, there are special reference libraries of great value for historical work. Something may often be accomplished by making out a list of desirable books and asking each pupil either to buy one or to contribute to the purchase of one: in the course of a few years a considerable library may thus be brought together. Every school board which is willing to buy chemical and physical apparatus, may be brought to such a state of grace that it will buy reference books.

The main necessity is that teachers should have it firmly fixed in their minds that it is as impossible to teach history without reference books, as it is to teach chemistry without glass and rubber tubing. This system may also be so arranged as to create in the minds of pupils a desire to possess and use books, which will do much to break the monotony of their lives and to cultivate the habit of judicious expenditure. The time has been when in the houses of many intelligent families, educated in the common-schools, and reading newspapers regularly, almost the only books were the Bible and a Patent Office Report. It is the duty of the schools to make the return of such conditions impossible. Where expensive collections of documents can not be had, the sets of leaflets, which are now issued in a variety of forms and on a variety of subjects, may be used, at a smaller expense.

Another sort of illustrative reading may take the form of special exercises in literature, such as the study of poems on American colonial life in connection with American history; or of Chaucer with

13

English history. We feel hesitation with reference to historical novels: the natural tendency is to skip the history in them or to receive a false historical impression if the history is accepted. Nevertheless, there are standard historical novels which will always be read, and which will always leave an approximately correct picture of the times which they describe. It goes without saying, that pupils should be encouraged to read general historical literature at home, outside of any immediate connection with their studies. Only about one-half of the students who enter one of our great colleges have read at least one work of such historians as Prescott, Macaulay, Irving, Green, or Bancroft.

32. Written Work.

The written exercises required in connection with history vary all the way from a page of a note-book to an elaborate study from the sources. In two ways such exercises tend to the education of pupils : they give excellent practice in the collection and selection of material, and they afford an invaluable training in judgment and in accuracy of statement. Besides the written recitations already described above (§ 28), some teachers require notes and abstracts of analyses to be made up from books. " Collateral readings in history are assigned and reported on. Another exercise is the so-called written analysis, in which having gone over the ground of the lesson a pupil is sent to the board and w.ites an analysis of the lesson ; his selection of topics is then criticized by the class, and the form of expression is altered until put into the . . . most striking phraseology. . . . This exercise in analysis I find of the utmost value ; it trains the children in discrimination between the essential and unessential, in putting facts in the right perspective ; it teaches them to handle books . . . its tabular arrangement shows at a glance the bearing of each part upon the whole. . . . The page of topics is also an essential help to the memory, hence is, psychologically, a valuable device for younger pupils." Another system is to call for " special reports," brief and summarized statements upon a subject specially assigned. Such work in most schools would, of course, be based on secondary authorities ; but the arrangement and the results should be the pupil's own. The subject of such a written report should be sufficiently minute, so that the pupil may learn all that is worth knowing in the authorities at hand (§ 33). One form of this written work may be the requirement to prepare a bibliography of all the references available on an assigned subject. This is particularly applicable to biographies of public men ; and the results thus obtained may be left on file and may be referred to for later reports. The method tends to train pupils to use bibliographical aids, the short-cuts to historical material.

The second general system of written work in connection with history is set forth in Resolution 23 : " That the teaching of history should be intimately connected with the teaching of English . . . by writing English compositions on subjects drawn from the historical lessons." In few schools has this connection between the two kindred branches been established. The necessary work of reading parallel references may thus be made to serve a double turn, and the amount of reading may be correspondingly increased. Your Conference need not dwell upon the importance of such a connection, as developing both the power of expression, and the power of dealing with historical material.

33. The Topical Method.

The third general system of written work is the preparation of topics ; Resolution 22 reads : " That the method of study by topics be strongly recommended, as tending to stimulate pupils and to encourage independence of judgment." Resolution 26 adds : " That in all practicable ways, an effort should be made to teach the pupils in the later years to discriminate between authorities, and especially between original sources and secondary works." It is not expected that pupils in grammar or high schools are to be historical writers, or that they are to suppose that they are carrying out historical investigation to its widest extent ; but we confidently and urgently recommend the use of this historical method because of its peculiar educational value. It is the system in use in German schools of a corresponding grade, and accounts in part for the development of historical investigation in that country.

One year of the eight-year course has been set apart for what has been called " the intensive study of history," i. e., the more minute and careful study of some limited period, with as much use of the sources as is practicable. (§ 15.) The topical system can, of course, be applied in that year, but it is applicable throughout the course, especially in the latter half. The first point to notice is, that the topical method requires the pupils to do part of the work, and, in well advanced courses, it may very sensibly relieve the teacher from the necessity of minute investigation of the whole ground for himself. In the next place, the topical method may be so employed as to introduce the pupil to the sources, which are the life of history.

Two sorts of work are combined under the single title of the topical method. In the first place it may be used as a system of division of labor, the topics taken together covering substantially the whole ground of the course ; and recitations may then be held upon the topics, taking advantage of the special preparation of one student on each topic. " In selecting topics, care should be taken to make them cover only one simple subject. Questions should not be assigned about which no definite information is to be had. . . . Biography lends itself easily to this method ; any number of subjects of about equal difficulty may be found, and it is easy to secure a lucid, well arranged report. Where the topics are numerous, the teacher owes it to his pupils to give them a good outfit of specific directions and specific references ; for an occasional theme it is an excellent plan to turn a pupil loose into a library ; but where he is expected to learn something valuable about his topic in a short time, he must not be discouraged by the mass of books ; he must have his clue. . . . The return of the work in the precise outward form required should be insisted upon, because it is of much importance to be able to put information into a shape useful to another person, and the labor of handling the papers is thus greatly reduced, There is plenty of room for personality in the choice of books and the selection and arrangement of facts. Great care must be taken to prevent the pupil from simply reproducing what he finds in one or several books. From the very outset the pupil should be taught always to append a brief bibliographical note, setting forth the source of his information and giving exact references to volume and page. Bright scholars may criticize each other's work ; and the selection of the best papers to be read in class will be a reward." The method thus described in general terms is widely applicable to schools of almost every grade in which history can be taught at all. Perhaps the principal objection is the necessary correction of the written work ; here, as in other written exercises, a great deal may be done by exchanging papers among the pupils and calling for criticism of pupil upon pupil ; or by taking up topical exercises and criticising them in class with the help of the class.

The second purpose of the topical method is the study of sources. Says a member of the Conference : " The original sources are often more delightful reading than the most striking descriptions of Gibbon, or Taine, or Macaulay, and in many cases quite as ready at hand. The real short-cut which leaves hundreds of volumes of formal history at one side, if we are really intent upon getting the greatest good from our work, lies through the study of the sources. Unconsciously moulded as these are by the spirit of the time in which they were written, every line gives by innuendo an insight into the period which the author certainly never intended, and which volumes of analysis can never reproduce. The mere information, too, comes in a form which we cannot forget if we try." No part of historical education does so much to train the pupil as the search for material, the weighing of evidence, and the combining of the results thus obtained in a statement put into a form useful to other persons. Collections of suitable material are already numerous, and are rapidly increasing. To make such a system successful it is necessary that no two members of a given class shall have the same topic; this precaution gives to the pupil the agreeable sense of a separate and independent piece of investigation. Of course the topics must be very limited in scope; the writing of elaborate theses and mono-graphs in the schools is not to be commended; all the good results can be had by a succession of brief pieces. The material to be used may comprise the local records, which, in the towns possess-ing them, have seldom been carefully used. Occasionally families have a little store of manuscripts; or such collections are to be found in local libraries. The main dependence, however, must always be on printed records such as the Colonial Records of the older States of the Union; the calendars of British State papers; the State and national statutes; the United States printed collections of documents; the correspondence and other writings of statesmen; elaborate biographies and reminiscences, town and county histories; periodicals and old newspapers. The work is within the reach of good teachers, without very elaborate or expensive apparatus.

34. Illustrative Methods.

All methods of teaching history may be made more effective by having the proper surroundings, and by making use of illustrations drawn from the experience of the community. An attractive class-room is an incentive to historical study. In many schools something may be done by encouraging the pupils to bring in historical pic-tures; these may be of every degree of value from rough wood-cuts taken out of daily papers to portraits and engravings of historical scenes, and photographs of famous places or buildings. In one school the teacher has a large collection of pictures cut from illus-trated newspapers and pasted on cards. In choosing text-books care ought always to be taken to see that its illustrations, if there are any, represent something real; pupils are sometimes quick to see historical inconsistencies. A picture in a well known historical text-book purports to represent Braddock's headquarters; but in the foreground is a flag-staff with the stars and stripes displayed. The use of the magic lantern is becoming more and more common as a means of instruction, and where schools have not the opportunity to make a collection of slides for themselves, they may often call in lecturers for occasional illustrated talks, or may avail themselves of University Extension or other courses of lectures.

Next in importance come accounts of historical places from those who have visited them. Any class may be interested in an account of the city of Washington and of the Houses of Congress in session, especially if illustrated by graphic aids. In many places, however, the historic scenes are at hand, and all that is necessary is to point them out to the class, although not every city is so fortunate as that which possesses the Washington elm, the Longfellow house, and the James Russell Lowell mansion. The study of history may also be made a means for those rambling excursions which should do much for the health of the children. Where historical places are lacking there are often interesting collections; the larger cities have art museums, which are invaluable for the light they throw upon ancient history; and many cities have libraries with rare and interesting books. Everywhere there is the opportunity of illustrating history and particularly civil government, by the local government of the place (§ 18).

Another means of illustration is to set debates on subjects which occur in the lessons. School debating societies are very common, and might be made still more instructive, if pains were taken always to set questions which permitted the debaters to use their own judgment and knowledge. An excellent device in such debates is to require each side to submit preliminary written briefs, with arguments arranged in logical form and provided with specific reference to authorities. Of a similar value are mock legislatures, parliaments, conventions, and diplomatic congresses, — an interesting form of object lessons. (§ 18.)

Finally, history ought constantly to be illustrated by reference to the lives of great men. This is the opportunity for ethical training. Boys who cannot understand the development of the Athenian constitution, and who painfully learn and easily forget the military details of the Greek wars, may be animated with interest over Themistocles, or Cicero, or Charlemagne, or Luther, or John Wilkes, or John C. Calhoun, or Abraham Lincoln. In Germany, the pupil "goes over universal history three times in as many different ways. The first time, all history is encompassed by what may be called the biographical method." Biography is not all of history, because even the incidents of great lives are important chiefly in their relations to each other; but biography clings to the memory, and a later, more systematic study will show the connection with national development.

35. Historical Geography.

"Geography, the twin sister of history, has, as yet, had but a cold reception in the historical family; only about one half the schools make the study what it should be, an essential and integral part of the study of every period." Our recommendation on this subject is set forth in Resolution 25, "That the study of history should be constantly associated with the study of topography and political geography, and should be supplemented by the study of historical and commercial geography, and the drawing of historical maps."

This resolution suggests three directions in which the study of geography may be made a helpful adjunct to history. In the first place, from the beginning of geographical study, attention should be paid to the physical outline of each country, not only with reference to its productions, but to the movement of races, the progress of settlement, and the establishment of centres of population. For instance, it should be shown how the commercial greatness of Chicago and of New York depend on a simple fact in American physical geography — their position at the head and foot of a system of water communication; the indented coast of New England should suggest how thrifty little sea-ports came to be established there; the relation of the Vosges Mountains to the Alps is a guide to the successive migrations of nations across Europe. From the beginning, the teacher should attempt to connect physical geography with the present political condition of the world; and, in like manner, the study of political geography should constantly bring in the physical features.

The second geographical method consists in putting before pupils for constant use wall-maps and historical atlases. So little is this necessity understood that in no other civilized country are good and cheap maps so rare; and our school atlases are notoriously inferior to those of France and Germany. In the use of maps, good or bad, there is an opportunity for the use of judgment; a mere reference to a place on a map on which the surface shows no physical relief does little to impress its position. For instance, the important geographical fact about the city of Rome is not that it lay in Latium, rather than in Etruria, but that it could control the trade of the Tiber valley, and, at the same time, was so far inland as to be free from attacks of pirates. The reason for its growth once learned, the site will never be forgotten. An excellent system in class is for a pupil to follow the recitation, pointing out on the wall-map the places as they are mentioned by the reciter.

A third and very efficient method of geographical training is the use of outline maps. "We buy outlines," says a teacher, "and strive to set forth upon them as many subjects as lend themselves to such modes of representation.   I should be at loss, without them, to make attractive the geography of Greece with its multitude of new names so hard to the junior mind, the migrations, the different eras of colonization, etc.   But with maps it becomes very pleasant work.   Maps are also especially interesting in showing the development and decay of the Roman empire, and the rise and growth of modern nations. . . . In every recitation in history every child has an open atlas upon his desk, and not only are all the places carefully looked up, but the effects of physical environments are constantly noted."   By outline maps is not here meant the exasperating system of skewering the boundaries of countries upon an artificial geometrical scaffolding; but the use of maps having printed upon them the simple outlines of the country, the pupil to insert important places in their proper relations. This system is not unreasonably expensive, and pupils should be taught to feel that maps thus made are not simply exercises to be thrown away, but that by preserving them they may bring together a little special geographical atlas of their own.   Mere copying from larger maps is an exercise without discipline, and is of no aid to the memory; in order to get the advantage of the geographical study each child must make up his map from a variety of sources.   Map making thus becomes a kind of topical work, but a sort in which most children find a peculiar delight and stimulus.

VII. Summary.

In conclusion, your Conference begs to recapitulate a few of the points in the above report which we wish especially to emphasize. We believe that the subjects upon which we have reported ought to receive at least as much attention as they now receive in the best and most carefully taught schools, and considerably more than in the present average schools.   A part of the time necessary for this change can be had by bringing the study of English and of geography into closer relations with the study of history.   We strongly urge that the historical course be continuous from year to year, and in this respect be placed upon the same footing as other substantial subjects.   We urge a closer co-ordination of the work in civil government and political economy with that in history.   We especially recommend such a choice of subjects as will give pupils in the grammar schools an opportunity to study the history of other countries, and to the high schools one year's study on the intensive method.

As to methods, we have to suggest only the use of the methods which, in good schools, are now accustoming pupils to think for themselves, to put together their own materials, to state their results, to compare one series of events with another series and the history of one country with that of another.

Finally, we urge that only teachers who have had adequate special training shall be employed to teach these important subjects.

Respectfully submitted,

CHARLES KENDALL ADAMS, *President of the University of Wisconsin*, Chairman.

EDWARD G. BOURNE, *Professor of History, Adelbert College.*

ABRAM BROWN, *Principal of the Central High School, Columbus, Ohio.*

RAY GREENE HULING, *Principal of the High School, New Bedford, Mass.*

JESSE MACY, *Professor of Political Science, Iowa College.*

JAMES HARVEY ROBINSON, *Associate Professor of European History, University of Pennsylvania.*

WILLIAM A. SCOTT, *Assistant Professor of Political Economy, University of Wisconsin.*

HENRY P. WARREN, *Head Master of The Albany Academy.*

WOODROW WILSON, *Professor of Jurisprudence and Political Economy, Princeton College.*

ALBERT BUSHNELL HART, *Assistant Professor of History, Harvard University*, Secretary.

APPENDIX.

ANSWERS TO THE QUESTIONS OF THE COMMITTEE OF TEN.

Specific answers to the nine questions may be found by referring to the report and accompanying resolutions as follows :

1. In the school course of study extending approximately from the age of six years to eighteen years — a course including the periods of both elementary and secondary instruction — at what age should the study which is the subject of the Conference be first introduced?

At about nine or ten years : *Resolutions* 13, 14 ; *Report*, § 6.

2. After it is introduced, how many hours a week for how many years should be devoted to it?

Not less than three exercises per week during eight years ; or, under special circumstances, during six years : *Resolutions* 14–17 ; *Report*, §§ 7–9.

3. How many hours a week for how many years should be devoted to it during the last four years of the complete course ; that is, during the ordinary high school period?

Three hours per week during four years of the high school course ; or, in special circumstances, three years : *Resolutions* 14–16 ; *Report*, §§ 8–10.

4. What topics, or parts, of the subject may reasonably be covered during the whole course?

This question is answered in the proposed curriculum : *Resolutions* 2–10, 14, 16 ; *Report*, §§ 10, 16–19.

5. What topics, or parts, of the subject may best be reserved for the last four years?

The opinion of the Conference is shown by the curriculum proposed : *Resolutions* 13, 14, 16, 28–30 ; *Report*, §§ 12–19.

6. In what form and to what extent should the subject enter into college requirements for admission? Such questions as the sufficiency of translations at sight as a test of knowledge of a language, or the superiority of a laboratory examination in a scientific subject to a written examination on a text-book, are intended to be suggested under this head by the phrase " in what form?"

Methods of college examinations are suggested in *Resolutions* 32, 33 ; *Report*, §§ 20, 21.

7. Should the subject be treated differently for pupils who are going to college, for those who are going to a scientific school, and for those who, presumably, are going to neither?

We are unanimously against making such a distinction: *Resolution* 31 ; *Report*, §§ 2, 11.

8. At what age should this differentiation begin, if any be recommended?

There should be no differentiation : *Resolution* 31 ; *Report*, §§ 2, 11.

9. Can any description be given of the best method of teaching this subject throughout the school course?

The subject is discussed in *Resolutions* 18–30 ; *Report*, §§ 23–35. The essentials are : trained teachers ; good text-books ; suggestive recitations ; outside reading ; written work, especially in connection with English composition ; topical study ; suitable illustrative material ; and historical geography intelligently taught.

10. Can any description be given of the best mode of testing attainments in this subject at college admission examinations?

A recommendation of examination questions requiring thought and the acceptance of satisfactory written work as a part of the evidence of preparation appears in *Resolutions* 32, 33 ; *Report*, §§ 20, 21.

11. For those cases in which colleges and universities permit a division of the admission examination into a preliminary and a final examination, separated by at least a year, can the best limit between the preliminary and the final examinations be approximately defined?

The Conference suggests that history be reserved for the final examinations : *Resolution* 34 ; *Report*, § 22.

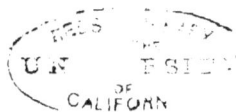

GEOGRAPHY.

PRESIDENT CHARLES W. ELIOT, CHAIRMAN OF COMMITTEE OF TEN, NATIONAL EDUCATIONAL ASSOCIATION :—

Dear Sir,—The members of the Conference on geography (embracing geology and meteorology) appointed by your committee, held sessions on December 28th, 29th and 30th, at the Cook County Normal School, as designated by you, and gave careful consideration to the questions submitted to them. They beg leave to submit the following report :—

RELATIONS OF THE SUBJECT.

It was found difficult to define strictly the scope of geography on account of its intimate relations with, and gradations into, geological, meteorological, zoölogical, botanical, historical, political, and other sciences. Geography is an important factor in all these, and they in turn enter as factors into a comprehensive study of it. It is impossible to draw any sharp divisional lines, and the Conference have found it practicable to indicate in a limited degree only, by suggestions, how far these several associated subjects should be brought into the study of geography, as such, and how far, on the other hand, the geographical element in each of these should be left to be taught in connection with them, as separate sciences. While it did not seem to the Conference advisable to greatly modify the range of subjects usually embraced under the term geography, they recommend a more distinct recognition of its different phases and some modifications of treatment for the purpose of giving these greater emphasis and more advantageous relations to other work, as indicated below.

FORMAL DIVISIONS AND DISTRIBUTION OF THE SUBJECT.

General Elementary Geography. There are important reasons for devoting the work of the earlier and intermediate years to those features of geography which will be most serviceable to the majority of pupils without regard to any sharp classification, because these are the only years during which many pupils remain in school. The earlier courses should, therefore, treat broadly of the earth and its environment and inhabitants. The instruction should extend freely into fields which are recognized as belonging to separate sciences in later years of study. It should deal not only with the face of the earth but with elementary considerations in astronomy, meteorology, zoölogy, botany, history, commerce, governments, races, religions, etc., so far as these are connected with geography. Unless this admixture of subjects is included under the elementary courses *(b)* of geography many scholars will not gain a knowledge of even the outlines of these important subjects.

Applied Geography. But when this common groundwork is laid, there is a distinct advantage in a gradual differentiation of the subject. Some of its phases may be best disconnected from the formal study of geography and taken up in connection with the subjects to which they are most intimately related. For example, the geographical element in history is best understood, appreciated, and retained in memory when taken in connection with historical study. The distribution of plants and animals will only have its fullest meaning when studied in connection with the nature of the plants and animals themselves ; that is, as a phase of botany or zoölogy.

Unfortunately our works in botany and zoölogy are very defective in this respect. The Conference would urge that this serious fault be remedied.

In general, all forms of applied geography are most advantageously taken in connection with their applications, provided that a general knowledge of elementary geography has been previously acquired, as indicated above.

Physical Geography and Physiography. On the other hand, the special subject of geography should take on a more advanced form and should relate more specifically to the features of the earth's surface, the agencies that produce and destroy them, the environing conditions under which these act, and the physical influences by which man and all the creatures of the earth are so profoundly affected. This has usually been designated physical geography. There is an advanced and modernized phase of it, however, which the majority of the committee prefer to designate physiography, not because the name is important, but because it emphasizes a special and important phase of the subject and of its treatment. The scientific investigations of the last decade have made very important additions to physiographic knowledge and methods of study. These are indeed so radical as to be properly regarded, perhaps, as revolutionary. Unfortunately they are not yet incorporated in textbooks, in any large degree, nor are they, even in scientific treatises, collected into a form readily available for the use of the teacher. As yet they are widely scattered through various scientific publications. But this condition will doubtless be improved at an early date. Meanwhile, it is thought best that physical geography should be taught, by the aid of the best elementary textbooks now available, as the last geographic course previous to the high school, and that there should be introduced into the high-

school course either physiography, geology, or meteorology as the
representative of the geographic line of studies, which may be broadly
characterized as that which relates to the physical environment of
man. Possibly more than one of these may be practicable in some
high schools, when alternative or elective studies are offered.

As this line of study develops into better form and expression,
physical geography will probably come to signify a stage of differentiation and a method of treatment intermediate between that of
common geography and that of physiography, and the latter will
represent that more advanced treatment which belongs to the higher
courses. But without regard to what may be the terminology of the
future (which is not very important in itself), the majority of the
Conference wish to impress upon the attention of teachers the fact
that there has been developed within the past decade a new and most
important phase of the subject, and to urge that they hasten to
acquaint themselves with it and bring it into the work of the schoolroom and of the field.

The ground to be covered by physiography, when introduced as a
high school study, may be indicated by the following topics : [1] The
wasting of the land surfaces, the transportation of the waste to the
sea, and its deposition on the marginal sea bottoms ; a brief account
of the more common minerals and rocks in their relation to wasting ;
the changes of river action during the progress of land denudation ;
the relations of lakes, waterfalls, divides and their migration, floodplains, deltas, etc., to the stage of river-development in which they
are observed ; the development of shore lines and the variation
of their features under the long continued action of the shore waves ;
the interruptions of the normal progress of denudation and shore
action by depression, elevation, or deformation ; and by volcanic
action or by climatic change, including briefly the effects of glacial
action. The various kinds of land forms, as plains, plateaus, mountains, volcanoes, should be considered in accordance with the constructional processes involved in their origin and with the system of
development above outlined ; and their distribution over the earth
should be briefly sketched. The better known land areas, and especially our home country, should be described in accordance with the
development of the various geographical elements of which they are
constituted. No attempt should be made to describe the whole
world in this way, because the subject is too large for high-school
treatment ; but the conviction that all land areas are constituted of
geographical elements in various stages of development should be

---

[1] The subject will be further developed under the head of method.

enforced by frequent mention of examples of different kinds in various parts of the world. Sufficient account of climate should be given to introduce an intelligent consideration of the conditions that determine the distribution of life ; but this should be made relatively subordinate to the main theme, namely, the geography of the lands.

The associated study of the oceans should be relatively brief. It should give a condensed account of the ocean basins, recognizing the deep continuous basins of the great oceans, the enclosed mediterraneans, and the continental shelves ; of the conditions of the ocean bottoms ; of the composition and deep-currents of the sea, and of the tides. The relation of these conditions to the distribution of oceanic life may be briefly introduced.

Unless an additional course on meteorology is offered, a sufficient practical use of the weather maps should be introduced into the course of physiography to furnish the scholars with a knowledge of the general principles of weather changes and forecasts.

Meteorology. Since the establishment of the national Weather Bureau, meteorology has not only been greatly advanced as a systematic science, but it has become a subject of wide popular interest. This, together with its importance as a factor of geography, moves the committee to recommend that meteorology be introduced as an elective study for half a year in the third or fourth year of the high-school course, when practicable. Elementary physics should precede it. It should be opened by local observations of the passing weather changes, accompanied by a study of a series of daily weather maps, and the application of physical principles to explain the general phenomena of the atmosphere should follow. Local observations should be carried further in this course than they extended in earlier years, especially regarding the sequence of phenomena in the atmosphere and the correlation of various weather elements. The study of weather maps, already familiar objects from the less systematic study of earlier years, should now reach to the clear understanding and description of the distribution of temperature and pressure, flow of the winds, and occurrence of clear, cloudy, rainy or snowy areas ; and to a careful induction of generalizations by which various phenomena are connected ; for example, the correlation of the direction and velocity of the winds with the value of the barometric gradient ; or of areas of high or low pressure with the spiral outflowing or inflowing winds and the areas of clear or cloudy and rainy sky. The effect of the progression of these areas of high and low pressure on local weather changes and their value in weather prediction should be made clear ; practical exercises should be given in this connection, as will be more fully explained in a later section. During the advance

of local observation and study of the weather maps, instruction
should be given on the more general relations of the science, in which
the following headings are the most important: Composition and
offices of the atmosphere; arrangement of the atmosphere around the
earth under the action of gravity; the nature of solar energy and its
distribution over the earth and through the year; the different action
of solar energy on air, land, and water; the mean annual and seasonal
distribution of temperature over the earth; the processes of local and
general convection; evaporation, humidity, clouds, rainfall; the distribution of atmospheric pressure, and the general circulation of the
atmosphere, as modified by the annual march of the sun north and
south, and by the influences of the continents; storms, both cyclonic
and local; weather changes and their prediction; climate, zones, and
their relation to habitation.

   Geology. So soon as it shall be practicable to introduce an effective course in modern physiography into the high school, it will
probably not be advisable to give a course in geology also, except in
special cases where the teacher is unusually well prepared to teach
the subject and the locality affords special advantages. At present,
however, the material and the methods of geology are better known
to teachers than those of either physiography (in the modern sense)
or meteorology, and its literature is in better form for school use.
Until, therefore, physiography and meteorology are developed into
good working forms and teachers are adequately trained in them, the
Conference recommend that geology be offered as an elective study for
a half year in the last year of the high school. Unless either physiography or geology is retained in the high school and given vitality
and efficiency, a serious danger threatens the whole geographic line
of study in the lower schools, for the great mass of teachers of
geography have not taken courses beyond the high schools, and in
the immediate future are not likely to go farther with their education,
and if they are not taught the elementary processes and principles of
these sciences there, they will have little real strength as teachers of
geography. They cannot go much beyond mere facts and formalities.
The high school must teach those things that are necessary to give
efficiency to teaching in the lower grades or that teaching will suffer,
for, great as is the work of the normal schools (and it should be
greatly increased and its value urged by every influence at command)
they cannot supply the great mass of teachers for the primary,
intermediate, and grammar schools. Temporarily, therefore, the
Conference recommend that geology be offered as an elective, in the
hope that soon physiography and meteorology may take its place,
leaving it to be transferred to normal schools and colleges.

As there must be a selection of topics, the committee recommend that the nature of the processes involved in the formation and modification of the earth's surface, essentially as indicated under the head of physiography, be regarded as having the most vital importance both to the general student and the prospective teacher. Practical instruction in the field on surface forms, on the formation and natural occurrence of rocks, and on fossils should form a part of the work. Especial attention should be given to an intelligent interpretation of the textbook, which is liable to be meaningless to the scholars without it, however well it may be written. This can be done best by local illustrations, carefully examined by the class, for the purpose of giving typical conceptions and by the study of cabinet specimens. The result of the course should be as apparent in an increased appreciation of the facts of geology as exhibited in the neighborhood of the school, as in a knowledge of the general truths of the science of world-wide application.

If, however, schools are not prepared to treat the subject with real intelligence and effectiveness, it is better not to offer it at all.

The natural order of geographic subjects seems, therefore, to be the following :

1. *Elementary Geography*, a broad treatment of the earth and its inhabitants and institutions, to be pursued in the primary, intermediate, and lower grammar grades. *General & Applied*

2. *Physical Geography*, a more special but still broad treatment of the physical features of the earth, atmosphere and ocean, and of the forms of life and their physical relations, to be pursued in later grammar grades. *agencies, environ. conditions*

3. *Physiography*, a more advanced treatment of our physical environment in which the agencies and processes involved, the origin, development, and decadence of the forms presented, and the significance of the features of the earth's face are the leading themes, to be pursued in the later high-school or early college years.

4. *Meteorology*, a specialized study of atmospheric phenomena, to be offered by schools that are prepared to do so properly, as an elective in the later high-school years.

5. *Geology*, a study of the earth's structure and its past history, to be offered by schools prepared to do so properly, as an elective in the last year of the high-school course.

The precise distribution of these divisions of the subject through the several grades of our schools can best be left to the judgment and discretion of those who have immediate charge of them, for their best

14

distribution depends, in a large degree, upon the preparation and ability of the teachers, the character of the school, the advancement and intelligence of the community (which greatly aids or retards the work of scholars) the local geographic surroundings, and the facilities for advantageous study both within and without the school. Each step should be satisfactorily taken before the next is attempted. A rigid system which forces a class over a given ground in a given time without regard to their ability to cover it properly will not be helpful to the best results. In general, however, it is the judgment of the Conference that too much time is given to the subject *in proportion to to the results secured*. It is not their judgment that more time is given to the subject than it merits, but that either more should be accomplished or less time taken to attain it. In general, they believe the progress of the work is too slow, and that it will be both more interesting to the scholars and more successfully done if pushed with greater vigor. The work should move on earnestly and at a pace that makes the progress obvious to the scholars. Interest lags when the advance is too slow. Dawdling and dwelling on trivialities are among the great mistakes of the schoolroom. They are especially vicious when mistaken for thoroughness. The committee believe that the real acquisitions of pupils may be increased twofold, or threefold, or fourfold, by right methods and by earnest judicious pressing of the work, and hence, that the time given to geography may be somewhat shortened and yet higher attainments secured, and that a portion of the time thus saved, may be devoted to natural and human history, wherein, if they are properly treated, the geographic factor will be brought into its natural place and functions, and the pupils taught that most important of lessons, the utilization of their geographic knowledge. The Conference regard the subject of geography of equal importance with arithmetic in the primary and secondary schools, and entitled to equal time, but they think that a like remark concerning greater results in less time is applicable to the mathematical work.

ORDER OF TREATMENT BASED ON MENTAL PROCESSES.

The foregoing suggestions relate to the succession of the formal divisions of the geographic line of studies and bear rather upon the arrangement of the school curriculum than upon the treatment of the topics involved. These formal divisions are based largely upon practical considerations and natural relationships, and take little account of the intellectual processes involved and their proper sequences. These latter, however, are the chief considerations in the mind of the conscientious and intelligent teacher, for they control the specific treatment of the subjects embraced in the study and determine the habits of thought, and the modes of the work of the pupils. The teacher, therefore, needs for his own use (not to give his pupils nor to put in the curriculum) a more analytical view of the subject based on the intellectual processes involved, a view which may be an ever-present guide in the arrangement of details and the treatment of the special points of the subject. The Conference offer, by way of suggestion, the following scheme. The appended remarks bear in part upon the educational philosophy entertained, in part upon the purpose of the work, and part upon the methods of execution. Reduced to a sentence the scheme is : first, see ; next, reproduce ; then study the productions of others, and, meanwhile, ponder and reason on all.

1. *Observational Geography.* In the judgment of the Conference, observation should go before all other forms of geographical study and prepare the way for them ; its object being (1) to develop the power and habit of geographic observation, (2) to give the pupils true and vivid basal ideas, and (3) to arouse a spirit of inquiry and a thirst for geographical knowledge. This work of observation should begin with those features that lie immediately about the pupils and so fall easily within the reach of their direct study and ready comprehension. In rural districts, the natural features of the surface will obviously form a large part of the study, while in cities, the artificial features must largely take the place of these. In the one instance, natural geography, as seen in the forms of the land, the hills, valleys, plains, meadows, divides, streams, lakes, etc., will predominate, while in the other artificial or humanistic geography will receive leading attention, as streets, railways, wharves, harbors, parks, plots, wards, etc. ; but something of both these groups of subjects may be found and utilized in both localities. Neither should be neglected, for the pupils need not only to acquire clear ideas of the things by which they are chiefly surrounded but type ideas of the things which characterize other localities and of which they need to form correct ideas without being able to see them. Observation, however, should not be confined simply to the passive fixed features by which pupils are surrounded. They should observe the agencies that produce surface changes, such as winds, rains, floods, thawing, freezing, cultivation, etc. The temporary streams that follow heavy rains represent on a small scale many of the natural processes by which surface features are produced. From these immediate agencies, the observations should extend to the phenomena of the weather and the climate, such as temperature, winds, clouds, seasons, etc. As a step toward the understanding of mathematical geography, so-called, the children should be led to observe the shifting of the sun north and south with

the seasons and to measure the amount of this by the length of shadows at noonday in the different months of the year. They should compare these by means of a record kept for the purpose. In like manner, they should observe the movements of the stars and other heavenly bodies. As a step toward the study of the distribution of plants and animals and an insight into their dependence upon temperature, soil, food, etc., the pupils should be encouraged to observe the differences of plants on uplands, lowlands, marshes, etc., and upon sandy, clayey, gravelly or stony ground, and to note the habitual dispersal of animals and insects in the neighborhood, and also their relations to each other, as in forming or frequenting forests, prairies, meadows, etc. As a step toward the study of the human elements in geography, observations should be made upon the population and its distribution, upon home occupations and productions, upon local political boundaries, as wards, school districts, city or town limits, etc., and upon the location of cities, villages, railways, canals, etc. Thus, by a little ingenuity and industry, a large part of the features that make up the substance of geography in the large sense may be found illustrated close at home, and, if suitably studied, the basis may be laid for clear conceptions of those features which lie beyond the range of the child's observation.

Observation should not only begin the work in geography but should continue throughout the entire course and beyond. If scholars are not educated so as to continually observe geographic features and note their significance whenever they are brought in contact with them, whether during school days or afterwards, the school work fails of its most important possibilities. The pupils' first observational work is necessarily of the simpler and more superficial kind. As knowledge and insight increase, they should see more and more of the geographic phenomena that come before them and see deeper and deeper into their significance and receive increasing pleasure and profit from them. To this end, every opportunity for observational work in geography should be eagerly embraced. Excursions for the special purpose should be made as frequently as practicable, formally or informally, in school hours and out of school hours, by classes and by individuals. Advantage should be taken of incidental excursions in which the class or any of its members participate. The little trips and longer travels of members of the class should be taken advantage of. Late in the course, special studies of certain geographic features may be taken up with success and profit.

2. *Representative Geography.* Immediately after the making of observations should come their reproduction in the form of descriptions, sketches, maps, models, etc. The instruction of the teacher

falls far short of its highest efficiency if the early work is merely observational and receptive. The great end of education is to create productive ability. One important form of this is representative production. Besides having value in itself, the description of features that have been seen and their representation by sketches, maps, or models reacts upon the observational work and induces a clearness, sharpness, and definiteness that it would not otherwise be likely to take. Not only this, but it leads the scholars to realize what maps, descriptions, etc., really mean. By this means, pupils are lead up naturally to an ability to read with vividness, ease, and full understanding, the maps and descriptions which constitute the medium of the larger part of their later studies, and such ability to read is of supreme importance in all subsequent work.

3. *Derivative or Descriptive Geography.* When pupils have gained true and vivid basal ideas by observation and have, by reproducing these, acquired a realistic sense of the meaning of maps and an ability to read them, in the full and proper sense of the term, they are prepared to pass on to a formal study of descriptive geography. In this, the observational and representative work of others than themselves is made the basis of study. The pupils are not now studying the earth's surface but " a description of the earth's surface." The work is not direct and immediate, but derivative and secondary. The pupils cannot carry their own observations over more than a very small fraction of the earth's surface and their work upon even this small portion must, in the nature of the case, be very imperfect. Their great dependence must, therefore, be upon the work of others, the work of geographical experts, and hence descriptive geography must embrace much the largest portion of their attention. The common mistake is that it embraces too nearly all of it, and the observational and reproductive efforts which are necessary to give the study of descriptions its greatest serviceability are neglected. These should be continued throughout the course running parallel with the descriptive study and supplementing and vivifying it.

4. *Rational Geography.* It has already been urged that the pupils should be induced to observe changes and processes as well as the simple passive facts of geography, and that there should thereby be laid the foundation for an understanding of the origin, the development, and the future history of geographic features. This is the introduction of rational geography, as distinguished from the mere noting and memorizing of facts. This phase of the subject which leads the pupils into the reason of things, should be assiduously cultivated, for it is the soul of the science. It should, however, be carefully adapted to the capabilities of the pupils, particularly in the

earlier stages of the study. They should not be forced beyond their capacity to comprehend the nature of the agencies that have rendered geography what it is. On the other hand, there is an equal danger of underestimating the capacities of pupils to see into the reasons for natural operations. It is as dangerous to allow their capacities to lie undeveloped as it is to overload them with reasonings they cannot understand, and to force them to carry these in a mere verbal form by an effort of memory. The reasonings should be such as they can follow understandingly, if not work out themselves. If they merely commit them to memory, they are as dead as other things simply memorized and lose entirely the rational element. It may not be wholly without value in some cases to give to children a statement of the causes of phenomena even though they are unable to understand the methods of their operation, but it should be clearly understood that this is not teaching the scholars to reason concerning phenomena, or even to follow reasonings concerning phenomena, but merely to memorize the reasons of phenomena.

It is not recommended that rational geography be disassociated from observational and descriptive geography, but rather, on the contrary, that it be intimately connected with these and that it be introduced so as to give them life and significance. To do this, skill and discretion must be used respecting the way in which the rational element is introduced and the extent to which it is carried.

Treatment in Relation to Mental Discipline.

It is an advantage to the teacher to carry the analysis and classification of the work in geography a step further in the direction of its psychological effects so as to make the point of view more exclusively and definitely the mental powers to be exercised and developed. But this should be understood as having reference solely to the teacher's aid and guidance in the arrangement and conduct of the work, and not as a formal division of the subject nor as a matter to be taught pupils. Clear and definite views of the cultural purposes of the work cannot be too strongly urged upon the teacher. Such views will not only be a guide to the proper method of treatment of the subject but will be constantly suggestive of the difficulties the scholars encounter, of the defects of their modes of thinking, and of the ways and means of obviating these. While various activities of the mind are called into exercise in geographical work, the committee would advise that the systematic development of three classes of these should largely control the arrangement of the work, viz., (1) the powers of observation, (2) the powers of scientific imagination, and (3) the powers of reasoning. The cultivation of the powers of observation is necessary to furnish clear, accurate, and realistic fundamental ideas and modes of thought. These, in turn, are necessary as a ground work for the training of the scientific imagination, for clear images are not likely to be formed of things not seen unless clear impressions are formed of things seen. The image-producing power is the only means by which the larger part of the matter of geography can be presented to the mind, and no effort should be spared to give it strength and vividness. Both clearness of observation and strength of imagination are essential as a basis for safe reasoning; for recourse must be had to both for the ground-work upon which reasoning proceeds.

Much that falls under this head has been implied in the foregoing discussion but, at the risk of some repetition, the following classes of topics are cited as suggesting the means of cultivating advantageously these powers. The first class may seem too obvious and familiar to need naming, even in outline, but the second is not so generally recognized as calling into exercise the imagination. The definite concrete recognition by the teacher of the necessary function of the imagination in the study of these topics and the specific application of methods suited to the development of clear and strong powers of image-production in the scholars is important to best results.

A. Under the head of resources for the culture of the observational powers will obviously fall (1) study of surface forms, such as hills, valleys, plains, plateaus, streams, lakes, shores, and all similar phenomena within the pupils' horizon. These may be approached, as already indicated, by observations on miniature forms of like nature, such as may be found in gutters, gullies, ravines, brooklets, ponds, "bottoms," etc.; (2) observations on the temperature and its relations to the direction of the sun's rays, the apparent motion of the heavenly bodies, as their circling round the poles, the rising and setting of some stars and not of others, the shifting north and south of the sun, moon, etc.; (3) movements of the atmosphere and their effects, rain and its effects, snow and its effects, fogs, clouds, etc.; (4) plant life and its dependence on heat, moisture, sunlight, etc.; the influence of soil, slope, etc.; (5) observations on animal life, of similar nature; (6) observations on man in the family, in educational, church, social, and business organizations, in city and town organizations, and so on up towards the larger human organizations and the forms of government. So also, observations on city and town plots with their street systems, railways, canals, harbors, their wards, school districts, etc.

B. Under work involving the culture of the imagination will fall the formation of concepts of all the larger features of geography and of all features beyond the range of observation; as (1) the river basins, the great relief systems, the continental divisions and sub-divisions, the ocean bottoms, the distribution of land and water, and, in a less pronounced way, the picturing of all geographical features not actually observed ; (2) modifications of apparent motions due to imagined changes of position of the observer on the earth's surface, such as the position at the pole, on the equator, on the different parallels, etc. ; (3) distribution of the meteorological agencies over the globe, as moisture, winds, climate ; the mental picturing of the great wind movements, the cyclonic circulation, the zones, etc. ; (4) distribution of plant life developed in the form of a mental picture in its relations to the earth's surface, to land and water, to altitude and climatic conditions, as distinguished from a mere memorizing of the facts of distribution without any such pictorial conception ; (5) distribution of animal life in like manner ; (6) distribution of races of men, forms of government, national territory, etc.

C. Both of the foregoing lists of topics furnish the ground-work for the culture of the reasoning powers if the question of causes and agencies is raised in connection with them. Why do the several features take the forms they do? By what agencies were they caused, and why did these agencies work in such ways? How did these forms originate? What are the causes of the winds, the clouds, the changes of temperature? Why are the animals and plants distributed as they are? Why were these cities located as they are? Why are these large and those small? Why do these railways take this course rather than another? And so on.

The Conference do not advise the disassociation of these processes for the specific development of these mental powers from each other in the practice of the schoolroom, but they do urge that teachers clearly recognize them as they are involved in their work and fully appreciate their importance. They should definitely associate the topics they are endeavoring to teach with the mental powers they bring into exercise, so that there shall be ever present in the mind as an object of endeavor not only the mastery of the subject-matter but the acquisition of improved mental powers.

This is not matter to be put before pupils, as they are not presumed to be studying psychology. Its value lies in its guidance of the teacher's conduct of the work.

METHODS OF PRESENTATION.

In the discussion of the previous topics, we have necessarily touched upon some of the most vital considerations that bear upon methods of teaching. This is especially true of those that relate to the order of arrangement of the work, the methods of approach to the different phases of the subject, and the mental powers to be cultivated. But in addition to these more general and fundamental suggestions there are considerations that relate to modes of presentation and appliances for illustrative instruction that require attention. The suggestions of the Conference must necessarily be incomplete, and, at the outset, they wish to disclaim any intention of limiting, even by suggestion, the modes of teaching to the methods here briefly outlined. The Conference hold it to be of first importance that every teacher should become so familiar with the subject as to be able freely to depart from any proposed method according as the special conditions of the school shall indicate. At the same time, the Conference feel that the following outlines of the manner in which different parts of the subject may be laid before a class may prove serviceable. Their effort is to suggest briefly and definitely certain modes of treatment of the various parts of the subject, believing that teachers can infer from these the manner in which other parts of the subject may be developed.

Preliminary Suggestions. Inasmuch as all success in teaching depends largely on the ability, training, and opportunities of the teacher, several rather miscellaneous recommendations are introduced, at the outset, relative to the organization and equipment of the school and the training of the teacher.

We urge that, in the selection of new teachers, only those be appointed who, by observation and by practice in recording and reproducing their work, have acquired a sufficient knowledge and skill to be able to carry out themselves the observations, recordings, mappings, and modellings that are expected of their scholars. We also recommend that familiarity with the modern aspects of physiography be made a requirement of all special teachers of geography, as soon as practicable.

We strongly urge that self-improvement be stimulated by special meetings of geographical teachers wherever these can be organized, and that the resources of the schools and of accessible libraries be utilized as fully as possible in the presentation and discussion by the teachers themselves, at these meetings, of various special problems connected with this specific line of work.

We recommend that schools be supplied (1) with large-scale maps of their own district and their own state ; (2) with the best obtainable series of general maps, prepared as far as possible on uniform scales ; the style of projection and the scale being indicated on each map ; (3) with a sufficient number of small globes to enable every scholar, sufficiently advanced, to study the globe individually, at one hour or another, during the day, just as a book might be studied ; (4)

with illustrations of various kinds as liberally as possible, including photographs, lantern slides, and means of projection ; (5) if possible, with a few models (whose scales should not be unreasonably exaggerated) representing the home district, if these can be obtained, or, if not, at least with typical models of some interesting regions of our own country ; (6) with books of reference on history, travels, natural history, etc., involving geographical elements and suitable for the use of both scholars and teachers, and in increasing numbers year by year ; (7) with a selected series of topographical maps for use in schools (see note below). In order that the expense incurred in procuring all these materials should not be too heavy, at any one time, it is suggested that it be divided and distributed over several years, rather than that the supply of materials be neglected. In many cases, the assistance of generous patrons of public schools may be enlisted to this end.

We recommend that each teacher keep a book of record, in addition to any records kept by scholars, and that in this the more general and important results of class work be set down for future. reference ; thus accumulating a fund of original information, largely the product of the scholars' own activities, which will be serviceable to them, later in their studies, and to their successors.

We urge that at all stages and in all parts of the study of geography the teacher, rather than the textbook, should lead the class. A good textbook is necessary to furnish maps and other material of study, to secure conciseness of definition, and to save time in study, after a proper introduction to its texts has been given by the teacher, and a good textbook should give a better presentation of the subject than teachers can usually be expected to command. So also, recitations based on textbooks are indispensable in order to secure precision of understanding and of statement on the part of the scholars. But every stage of the subject should be naturally introduced and illustrated by the teacher, and the textbook should be kept

NOTE.—Regarding a series of topographical maps for use in high schools, the Conference voted that the chairman should appoint a committee whose duty it should be to select from topographical maps of the United States Geological Survey such a series as shall best illustrate the principal topographical forms of our country, and also to select from the charts of the Coast and Lake Surveys a series which shall best illustrate the principal features of our shore lines; and that high schools be urged to purchase these series of maps, together with the topographic maps of the district in which the school is located, if such have been made. When this committee reports, it is probable that the list of maps which it selects will be published, together with the prices at which they can be obtained. Professors William M. Davis, Charles F. King, and George L. Collie were appointed as such committee.

in its proper place as an aid and not as a master, and mere lesson-hearing should never be allowed to replace actual teaching.

It is scarcely necessary to say that the simple memorizing, or the slavish following, of the textbook should be avoided, and the work adapted to the particular class of pupils under instruction and to their geographic surroundings. In departing from the textbook, however, the opposite mistake of consuming undue time in giving the scholars what the textbook would give them in better form, and in dwelling on trivial local things, or on mere illustrations that are not — necessary to develop the essentials, or on simple entertainment, or on carrying out a mere ideal method, should be avoided. The work should be important and the matter valuable, either in itself, or as a means of reaching that which is valuable. The leading up to a subject, and the leading out into it, should be such as to aid the pupils in making the highest and best use of the textbook and of all geographical literature with which they come in contact.

Modelling, drawing, and other graphic modes of expression are fully recognized as indispensable means of aiding the imagination, intensifying thought, and strengthening memory. But these means should be kept subordinate to the study of the subject itself. They may be made ineffective and even harmful by degrading them to the drudgery of mere imitation, or the simple copying of other maps or models.

The habit of making use of geographical knowledge in all studies to which it is applicable and the practice of constantly locating places on maps should be encouraged. In all reading, especially the study of history, travels, explorations, and other treatises including geographic descriptions, the places mentioned should always be carefully located.

The desirability of a better execution of maps for school purposes is urged, as also the use of both the English and metric scale. A statement of the projection employed in each map is desirable. It is especially urged that relief maps should be reduced as nearly to natural scale as possible, and that, in all maps, the representations should be as realistic as practicable, and the coloring and lettering, — while clear and distinct, should be subordinate to the geographic features.

Topical recitation and study should be used as freely as practicable, and the subject developed by comparison of observations, by discussions, and by readings from all sources available, and by the introduction of all kinds of illustration. A larger use of works of travel adapted to the capacity of the pupils is strongly recommended.

The teacher can economize time in recitation by using the facts

gained by a study of the assigned lesson as a point of departure for
the purpose of leading on to additional facts and causes and
results, for making comparisons, and for stimulating fresh thought
upon the subject, instead of going over the subject solely to test the
pupils' memory and faithfulness. As an illustration, the class having
learned what they can about the Mississippi River, instead of spending half an hour asking pupils in turn the length of the river, where
it rises, between what states it flows, and into what body of water it
empties, the teacher and the class may take an imaginary ride from
the Falls of St. Anthony down the river, and develop the facts
connected with its course and their applications in a graphic and
realistic way from the imaginary deck of a steamer.

We urge upon teachers the free use of the crayon and blackboard.
The simplest illustrations are of the greatest help, as, for instance,
sketches of mountains, lakes, bays, etc., a few lines to show the
comparative size of mountains, fanciful shapes of countries, sketch
maps of countries, or parts of a country, localities of coal, silver,
gold, or copper fields, simple sketches of plant and animal life, belts
of forests and deserts, etc. The outlines of a country painted upon
a cloth blackboard, in oil, form an invaluable and inexpensive piece
of apparatus which can be used by the teacher while imparting
information, and by the pupil in recitation.

Charts, which can be readily made upon manilla paper with the
rubber pen, are of great assistance in preserving illustrations for use
from year to year.

The descriptive matter which is generally given in regular
geographical textbooks is too condensed and often too dryly stated
to awaken the highest interest in children in the intermediate and
grammar grades. The matter given in most works of travel and in
geographical readers is better adapted to the understanding and
appreciation of young pupils. In most of these books, the personal
element interests the young minds and awakens their closest attention.
Within a few years " geographical supplementary reading " has been
provided in such abundance that every teacher has large opportunities
of selection in this line of reading, and the free use of this is
recommended.

Methods in the Lowest Grades. While the simpler facts of a
geographical nature cannot be introduced too early in a child's
education, it is not recommended that the formal study of geography
as a separate subject, however elementary, be undertaken in the
lowest grades. But the habit of observation should be stimulated as
soon as the child enters the school and its development constantly
encouraged. The plan of the schoolhouse and schoolyard and the

geographical surroundings of the school furnish immediate opportunities for this work of observation in the geographical line. The
power of verbal expression, which should receive attention at the
outset, and facility in writing and reading, which comes later, are
developed most naturally in connection with subjects that lie within
the observation of the child, and many of these are geographical.
Narratives involving travel and descriptions of foreign countries and
peoples may be included as properly in the reading matter of the
school as they are in the stories which children delight to hear at
home. Inasmuch as the first years of the school work are, for
the most part, years of preparation for the work to follow, it is
of the utmost importance that good intellectual habits be formed.
Correct observation and accurate statement of simple facts, concentration of thought on simple subjects which easily absorb the
attention, and precise memory of matters which readily remain
in the mind are modes by which, through the aid of geographical
surroundings, good basal habits of mental action may be developed.

The meaning of a map can be gradually developed in the minds of
pupils in the third and fourth grade by having the children, with
some help from the teacher, first draw a simple plan of the schoolroom, marking the places of the doors, windows, and the teacher's
desk ; then add, on the same scale, the pupils' desks, and then other
fixed objects. After this has been done, a sketch map of the school
yard and the streets, or roads, in the vicinity may be made. The
teacher may first draw on the blackboard while the pupils draw on
paper, adding line after line, and naming each as it is drawn. When
the sketch is finished, let a pupil point out on it how he would go
from the school to his home and tell the points of interest or
importance passed on the way. In this way, lines begin to have a
representative value in the mind of the child. From the map of the
home locality, the teacher may proceed to the making of a map of
the country, state, and grand division, always emphasizing the
meaning of each line used. If the teacher can show pictures of
places never seen by the class, as a valley through which a river
flows, and will then make maps of the same, it will help the pupils to
understand maps still better.

The class may then be taught to read or interpret maps of different
kinds, to explain the use of color, of shading, of parallels, of scale,
etc. The meaning of scale can be impressed upon the young child by
the teacher by first drawing a map in a rectangle divided into square
inches whose sides represent, for instance, just 1000 miles. Then
draw the same map in a smaller rectangle and ask the children
questions in reference to the squares, length of lines, etc.

After children understand the significance of color on physical maps, their attention can be called to the use of other means of representing the same facts, as by shading, hachures, and contour lines.

Mapping as a means for the reproduction and graphic illustration of facts learned, and to aid the memory, is of the greatest importance. When the outlines are only a groundwork for the plotting of the significant matter, time may be saved by procuring these already printed, or manifolded by some of the many cheap methods now in use. These can then be filled in with lines and words to represent the points under study as elevations, drainage, productions, exports, commerce, etc. The filling in may be done gradually at the end of each lesson, thus forming what may be appropriately called a "progressive map."

Methods in the Intermediate and Grammar Grades. As the work advances to the formal study of geography, every new branch of the subject should be naturally introduced by easy transition from what has gone before or from some new quality of local observation. No new step should be taken until the class is clearly ready to take it. The art of the teacher should be so exercised that the class is lead towards the next division of the subject before the preceding one is passed, and, if possible, questions should be elicited from the brighter scholars whose answers will anticipate the subject next to be considered. The intelligence of the children will be an important element in determining the progress of study. Great care should be taken to develop the use of local opportunities in such order as will best open the more advanced parts of the subject. A varying emphasis must be given to different subjects according to the need of the class.

The greatest care should be given to secure clearness of ideas. For this reason, we recommend again that observational study should form the beginning of every new division of the subject, if it can be done, and that the exercise of the imagination of remote objects should always be preceded, if possible, by the exercise of the observation of similar facts near at home. The expert teacher will nearly everywhere find that the variety of available material increases as practice in this method is continued.

In view of what has already been said under previous heads, we do not feel that it is necessary to enter further into detail as to methods of teaching common geography or the common phases of physical geography, especially as they are somewhat fully set forth in available treatises, but in view of the new factors in physiography and meteorology, we have entered into a somewhat full sketch of methods of treatment of those subjects.

Methods in Physiography. Inasmuch as meteorology is considered under a separate heading, and as oceanography can seldom receive close attention, we shall here confine ourselves to a consideration of the physiography' of the land.

The method adopted in teaching this subject in the high school should be such as to bring out clearly its leading educational values : first, the understanding that it gives of the forms of the land at home and abroad as dependent on the stage of advance of various processes ; second, the practice that it requires in the conception of the many variable and interacting agencies on which the forms of the land depend.

In order to secure the successful application and illustration of the principles of physiography in the home district, we advise that the teacher of this subject should, if possible, have had some outdoor experience in geological field work, as it is only through such experience that local illustrations can be utilized to the fullest advantage and a sufficiently practical turn can be given to the study.

To reach the best results, we advise that the following classes of materials be supplied as liberally and utilized as fully as possible :

Maps : Not only the physical maps of the larger land divisions, already introduced in more elementary teaching ; but also special maps of restricted areas on large scale, illustrative of typical land forms, such as it is the intention of the Conference to select and recommend for use, through its sub-committee, as referred to on page 135 : the object gained by these large scale maps being the actual representation of the actual forms of the land, instead of the mere indication of the locality where certain forms occur, as is the case with the use of small-scale maps.

Illustrations : Not so much of different places, as of different kinds of places ; the effort being to present a systematic series of the different classes of land forms. These may be secured in part from illustrated newspapers and magazines ; still better in photographs and lantern slides ; some form of lantern for projection being essential to the attainment of the best results. The collection of illustrations should be gradually extended and improved from year to year. The use of colored chalks on the blackboard may be made very effective in representing maps, sections, ideal diagrams, birds-eye views, etc.

Models : While elaborate models and relief-maps are too expensive for general use, effective reliefs of diagrammatic style are less costly and should be introduced. Diagrammatic models should be made by the teacher ; for it is fair to expect that the skill manifested by young scholars in making their sand and clay reliefs should be far enough developed in the teacher of physiography to produce original models of typical land-forms in their physical relations. When made with some attention to artistic finish such models are of great assistance in teaching.

Books: Use should be made as far as possible of the descriptions of classic examples of land-forms in books of travel, survey reports, and scientific periodicals, such as are generally accessible in the libraries of the larger cities. A collection of extracts from these sources, made by the assistance of the scholars, may be gradually accumulated in such variety as to be of much service.

Other Materials: A collection of common minerals and rocks should be made use of in describing the constitution of the crust of the earth on which the carving of the destructive forces of the weather produces the land-forms on which we live. Care should be taken not to extend this collection unnecessarily and to exclude from it all misrepresentative specimens. The weathering of rocks and the production of soils should be illustrated by a special suite of specimens, selected from the school district, if possible. Characteristic varieties of glacial drift deserve especial attention in the northern states. Weather maps should be secured from the nearest publishing station of the Weather Bureau, carefully preserved from year to year, until examples of different weather types are obtained in sufficient variety; the treatment of these maps having been explained in other sections of this report.

In offering the following suggestions regarding the conduct of the course in physiography, we repeat the caution already expressed regarding the intention of such suggestions. It is not in the least our purpose to constrain any teacher from the greatest individual freedom in his work; indeed the higher success that we desire to see can be reached only when the teacher is free to apply his own manner of representation, explanation, and illustration. Yet we conceive that the following indications of the manner in which the subject may be presented will be of service to some superintendents and teachers in making our measure of the subject and its educational value more explicit. For the sake of brevity we shall consider only that part of the subject that is concerned with the development of land-forms.

The general conception of the wasting of a land area and the ultimate production of a lowland of denudation from whatever form the area had in its earlier stages, deserves early and deliberate illustration. Around this fundamental conception, the teacher may group a variety of facts, both local and general, concerning the rocks and their structural relations in the earth's crust, on the one hand, and the weather and its summation in climate, on the other hand. However hard its rocks, however dry the climate, a lowland of faint relief is the ultimate form of every land area under the slow wasting of its surface; and during all the progress of this wasting, a systematic sequence of forms is exhibited. The essential elements in the study are thus introduced early and in their simplest form; the slow but continuous variation of land forms under these processes; the long duration of time that must be considered, even if not conceived. Every part of the land surface represents some stage in the course of its progress from its beginning in constructional uplifting or accumulation, towards its end as a completed lowland of denudation. Every part of the district around the school must be regarded in its true light as partly advanced on its way to extinction under the ceaseless attack of the weather.

The particular consideration of rivers, under whose guidance the waste of the land is carried to the sea, may be advisably introduced as the next general heading; because, from whatever constructional processes of accumulation or uplift a region had its beginning, there are certain general features of river-life common to all regions, and these may be conveniently presented before the different structural kinds of land forms are taken up. This serves not only to impress upon the scholars the systematic sequence of form-changes during the progress of general denudation, but also to emphasize the many features of the land that are associated with the development of its drainage. Throughout this division of the subject, particular care should be taken to bring the class into sympathy with the subject, by forgetting for the moment human measures of time and looking at rivers in the way rivers would look at themselves. Thus are examined the conditions that determine the original drainage area of a river, the location of its enclosing divides, and the arrangement of tributary branches; then the quick deepening of its valleys and the drainage of any lakes in which its waters may be at first detained; and, at the same time, the development of additional young side-streams, the accompanying subdivision of the drainage area, and, occasionally, the rearrangement of discharge by the shifting of divides under the action of active competing streams; with the rapid deepening of the valleys comes at first the development and later the extinction of the water falls; with the widening of the valleys comes the slow spreading out of land-waste in floodplains where the mature streams meander, and in deltas, where the streams branch out in "distributaries." Late in river-life, when the inter-stream hills are wasted away, the old streams wander sluggishly almost at will along ill-defined courses, slowly doing the little that remains for the completion of their life-work. During the advance of this consideration, specific examples may be given of rivers in one or

15

another stage of development from various parts of the world, thus
utilizing the maps and illustrations above described. The relation of
the development of a river to the opportunity for occupation of its
basin, or use of its current by man, supplies many interesting subjects
for detaining the attention and extending the understanding of the
class.

The river-lesson may be extremely valuable in giving life and
meaning to the commonplace facts of geography ; and especially in
bringing the class into appreciative relation with such rivers and
streams as they may see about their homes. A comparison of these
home examples with others more distant but in similar stages of
development, or a contrast with others in dissimilar stages of
development, offers an admirable means of acquainting scholars with
the general facts of geography. (The citation of many illustrations
of river development impresses scholars with the reality of the
changes of land forms, and with the systematic sequence of these
changes. The face of the earth thus comes to have a new aspect,
and a long step is made toward that intimate acquaintance with the
life of inorganic nature which this subject strives to promote.)

After gaining an understanding of changes in the life of an undis-
turbed river, the effects of elevation, depression, or deformation of
the land, or of climatic changes may be introduced. With their
introduction, an important step is taken toward the more complicated
conditions of nature ; at the same time, the subject becomes somewhat
more difficult from the necessity of maintaining a greater number of
factors in mind while interpreting the relations of rivers having more
or less disturbed development. Yet with a deliberate and well-
illustrated approach to this division of the subject, it should present
no serious difficulty to high-school classes.

The consideration of regions of different structure, and hence of
different surface expression, advisably follows the preceding account
of river development. While the general arrangement and form
of valleys has there been explained, the form of the hills, plateaus,
ridges and mountains between the valleys now becomes the leading
object. The explanations of geological structure here required will
present no difficulty, if the teacher has a personal knowledge of
such subjects from field experience ; but otherwise it is doubtful if
this plan of treatment can be usefully introduced into the high-school
course. In illustration of what is here intended, we may briefly refer
to the group of plains and plateaus, characterized by possessing a
horizontally stratified structure. These may be first considered
according to the condition of their accumulation ; as marine plains,
lacustrine plains, fluviatile plains, lava plains, snow plains, and

dust plains. Second, according to the manner in which those formed under water have become exposed as dry land; as by upheaval from beneath the sea, by down-cutting of lake outlets, by evaporation of lake waters in arid climates, by melting away of the ice barriers of glacial lakes. Third, according to the expression of surface form as dependent on complication of structure, altitude above sea-level, stage of development, condition of climate. Fourth, according to the distribution of plains and plateaus of different kinds; thus we find a young marine plain in Florida, an old marine plain, much dissected, in West Virginia; a young lacustrine plain in Minnesota and Dakota, an older lacustrine plain in the Green River Basin of Wyoming; a young lava plain in the Snake River Basin of Idaho, an older lava plain in West Scotland, and so on. Mountains should receive similar treatment. Features of glacial origin deserve especial attention in the northern states. Experience shows that when the subdivisions of the land are thus rationally explained, their peculiarities are much more easily remembered, and their relations to habitation and productions are much more fully appreciated. Just as in botany and zoölogy, where no attempt is made to describe all the forms of plants and animals and their distribution over the earth, but where the scholar is shown the more important forms, with their correlations, as determined, not by apparent similarity, but by development; so in physiography, it is not advisable to attempt an account of all parts of the earth, when only the slightest attention could be allotted to each; it is better to give careful attention to the more significant parts, and to study these in their natural relations, introducing a sufficient number of examples to give a good idea of the distribution of various forms, and of their relation to habitation and production. By these means, a better idea is gained of the features of the earth's surface, and the scholars are enabled afterwards to recognize and enjoy the expression of the face of nature when they are moving about over the world in later life.

Methods of Teaching Meteorology. (a) *Intermediate or Grammar School Course.* The simplest facts concerning the weather may be introduced into observational studies as early as the teacher desires. These should be followed by simple instrumental records in the fourth or fifth year, never so complex or frequent as to be burdensome, so that when the sixth and seventh year of school is reached, the scholar will have gained an elementary but practical and familiar acquaintance with the use of the thermometer, the wind vane, and the rain-gauge. The barometer and hygrometer should be introduced, if possible, but not so early as the simpler instruments. Habits of punctuality, care, neatness, and system may be taught by keeping a record, and excellent arithmetical practice may be given in determining averages and totals; but the teacher should take care that the scholars' attention be directed to the phenomena of atmospheric changes, as well as to their intrumental records.

Accompanying the local observation of weather elements, a simple study of weather maps should be introduced; but this should progress very slowly, in order that the best value may be derived from it. The following suggestions may be of service in this connection. Assuming that the school can receive a supply of daily weather maps for at least a part of the school year, and that it has access to maps received in earlier years: let the teacher select several of the older maps on which the winds over the country east of the Rocky Mountains happened to be moving in a systematic manner, for example, a great volume of southerly winds moving northward from the Gulf up the Mississippi Valley and inland from the South Atlantic Coast, while westerly winds are advancing across the great plains; or a broad sweep of westerly or northwesterly winds spreading all over the eastern half of the country, as during a cold wave. Draw the wind arrows in heavy black lines, for easier seeing; such work as this may often be entrusted to advantage to some of the better draftsmen among the scholars. In order to enforce the idea that the whole lower part of the atmosphere is moving, and not simply the winds at certain stations of observation, draw many intermediate lines, accordant with the directions of the wind arrows; the length, or heaviness, of these lines may be made to indicate the velocity of the winds. A series of charts may thus be prepared with little trouble, from which an effective presentation of some of the greater facts of meteorology can be easily and clearly made. These maps may be used as the basis of exercises in writing; the description of their wind movements deserves careful statement. When the spiral winds about areas of high pressure and of low pressure are included in the series, the scholars will find all their powers of verbal description called on to enable them to state the facts properly. The continued use of the maps will also serve to impress many geographical facts on the memory.

Areas of cloud and rainfall may be treated in a similar way; and their contrast with adjacent areas of fair or clear sky afford much material for study and description. The presence of clear weather in one region, while heavy rains are falling in another, is thus taught in a simple and effective manner.

The distribution of temperature should be introduced, first, by entering the thermometer readings at the various stations on the map in strong figures, so that a class may easily see them; and then asking for verbal statements concerning the warmer and colder parts of the country. By selecting maps in which temperature contrasts are distinct, many interesting exercises may be developed in this manner. When the idea of distribution of warmer and colder areas is gained, it may be suggested that one of the class draw a line to separate all that region which is warmer than 60°, for example, from the region colder than 60°. Similar lines may be drawn by other scholars on other maps. Summer and winter maps may be compared. When the lines are familiar, they may be named "isotherms." If the subject is one in which the teacher takes especial interest, and which therefore properly receives more extended treatment than it might otherwise, an additional exercise may be made on a series of lines at right angles to the isotherms (the lines of temperature-decrease, or the "thermometric gradient" lines) along which the most rapid decrease of temperature would be experienced. Their trend is generally northward, but on certain occasions their course is peculiarly deformed eastward or westward.

Barometer readings should be treated in the manner outlined for temperatures. The small difference of their values will soon be noted; and the frequent occurrence of limited oval areas of slightly higher or lower pressure than that of their surroundings will soon attract the attention of the scholars. As with temperature, so here, an examination of the curved lines at right angles to the isobars, along which the pressure decreases, will prove instructive; these lines will converge towards the centre of low pressure areas, and diverge from the centre of high pressure areas. When the isobaric lines are close together, the lines of pressure-decrease should be drawn heavier, to indicate a rapid decrease of pressure. The rapidity of decrease of pressure, as indicated by the closeness of adjacent isobars, should be compared on different maps. When the rate and direction of decrease of pressure can be talked about familiarly it may be spoken of as "barometric gradient." By slow and patient work, even this relatively advanced idea will be grasped by children in the grammar school; but to attain success, it is of the utmost importance that the work should progress no faster than the scholars ask for it by their behavior with the maps. It would be better to have the work thus far outlined extended over occasional exercises for a year than to hasten too fast, making apparent but unreal, unsubstantial progress.

When examples of winds, temperatures, clouds, rainfall, and pressures have been given in sufficient number, a combination of two elements, as wind and pressure, may be introduced; and here, in particular, the scholars should be given time to discover for themselves the simple relations existing between two such elements. We are persuaded that the error is commonly made, in schools where weather maps are used, of going too fast under the lead of the teacher's brief explanations, perhaps because the teachers themselves are not yet familiar enough with the great lessons that the maps may give; thus not only passing over many matters with insufficient understanding by the scholars, but also preventing the practice in discovery which here develops so great an interest among children when they are in a properly awakened state, and which gives well-trained scholars so strong an encouragement in their studies. The teacher should supply maps in a proper order, he should guide the advance of the class by judicious questions; but he should leave them to find out the simple meteorological laws, such as those which associate the movement of the winds with the distribution of atmospheric pressure; the variation of temperature with the direction of the winds, etc. In this way, the following principles may be established: The winds flow towards the regions of lower pressures, but they generally turn a little to the right of the lines of pressure-decrease, that is, to the right of barometric gradient. The winds blow faster when the pressure decreases rapidly, and calms or light breezes prevail where the pressure is comparatively equable. The winds blow in left-handed curving spirals in areas of low pressure, and in right-handed outward spirals in areas of high pressure, and they are generally stronger in the former than in the latter. Southerly winds cause a rise of temperature; northerly winds cause a fall of temperature. Areas of low pressure are generally cloudy, with rain in summer, and with rain or snow in winter; areas of high pressure are prevailingly clear with warm days and cool nights in summer, and with cold weather and extremely cold nights in winter. These areas move in a general eastward course over the country, carrying their changes of wind and weather with them, in such a manner that the stationary observer suffers changes from clear to cloudy weather, and from warm southerly to cool northerly or westerly winds as they pass. Thunderstorms of summer time generally occur in the southeastern quadrant of low pressure areas.

During the advance of this work, current weather maps may be introduced to give exercise on the problems in hand, whenever they serve the purpose well. A connection may thus be made between the local weather noted at the school and the general atmospheric conditions over the country; and a passing rainstorm, or, a strong change of temperature, may be thus traced with great interest and profit. All through the work, continual practice should be maintained in formulating and-writing the conclusions reached by study. As the study advances, these written records become, in effect, so many compact generalizations in which the scholars' inductions are preserved. The training of mental powers and the encouragement given to persevering and intelligent study are not among the least of the results gained from work of this kind.

Without going further through an account of elementary exercises, based on the weather map and illustrated by local weather observations, we may add a few examples of subjects that may be borrowed from meteorology for the aid of descriptive geography. The prevalence of westerly winds and the general advance of areas of high and low pressure from west to east may be mentioned as one of the strongest characteristics of the middle temperate zone; and in contrast, the oblique northeast and southeast trade winds, blowing steadily, with few stormy interruptions, may be instanced as a prevailing characteristic of the torrid zone. The greater intensity of weather changes may be pointed out as a feature of winter, when we experience something of frigid conditions; the less intensity of weather change is a feature of summer, when we are visited by almost torrid heat. The general increase of rain or snow within areas of low pressure, as they approach the Atlantic Coast, may be used to explain the aridity of our western interior region, and of other continental interiors. The smaller variations of temperature near the coast, and particularly on the Pacific Coast, than in the upper Mississippi Valley, may be employed to teach one of the greatest climatic contrasts of the world.

(b) *High School Course.* The course in meteorology in the high school should be directed quite as much towards a training in the methods of logical investigation, as towards imparting information concerning the science. It should not be attempted until after a course in physics is passed. For the sake of brevity, only the shortest outline of the work can be introduced.

Facts of local observation about the school and of extended observation through the weather maps bring almost continuous but variable movements of the atmosphere before the class. The correlations discovered from the weather maps in the grammar school, now reviewed, show a clear connection between the movement of the winds and a variety of the other weather elements. Let it therefore be suggested that the cause of the winds be the main line of study, leaving the associated phenomena to be examined and explained in their natural connection with the winds.

Recalling the teaching of physics, it appears that no cause for atmospheric movement is so available as convection, that is, a gravitative circulatory movement, excited by differences of temperature.

Under assumed conditions as to temperature, the resulting distribution of atmospheric pressure and flow of the winds may be deduced in accordance with accepted physical principles, and this process may be at once contrasted with the inductive process by which the correlations of the weather maps were established. It may be then stated that if the distribution of temperature over the earth were known, the general circulation of the winds and the distribution of pressure could be predicted, and, according to the closeness of agreement afterwards found between these predictions and the facts, the theory of the convectional cause of the winds would be accepted or rejected, thus introducing the class to a rational method of scientific investigation, applicable in all manner of studies, as well as in meteorology.

On perceiving the direction thus given to further inquiry, the study of the control and distribution of atmospheric temperature is naturally taken up, because it is manifestly needed before further advance can be made. Under this division of the subject the teacher is advised to make clear the distinction between radiant solar energy, which traverses the celestial spaces in all directions from the sun, and of which a very small part reaches the earth, and the heat produced when this energy is acquired or absorbed by terrestrial matter. Interesting illustrations of physical processes are found in this connection; the different rates of absorption of radiant energy by air, water, and land, the control of temperature by specific heat, latent heat, dynamic cooling of ascending air currents, etc., etc.

The distribution of temperature on annual and seasonal isothermal charts may next be studied, noting the prevailingly high and uniform temperatures of the torrid zone, the variable temperature of the temperate zone, and the prevailingly low temperatures of the frigid zones; noting also the small variations of temperature from season to season on the oceans, even in relatively high latitudes, while the lands of the temperate zone have extremely variable temperatures.

In accordance with the theory of convectional circulation, it is now possible to predict the distribution of pressure and the flow of the winds, on the assumption that they are entirely the product of differences of temperature maintained by the sun. The predictions should be carefully formulated and entered on a blank map of the world. A series of annual and seasonal charts of pressures and winds should then be compared with the predicted consequences of the theory. It will be apparent that the theory is incomplete, because there are many differences between its predicted consequences and the facts; but all these differences are explained when adequate account is taken of the effect of the earth's rotation in deflecting the winds from the gradients and in rearranging the distribution of pressures. A good understanding of the general circulation of the atmosphere and its seasonal variations may thus be gained. Both the value and the danger of the deductive method, and the importance of continually confronting the consequences deduced from theory with the results of observation may be impressed by this lesson.

On attaining a rational understanding of the prevailing winds of the world, the consideration of atmospheric moisture and clouds may be introduced before the study of storms and rainfall is approached. In connection with the formation of clouds, the effects of the liberation of latent heat during the condensation of vapor should be deliberately examined, as a matter of much importance in the larger processes of convection.

Tropical cyclones offer the best introduction to the study of the stormy interruptions of the general circulation of the atmosphere. These cyclones are well-defined phenomena, closely studied in certain tropical seas, and of serious importance as dangers to navigation. The place and season of their origin and the manner of their action point to the conclusion that they are violent convectional whirls, turning in consequence of the earth's rotation, and supplied with much of their energy from the latent heat of the vapor that is condensed to furnish their heavy rains. They exhibit in a small way many features already familiar in the general circulation of the atmosphere around the poles. On coming next to cyclonic storms, and the anti-cyclonic areas of temperate latitudes, which together constitute the regions of low and high pressure in our weather maps, the presumption that they are convectional phenomena is naturally conceived, because convection has been previously found to be so sufficient a cause of the general circulation of the atmosphere and of tropical cyclones; but on perceiving that our cyclones and anticyclones are more frequent and more violent in winter than in summer, their convectional origin cannot be taken for granted, and other causes for their action must be examined. The science of meteorology is at present undecided on this question; although the weight of evidence leans towards explaining the cyclones and anticyclones of the temperate zones as an effect of irregular movements in the general circulation, rather than as independent, spontaneous, convectional phenomena. The absence of a demonstrated settlement of this question is not held to be good reason for excluding the discussion of the causes of these most interesting and important phenomena from the range of high school study. Students should as carefully learn to hold open opinions on disputed subjects as they are led to believe firmly in the demonstrable propositions of geometry. In all argumentative studies, the evidence leading to the conclusions, and not simply the conclusions, should receive careful consideration.

The cyclones and anticyclones of our latitudes are found of great importance not only in explaining the changes of weather — as has already been made familiar from earlier study — but also in the determination of the occurrence of local thunderstorms and tornadoes ; for these are determined for the most part by instability produced by the importation of warm and cold currents about the areas of low and high pressure.

The distribution of rainfall is best introduced after the explanation of winds and storms, both general and local. It may be used in confirmation of the explanations already given of the winds — the migrating equatorial rains of the doldrums ; the dry belts of the trade winds, except where they blow against mountains, the stormy rains of the westerly winds in temperate and higher latitudes ; the subtropical winter rains — all these follow as corollaries of the movements already recognized.

A general review of the subject may be made under the heading of climate, where the various phenomena hitherto studied separately may now be grouped geographically, and considered especially with regard to their influence on the development of organic life, and on the habitation of various regions by man.

EXAMINATIONS FOR ADMISSION TO COLLEGE.

The Conference adopted the following expressions of judgment as to the terms of admission to colleges : —

In view of the fact that our high schools, in fulfilment of their obligations to the majority of their pupils, must shape their work so as to give the best available preparation for the average duties of life without regard to college study ;

And that most high schools cannot maintain several distinct courses without weakening all, in greater or less degree, by undue division of instruction and equipment ;

And that it is desirable that all pupils who have finished a high-school course of the better order should be able to enter college without serious embarrassment from lack of adjustment, even if they shall come to desire to do so only at or near the end of their course in high schools, as is so often the case ;

And in view of the fact, on the other hand, that it is desirable that college graduates, as prospective principals, teachers, and patrons of the high schools, should be familiar by personal experience with as much of the high-school course as practicable, rather than a special phase of it only, and so should be in working sympathy with it ;

And that, for many additional reasons, it is desirable that there shall be the closest practicable relations between the colleges and high schools, therefore,

Resolved, that it is the sense of this Conference that the colleges should accept as preparatory work, in such due measure as a fair estimate of of their value shall permit, all studies which the high schools are compelled by their conditions to teach, and that, in arranging their requirements for admission, the colleges should make provision for a number of alternative subjects or adaptive studies sufficient to permit the high schools to subserve their primary functions and at the same time prepare their students for college without disadvantageous dispersion of effort;

Resolved, that physiography, geology, and meteorology should be given, in the terms of admission to college, values equal to the full extent of the work expended in their pursuit.

While urging the acceptance of physiography, geology, and meteorology for admission to college, the Conference do not urge that they should be required. 'In examinations for admission to college, the Conference suggest that physiography be given preference over other branches of geography, and that political geography be required in connection with history.

Concerning the class of questions most suitable for testing attainments, this being a subject submitted to the Conference, we suggest two criteria which should be met. The questions should be (1) such that no student who is not familiar with them can be supposed to have an adequate preparation, and (2) such that no student who has an adequate preparation can fail to exhibit it by means of them (time and other necessary conditions being granted). These criteria, we think, will be best met by the selection of broad but fundamental topics, rather than by narrow and special questions on which the student might fail although well trained on the subject in general. In attempting to treat the fundamental topics recommended the candidates will show the precise character of their command of the subject. If that is loose and superficial it will appear in their papers; if it is thorough and precise, that will appear; if it is a mere memorized knowledge of facts, that will be shown; if it is a keen analytical perception of causes, agencies, and processes, that will be indicated. When such topics are set, the candidates cannot either succeed or fail by the mere hazard of questions. Their opportunities are ample. And if the judgment on their papers rests, as it should, on the nature of the knowledge and training shown, and not simply on the fact that something has been written, a true estimate may be formed. "Catch questions" have no place in an examination for college. Among the

topics that may be employed in such an examination, the following
are selected as illustrations: Forms of projection used in maps;
interpretation of topographic maps (as a part of the required work in
physiography); the natural history of a river or a land area; the
topography of a familiar district expressed by sketch maps and by an
outline of the region and history of its topographic features; the
significant features of one of the continents and of its drainage systems; the physical features of the United States; the character of
ocean basins; the relation of the true continental border to the water
line; the essential facts of the distribution of rainfall, of temperature,
of atmospheric pressure, and of atmospheric circulation; the character and distribution of glaciers; the distribution of volcanoes, of
deserts, and the significance of the latter; cyclones and anticyclones;
the distribution of plants and animals.

It is with the deepest regret that the Conference are called upon to
report the death of one of their number, Mr. Delwyn A. Hamlin,
Master, of the Rice Training School of Boston. Mr. Hamlin met
wi᷍   Committee at Chicago, and was in full harmony with the
ge᷍   ᷍   ᷍ of this report. His death, May 25th, occurred before
the᷍   ᷍ were attached to the revised report.

Pr᷍   sor Edwin J. Houston dissents from some of the recommen-
dati   of this report.

A.l of which is respectfully submitted.

> T. C. CHAMBERLIN, *University of Chicago,*
> *Chicago, Ill.*
>
> GEORGE L. COLLIE, *Beloit College, Beloit,*
> *Wis.*
>
> W. M. DAVIS, *Harvard University, Cambridge,*
> *Mass.*
>
> *DELWYN A. HAMLIN, *Master of the Rice,*
> *Training School, Boston, Mass.*
>
> MARK W. HARRINGTON, *The Weather Bureau,*
> *Washington, D.C.*
>
> CHARLES F. KING, *Dearborn School, Boston,*
> *Mass.*
>
> FRANCIS W. PARKER, *Principal of the Cook*
> *County Normal School, Englewood, Ill.*
>
> ISRAEL C. RUSSELL, *University of Michigan,*
> *Ann Arbor, Mich.*

* Deceased.

To the Committee of 'Ten,
PRESIDENT CHARLES W. ELIOT, *Chairman:* —

Dear Sir, — I sincerely regret my inability to agree with the Majority Report of the Conference on Geography (including Geology and Meteorology) appointed by your Committee to meet at the Cook County Normal School, Chicago, Illinois, on December 28th, 29th and 30th ult. I, therefore, respectfully beg leave to submit the following Minority Report, containing a brief statement of some of the respects in which I differ from the conclusions reached by the rest of the Conference as embodied in their Report.

I have before me two Majority Reports; the first, consisting of some fifteen pages of typewritten matter, fairly embodying the conclusions reached by the majority of the Conference during the conference; the second and later report, consisting of some forty-six pages of typewritten matter, containing suggestions afterw—d—made by the members individually. In my judgment the ner   litional matter is so badly interwoven into the body of the   , as to produce a lack of precision, which renders it diffi   it,   respects, to ascertain exactly what conclusions have been r   ed by the gentlemen signing it. The recommendations of the two   orts, however, are essentially the same.

While the Majority Report contains much excellent material, I am, nevertheless, reluctantly compelled to differ from many of its fundamental conclusions and suggestions.

I agree with the statement in the Majority Report that "It did not seem advisable to greatly modify the range of subjects us: embraced under the term geography." Unfortunately, what I most strongly object to in the Report, is the fact that it greatly, and I think unwarrantably, modifies such range of subjects.

The Majority Report states "The natural order of geographical subjects seems, therefore, to be the following:

1. "*Elementary Geography*, a broad treatment of the earth and its inhabitants and institutions, to be pursued in the primary, intermediate and lower grammar grades."

2. "*Physical Geography*, a more special but still broad treatment of the physical features of the earth, atmosphere and ocean, and of the forms of life and their physical relations, to be pursued in the later grammar grades."

3. "*Physiography*, a more advanced treatment of our physical environment in which the agencies and processes involved, the origin, development, and decadence of the forms presented, and

the significance of the features of the earth's face are the leading themes, to be pursued in the later high-school or the early
college years."

4. "*Meteorology*, a specialized study of atmospheric phenomena,
to be offered by schools that are prepared to do so properly, as an
elective in the later high-school years."

5. "*Geology*, a study of the earth's structure and its past history,
to be offered by schools prepared to do so properly, as an elective in
the last year of the high school course."

The proposed distribution of these subjects in point of time is as
follows: viz., 1 and 2 are to extend through all the primary, intermediate and grammar grades; 3, 4, and 5 are either assigned to the
later high-school course, or are to be elected during the last high-
school or early college year.

The break thus introduced in the sequence of geographical studies
is, in my judgment, exceedingly inadvisable. The advantages of the
continued study of any subject are generally recognized by educators.
If an intermission of several years in the geographic studies is permitted, between the grammar grades and the latter part of the high-
school course, much time will necessarily be lost in again bringing
the mind of the student to the point it reached when it temporarily
abandoned these studies.

But, apart from this, the proposition to replace the general subject
of physical geography in the high school by specialized branches of
the science, appears to me to be one of the worst features of the
Majority Report, and its adoption, I believe, would work an irreparable
injury to the intelligent study of natural science not only in the
schools, but also in the colleges and universities.

The peculiar fitness of physical geography for the presentation and
classification of geographic facts is well known. Under its generalizations, the numerous, and, to the child, the often disconnected facts
of geography fall into orderly groupings, and much that has hitherto
perplexed and harassed its naturally inquisite mind, first finds
intelligent explanation.

In my long experience as a teacher of natural science, I have
found the study of physical geography always to attract, and often
to charm the mind of the student. Moreover, physical geography
forms the natural introduction to elementary natural science, since it
treats of the causes and effects of the things that are constantly
before the child's observation. Here is taught, or should be taught,
the mutual interdependence of the three dead geographic forms, the
land, the water and the air, and the two living forms, plant and
animal life. The proposition to change all this for the doubtful and

untried advantages of a so-called new study is, I think, unwarranted ⟩ and means retrogression and not progression.

A tendency unfortunately exists in educational circles to decry all that is old, and to laud and magnify all that is new. Such is the fruit of specialism, not of broad culture. The minds of the geologist and meteorologist, in my opinion, are too evident in the recommendations of the Majority Report. The advantages of the special departments of geology and meteorology have, I fear, been so magnified as to prevent the intelligent consideration of the remaining branches, the study of which is equally necessary for the broad culture of the child.

While I agree with the Majority Report that the work of the earlier and intermediate grades should deal " Not only with the face, of the earth but with elementary considerations in astronomy, meteorology, zoölogy, and botany, etc.," I do not do so entirely for the reason assigned ; namely, that " Unless this admixture of subjects is fairly included under the elementary courses of geography many scholars will not gain a knowledge of even the outlines of these important subjects," but mainly because I regard elementary geography as practically identical with elementary natural science, which I firmly believe should form as essential a part of primary education as either language or number. The child, in my judgment, should be taught the elementary facts of natural science along with its letters. The study of nature should form a large part of its first school work, if, indeed, not the only part.

That characteristic of childhood which finds expression in intense curiosity as to the why of the things it sees around it, and which leads it, when intelligent, to pour into the ears of its unwilling adult auditors, a deadly fusilade of questions that too frequently discloses their ignorance, can, if properly directed, be made in the study of elementary geography of considerable importance to early education. Children are close observers and possess the faculty of imagination to a degree much greater than is generally credited. Let then the first lessons of the child be limited to the things it can see and handle, and much will be done to ensure success.

I would recommend that in elementary geographical work, no textbooks be permitted to be used ; at least, no books such as those in general use, and that only those parts of the earth be studied where the child lives, and only those things on such parts with which the child is brought into actual contact, either in the house, along the streets or roads, on the playground, or in the school room. Such a study of geography will naturally prove of great benefit to the child, and will form the best method of ensuring interest in its studies, because it deals with objects that come within the range of its observation.

I entirely disagree with the Majority Report in the following statement regarding the time now devoted to the study of geography and the results of such work ; viz.,

" In general, however, it is the judgment of the Conference that too much time is given to the subject *in proportion to the results secured*. It is not their judgment that more time is given to the subject than it merits, but that either more should be accomplished or less time taken to attain it."

In the first place I respectfully submit that the statement is no truer of geography than of any other study of the lower grades. Indeed, I doubt if it is as true of geography as it is of either number or language. The excellent work in geography that is now being done by a large proportion of the lower grades of schools, generally throughout the United States, will, I feel assured, in its results, compare favorably with those attained in either number or language.

For the general purposes of classification, the studies of the lowest schools may be conveniently arranged under the following general heads ; viz., physical science, number and language.

I would introduce physical science in the lowest schools by the study of geography, which in its earliest stages should be strictly limited to observations of the simplest natural phenomena. As already remarked in its earliest stages, geography should be limited in place, to a description of that part of the earth where the child lives, and in subject matter, to those things which it sees, handles, and compares.

I would earnestly recommend that the child's first lessons in language be given through the medium of natural science thus introduced by elementary geography. I believe that a great advantage would be derived in so teaching a child language in connection with the studies in physical science. And this without that " Dawdling and dwelling on trivialities" which I agree with the Conference in unqualifiedly condemning. On the other hand, however, I would not urge undue pressing of the work, " In order that the time given to geography may be shortened." In all early school work it is best to make haste slowly.

But, apart from this, I do not believe that geography, as a branch of elementary natural science, can advantageously be crowded into fewer terms by devoting to it a greater number of hours per term. Whatever may be the advantages derived from such a plan in either number or language work, I do not believe that they exist in elementary science work. Early scientific ideas to become well grounded should be of gradual growth. Like all ideas based on observation, time forms an important factor in their acquirement; time for the observations to be made; time for them to be thoroughly absorbed; time for them to be intelligently observed, and time for the correct conclusions to be reached. In mere memorizing studies, hurry may possess advantages, but in elementary scientific studies the time element is of prime importance.

It is not, however, in the lower grades only that the Committee express their belief that too much time is expended in teaching geography. They urge the same as regards the higher grades. It is indeed especially in the higher grades, in the study of physical geography, that they believe marked changes are necessary; and this, as I understand it, is a result of the experience or belief of at least a majority of the Conference, that not only the study of geography in general, but of physical geography in particular has failed to awaken the interest or arouse the enthusiasm of the pupils. An experience of nearly twenty years in teaching physical geography, I am happy to say, is directly at variance with this conclusion. On the contrary, I have invariably found this study to awaken the liveliest interest and not infrequently to arouse marked enthusiasm. Nor do I believe that the general experience of teachers in this respect would bear out the opinion expressed by the Majority Report. Should, however, the facts be as claimed in some localities, for I cannot credit such to be generally true, it would seem that this deplorable state of affairs is due to that very lack of definiteness and want of logical order of sequence, which I regret to believe characterizes both the matter and the recommendations of much of the Majority Report.

I would suggest the following topics as properly coming under the head of general geography; viz.,

1. Elementary geography, consisting entirely of the simplest facts of physical geography.

2. Descriptive geography.

3. Mathematical geography.

4. Political geography.

5. Physical geography, including a systematic classification and co-ordination of the more or less disconnected facts studied under heads 1, 2, 3, and 4, including the new facts that will necessarily present themselves as a result of such classification and coördination.

I would, as already stated, limit the early study of geography to the simplest elementary ideas of physical geography.

16

As the child advances in its observations of the earth immediately around it, the study of descriptive, mathematical, and political geography should begin; that is to say, after elementary natural geography has been sufficiently taught, the other branches of geography are to be studied together. In this respect I quite agree with the ideas advanced by the Majority Report. I feel convinced, however, that not only should geographical studies continue through all grades to the high school, but also that physical geography should be taken up during the first year or two of the high-school course, rather than during the last year. I believe this because I am convinced that the study of physical geography is necessary to properly generalize and systematize the heterogeneous collection of facts embraced under ordinary geography, and I believe that this should be done immediately at the close of such general geographical studies and not only along with them.

In the intermediate grades considerable attention should be given to maps and map drawing. In all cases, however, such studies should be preceded by ideas of relative size and direction. The meaning of parallels and meridians should be thoroughly taught before any extended work is attempted on maps. For this purpose the use of a spherical blackboard, or a large blackboard or blackened sphere so prepared as to be readily used with chalk is recommended. Smaller, individual, spherical blackboards can also be advantageously employed for individual use by the pupils.

I heartily agree with the Majority Report as regards the value of the repeated use of maps, and of the necessity for teaching the child how to interpret them intelligently.

As regards the presentation of physical geography I would suggest the following arrangement of topics, based mainly on Guyot's plan, as being, in my experience, an order of sequence that has invariably given good results.

1. The Inside of the Earth.
      The Heated Interior and its Effects.
2. The Outside of the Earth.
      a. The Land.
      b. The Water.
      c. The Air.
      d. Plants.
      e. Animals, including Man.

In teaching these topics I would suggest the following order:
1. What is it?   Definition.
2. Where is it?   Distribution.
3. Why is it?   Cause.

1. *What is it ? Definition.* — In physical geography, as indeed in all studies, definite ideas must be had as to what the thing studied is. Clear and concise definitions should be given, the definitions, as far as possible, being vitalized either by the thing itself, or by a picture of the thing, if the thing itself cannot be readily obtained.

2. *Where is it ? Distribution.* — Clear ideas of the distribution of the five geographic forms is a matter of prime importance in the study of physical geography, in order that the effects of each form on the other can be thoroughly understood.

It is under this second head that the knowledge of map drawing, already taught in the lower grades, can be applied as follows :

The student should be required to draw an outline map of the earth, preferably on a Mercator's projection, and to represent thereon, *as they are studied*, the distribution of the different classes of features or forms.

If the work under this second head be intelligently directed, most of the facts already acquired in the lower grades can now be grouped or arranged in a systematic form, and, when complemented by the third step, will be raised to the dignity of a science.

3. *Why is it ? Cause.* — The study of the causes that have produced the present features of the earth, or are now modifying them, constitute an exceedingly important part of physical geography, and should be carefully insisted on ; indeed, the effects of these causes should be taught throughout the entire course of geography, from the primary grades to the end. The extent, however, to which effects should be traced to their causes will of necessity vary with the work of the different grades. It is in this final study of the subject in the early high school years that the relations between causes and effects should receive their most extended treatment.

I agree with the Majority Report as regards the importance of the study of the causes that have produced and modified or are now modifying the physical features of the earth. I would not, however, limit the study of these causes in the high-school course to what the Report calls physiography, which is practically limited to the land areas, but would extend it equally to the ocean and atmosphere and to the life of the earth generally ; for, if the study be thus limited to the land, and is not equally extended to the effects such changes in the land and water areas have on climate and especially upon plant and animal life, it loses much of its broad cultural value.

A study of physical geography based on the scheme I have outlined cannot, in my judgment, fail to possess great attractiveness to the student, and to prove an important factor in ensuring broad mental culture.

Whatever differences of opinion may exist as to the proper methods of teaching geography in the primary grades, I think there should be no doubt as to the method best suited to the high-school grade. Here I would invariably begin each topic by a concise and accurate statement of the principles which modern science has discovered concerning it. If science is not agreed as to such principles, I would give the general consensus of opinion, carefully avoiding controversial matter, except in the highest grades of the work.

Having concisely stated the principles, I would show how such principles can be deduced from the observations already made by the student, either from the standpoint of work actually required in the lower grades, or, in the absence of this, from the observations it may reasonably be assumed the student has made for himself, outside of school work, pointing out how the interpretation of such observations necessarily leads to the scientific law already stated, supplying where necessary the missing links. In this manner the law as stated may be shown to be presumably correct. I think this preferable to any attempt to make the students deduce the law themselves. In other words, the scheme proposed would not attempt to build up the science by observations, but rather to make the observations confirm the already deduced law.

Moreover, in their recommendation to place additional subjects in the requirements for admission to college, the Conference go beyond the purpose for which they were appointed; viz., " To consider the proper limits . . . . the best method of instruction, the most desirable allotment of time for the subject, the best method of testing pupils' attainments therein . . . . of each principal subject which enters into the programme of secondary schools in the United States and into the requirements for admission to college." The Conference exceed their powers:

1. In proposing new studies for the secondary schools.

2. In naming subjects not required for admission to colleges.

3. In recommending the dropping of a subject now specially mentioned as one of the requirements for admission to many colleges.

Among the colleges that require physical geography in their entrance examinations I would mention the following: namely, the Sheffield School of Science, the Boston Polytechnic Institute, Princeton University, University of Kansas, Cornell College, Iowa, University of Wisconsin, Swarthmore College, University of Pennsylvania, University of Michigan, Cornell University, etc., etc.

The Majority Report is characterized by a curious and persistent insistance as to the peculiar claims of physiography, which it styles advanced and modernized physical geography.

I radically disagree with the recommendations of the Majority Report in this respect. It is not that I object so much to the use of the term physiography, since I agree with the Conference that names are of little importance, provided their significance is fully understood. To my mind, however, the word physiography is vague and misleading. Its meaning, as indicated by its etomology, is a drawing of nature, and this is the sense in which Huxley employed it to cover the subject matter of a certain course of lectures, on natural phenomena in general, and on the basin of the Thames in particular. Unless it is specifically stated as to what the natural drawing is, no precise meaning is conveyed by the word.

The meaning of physiographic as an adjective is more definite; for example, physiographic geology. But even here authorities are at variance. Dana limits the scope of physiographic geology "To a general survey of the earth's surface features." Clearly, however, such a limitation is not intended by the Majority Report, which would include dynamical geology. The Majority Report would make physiography include not only a survey of the earth's present features, but also an account of the agencies or forces that have produced or are now producing or modifying such features. But this is what Prestwich calls physical geology, by which he means Physical and Stratigraphical Geology as distinguished from Paleantological Geology; the one deals with inorganic and the other with organic matter.

Geike defines physiographic geology as "That branch of geological inquiry which deals of the evolution of the existing contours of dry land," and this it would appear comes nearest to the meaning given to physiography by the Majority Report.

But it is primarily the study of geography and not geology that the Conference is considering, and, if a new term is needed, it would seem that physiographic geography would be indicated. The existence of the well-known term physical geography, in my opinion, renders the coining of the new word inadvisable.

The uncertainty surrounding the name physiography is recognized by the Century Dictionary, as is shown by the following definition; viz., "A word of rather variable meaning, but, as most generally used, nearly or quite the equivalent of physical geography."

Let us now look into the Majority Report as regards its recommendations for the high-school course.

Concisely these recommendations are that physical geography be dropped out of the high-school course, and be taken up in connection with elementary geography as now taught in the secondary and elementary grades.

It is proposed to replace physical geography by:
  1. Physiography
  2. Meteorology.
and, provisionally,
  3. Geology.

In order to criticize intelligently this selection of topics proposed for the high-school course, a brief review of the topics included under the head of physical geography may be of value. Physical geography treats in general of the distribution, etc., of the land, water, air, plants and animals.

Tabulating the many branches of science which come under this very general heading, we have the following; viz.,

PHYSICAL GEOGRAPHY	1. Land	a. The interior of earth	1. Volcanology.		
			2. Seismology.		
		b. The crust of earth	1. Formation & changes — Physiography.		
			2. Land masses.		
			3. Relief forms	Orography.	
				Topography.	
	2. Water	1. Continental	Oceanography or	Hydrography.	
		2. Oceanic	Thalassography		
	3. Air	1. Climate	— Climatology		Meteorology.
		2. Winds & storms	— Anemography		
		3. Precipitation	— Hyetology		
	4. Plants	Botany or Phytology		Biology.	
	5. Animals —	Zoölogy	Zoölogical geography		
			Ethnography		

In place of the varied topics thus embraced under the term physical geography, portions from nearly all of which have already been necessarily introduced into the studies of the lower grades, we have the exceedingly limited range of topics embraced mainly under a subdivision of the land; viz., that relating to the formation and changes of the crust, or physiography.

It is true that the study of the water, as far as relates to the actions of rivers, lakes, glaciers, etc., is included among the causes of these changes, but their study is only incidental.

I have not included geology in the above tabular review, since, generally speaking, geology may be regarded as practically treating of the same topics as physical geography, with, however, this distinction; i. e. that geology is properly limited to a study of the earth as it was, and physical geography to the earth as it is.

That I am correct in my estimate of the limited scope of physiography, as the Majority Report understands it, will, I think, appear from the following extracts from the report itself;

On page 5, "But this would be made relatively subordinate to the main theme, namely, the geography of the lands."

Again on page 7, "As there must be a selection of topics, the Conference recommend that the nature of the processes involved in the formation and modification of the earth's surface, essentially so indicated under the head of physiography, be regarded as having the most vital importance, both to the general student and to the prospective teacher."

Or on page 8, "Physiography, a more advanced treatment of our physical environment, in which the agencies and processes involved, the origin, development, and decadence of the forms presented, and significance of the features of the earth's face, are the leading themes."

Or again on page 27, "We shall here confine ourselves to the physiography of the land."

And again on page 30, "For the sake of brevity, we shall consider only that part of the subject, that is concerned with the development of the land forms."

As far as I have been able to understand the so-called advanced and modernized physical geography, it is fairly crystallized in the following phrase, taken from page 30, of the Report:

"Its progress from first beginning in constructional uplifting, or accumulation, towards its end in a completed lowland of denudation."

I believe no further comment is necessary in this connection unless it be to review the very curious reason assigned for the introduction of physiography into the high-school course (see page 7):

"Unless either physiography or geology is retained in the high school and given vitality and efficiency, a serious danger threatens the whole geographic line of study in the lower schools, for the great mass of teachers of geography have not taken courses beyond the high schools, and in the immediate future are not likely to go further in their education, and if they are not taught the elementary processes and principles of these sciences then they will have little real strength as teachers of geography." The Conference have curiously confounded the functions of the high school with that of the normal school. Comment is unnecessary.

As regards the advisability of introducing meteorology into the high-school course in place of physical geography, the same general objections can be urged as in the case of physiography; viz., the replacing of a special for a general study.

It would in my judgment be bad enough if it were proposed to substitute the general subject of the atmosphere and its phenomena for the more extended subject of physical geography; but to propose a substitution of the highly specialized subject the Committee desire to make of meteorology, namely, the weather and its attendant phenomena, is, I feel sure, a great error, and one calculated to work much harm to that part of the school system on which the college and university depends so largely for its students.

I will not attempt here to point out the fact that the distribution of the topics proposed under meteorology is somewhat illogical as regards order of sequence and, therefore, not calculated to insure the best results; for, this is unnecessary, being secondary in consideration to the objection urged against the subject itself.

I agree with the recommendation of the Majority Report " That it is the sense of this Conference that colleges should accept as preparatory work, in such due measure as a fair estimate of their value shall permit, all studies which the high schools are compelled by their conditions to teach, and that, by arranging their requirements for admission, the colleges should make provision for a number of alternative subjects or adaptive studies sufficient to permit the high schools to subserve their primary functions, and at the same time prepare their students for college without disadvantageous dispersion of effort."

I do not, however, agree with them " That physiography, geology, and meteorology should be given in the terms of admission to college values equal to the full extent of the work expended in their pursuit;" for this, in my judgment, would be giving separate credits for, in many respects, two closely allied subjects; namely, physiography and geology.

. Nor can I see any valid reason why so comparatively special a subject as that of physiography should be given any preference over any other special branches of geography.

I desire in this connection to call the attention of the Committee of Ten to the fact that for some reason which I am unable to comprehend, the Majority Report fails to make any provision whatever for the studies of botany and zoölogy, or generally for the subject of biology. Why the particular branches of physical geography recommended have been selected to the exclusion of the remaining branches is difficult to say.

In conclusion, I desire to take direct issue with the statement repeatedly made during the Conference, and contained by inference in the Majority Report, that all existing works on physical geography are practically useless because insufficiently modernized and advanced.

The magnificent works of Humboldt, the valuable comparative geography of Ritter, and the classic writings of Guyot, treat of physical geography or geophysics in its truest, broadest sense, and need far better argument and more convincing reasons than those advanced by the Majority Report, in order to be successfully relegated to obscurity.

It may be interesting here to note how exceedingly new is the modernized and advanced physical geography referred to in the Report, that the Conference express their conviction that, in all probability, it cannot be taught except by the happy few who have mastered it, and that the Conference, therefore, gravely recommend that until Physiography be put in accessible form the study of geology, pure and simple, be substituted for it. That they should be willing to recommend the displacement of a well tried branch for the sake of a branch they acknowledge cannot yet be generally taught, can hardly be regarded as partaking of that broad, liberal spirit in modern educational matters so necessary for true advance.

EDWIN J. HOUSTON.

Central High School, Phil., Pa

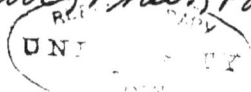

17